Strategic Policy Options for Bracing Nigeria for the Future of Trade

Gbadebo Odularu
Editor

Strategic Policy Options for Bracing Nigeria for the Future of Trade

palgrave
macmillan

Editor
Gbadebo Odularu
Department of Economics
and Finance
Bay Atlantic University
Washington, D.C., USA

ISBN 978-3-030-34551-8 ISBN 978-3-030-34552-5 (eBook)
https://doi.org/10.1007/978-3-030-34552-5

This Palgrave Macmillan imprint is published by the registered company Springer Nature Switzerland AG
The registered company address is: Gewerbestrasse 11, 6330 Cham, Switzerland

Foreword

Bracing Nigeria for the future of trade underscores the increasing need for enhanced capacities and partnerships in digitization as the essential ingredients for a successful transition to a digital economy.

Thus, the need for a broader digital trade facilitation policy reform lies at the heart of the rationale for this publication. It is crucial nonetheless to note that the chapters in this book discusses the roles of digital trade tools and relevant trade policy instruments in transforming the national and regional business and commercial landscape. However, much more work remains in order to optimally unlock the massive potential of private businesses, finance and investments in realizing the future of trade in Africa. This requires the convening roles of international organizations to leverage blended finance innovations as well as other public-private interactions for fostering digital trade.

The book presents perspectives on collaborative efforts across national, regional and international levels in articulating and implementing strategies on bracing Nigeria for the future of trade. A common thread in these chapters is an approach that values how maximum returns generate appreciable trade and development outcomes.

A holistic look at the chapters shows how they reinforce each other, articulate relevant challenges and priorities while providing strategic innovative policies from a wide range of perspectives.

Generally speaking, this book presents a whole ton of workable policy recommendations that lend themselves to making informed decisions that align trade to policy direction and positioning.

I hope this book will contribute to knowledge sharing and spark novel ideas to help stimulate future actions by Nigerian and African policy makers. In addition, this book provides innovative solutions which are urgently required for bracing Nigeria for the future of trade. SERAP LLC is committed to supporting Nigeria and other African countries to facilitate collaboration with development partners towards accessing a repository of resources, networks, strategies, innovations, policies, knowledge, best practices, and lessons learned by other countries in preparing for the future of trade.

Washington, D.C., USA

Sebnem Sahin, Ph.D.
Lead, Development Economist—Free Lancer
IFPRI, World Bank and the OECD

President and Founder, SERAP LLC

Socio-Economic Research Applications & Projects LLC
http://www.serapllc.com

Advisor, Infinite-Sum Modeling Inc.
http://infisum.com/index.php/2018/08/07/sebnem-sahin/

Adjunct Professor, Bay Atlantic University
Washington, D.C.
https://www.bau.edu/faculty/

Acknowledgements

Hearty appreciations and all praises go to God Almighty who is the source of all knowledge and wisdom. This publication is motivated by the robust career experience gathered from reputable organizations such as the World Trade Organization (WTO), United Nations Economic Commission for Africa (UNECA), United Nations Institute for Development Economic Planning (UNIDEP), International Food Policy Research Institute (IFPRI), United States Agriculture Department (USDA), Trade Policy Training Center in Africa (TRAPCA), Trade Policy Research and Training Program (TPRTP), University of Ibadan, University of Sunderland, Covenant University, Bay Atlantic University (BAU), Socio-Economic Research Applications and Projects (SERAP) and the Forum for Agricultural Research in Africa (FARA).

Adapting an old adage, it takes a collaborative efforts and strategic partnerships to write an excellent trade policy research book of this nature. In view of this, a special thank you goes to this book's authors and contributors.

This publication would have not been possible without the valuable support from my lovely family for providing the enabling environment for the commencement and completion of this book project. I also express my gratitude to my good friends, especially Prof. Bamidele Adekunle (University of Guelph, Canada). Lastly, we (the editor, authors and contributors) gratefully acknowledge the support and cooperation provided by Elizabeth Graber, Sophia Siegler, Susan Westendorf and the entire Economics Acquisition Team at Palgrave Macmillan, US.

CONTENTS

Notes on Contributors

Abiola Abidemi Akinsanya is currently a Commercial Officer in the Department of Trade, Federal Ministry of Trade and Investment, Nigeria, with over twelve years' experience in international trade. She has participated in the design of some of Nigeria's trade policies and her policy advice has helped to enhance Nigeria's bilateral trade with trading partners. Some of her achievements include being on the trade experts' team of Mr. President's delegation to Rwanda, Malawi and Botswana. Abiola holds bachelor's degree of Political Science from the University of Ado-Ekiti (UNAD), Nigeria; a master's degree in Diplomacy and Trade, Monash University, Australia; and a diploma from the Institute for International Trade, University of Adelaide, Australia. In her leisure time, Abiola loves to travel to explore new cultures and cuisines.

Ndah Abu Ali Assistant Director (Commercial) has over 14 years of experience in international trade negotiations (WTO, Regional/Bilateral Trade Agreement) trade-related issues and with a proven tracks records of providing policy analysis and briefing for top level management within the Federal Ministry of Industry, Trade and Investment. He has obtained some levels of capacity in terms of knowledge of multilateral trading system obligations and matters under negotiation in the current round of the Doha Development Agenda, namely, Non-Agriculture Market Access (NAMA), Trade Facilitation and the development dimension. He is passionate about championing Africa's cause for development through an ambitious regional integration agenda in terms of industrialization, boosting intra-Africa trade, trade facilitation, harmonization of trade policies and practices, and effective participation in the multilateral trading system. With good understanding on some challenges be faced by developing African countries' including supply-side constraints, limited value-addition, and over-dependence on primarily commodities for export, infrastructure gaps, poor trade facilitation implementations and problems on the ease of doing business. Over the past few years, he has been working as the Deputy Chief of Party (Assistant Project Coordinator) for a World Bank Project aimed at increasing firm's growth and employment in the participating firms.

Jonathan Adeyemi Aremu is a Professor of International Economic Relations at the Covenant University (CU), Ota, Nigeria and a Consultant, at ECOWAS (Economic Community of West African States) on Common Investment Market (ECIM), Abuja. Aremu (a) retired from the Central Bank of Nigeria as an Acting Assistant Director of Research in 1992; (b) among his outstanding publications on trade and investment is his book on *Attracting and Negotiating Foreign Direct Investment with Transnational Corporations in Nigeria* (2005). (c) He is a life Member of both Nigerian Economic Society and Nigerian Society of International Law as well as Facilitator of Trade, Investment and Competitiveness of Nigerian Economic Summit Group.

At ECOWAS level, Aremu was (a) appointed by European Union (EU) through Bizclim, as the Monitoring Expert on the Establishment of an ECOWAS Investment Guarantee/Reinsurance Agency, in 2011, and the Financial Expert to draft ECOWAS Community Investment Code and the Investment Policy Framework in preparation for the ECIM in the Region; (b) Member of Thematic Group on Investment in the Economic Partnership Agreements (EPAs) negotiation between European Union (EU) and ECOWAS Community; (c) the Lead Consultant on the ECIM for the region (to coordinate the establishment of ECOWAS Payments and Settlement System, ECOWAS Capital Market Integration, Common Investment Code and Policy, among others); (d) a Member of ECOWAS Tax Harmonization Committee of Experts; (e) Expert that conducted a Study on ECOWAS Trade in Services Policy Review, assisted by UNCTAD and GIZ and (f) Technical Consultant to the Federation of West African Chambers of Commerce and Industry (FEWACCI). At Continental and International levels,

Aremu is a (a) National Coordinator/Country Team Leader of UNIDO Investment Survey in Nigeria; (b) among the experts that developed a Trade Policy for Nigeria in 2012; (c) Member of the Technical Working Group (TWG) on the Nigeria Impact and Readiness Assessment of the African Continental Free Trade Area (AfCFTA). (d) Member of the technical experts that developed the Pan African Investment Code (PAIC) for African Union (AU) in 2016 and (e) Member of the Technical Working Group of the AfCFTA Unit of AU responsible for the development of the on-going Protocol on Investment in the next phase of the AfCFTA; (see UNECA Publication on Assessing Regional Integration in Africa (ARIA): Next Steps for the AfCFTA, July 2019).

Munaya A. Asiri is a trained economist with Bachelor's and Master's in Economics. Her work experience cut across being a statistical specialist at the General Authority for Statistics since April 2019. She is also a lecturer at Al Imam Mohammod University. She has volunteered in many national and international activities among which is the US Food Bank initiative.

Emily E. Ikhide is a Research Fellow in the Department of Research and Training of the National Institute for Legislative and Democratic Studies (NILDS). She holds a doctorate degree in Development Finance from the University of Stellenbosch, Cape Town, South Africa and master's and Bachelor's degrees in Economics from Universities of Botswana and Namibia, respectively. During her Ph.D., she focused on financing options for energy alternatives and economic growth in Nigeria. Dr. Ikhide had worked with the Nigerian Government at the Federal and State levels, including a position as a Strategic, Monitoring and Evaluation Officer in the Office of the Governor of a state. Her research interests include development finance, energy economics and macroeconomics, and her papers have been presented at several international conferences. Dr. Ikhide has participated in a number of research projects and won research and travel grants. She is currently leading a team to investigate the impacts of the National Food Security Program in Nigeria under the PEP PAGE II Research Grant.

Gbadebo Odularu teaches Economics and Finance at Bay Atlantic University, Washington D.C. He is the Senior Technical Consultant at Socio-Economic Research Applications & Projects, Washington, D.C., USA. He is also affiliated with the Center for Research on Political

Economy (CREPOL), as well as the American Heritage University of Southern California (AHUSC), USA. He works closely with national, continental and international partners to provide evidence-based policy tools for fostering digital economy towards realizing the United Nations Sustainable Development Goals (UN SDGs) 2030. His most recent book is *Trade Facilitation Capacity Needs* (Palgrave Macmillan, 2019).

Oluwasola E. Omoju is a Research Fellow at the National Institute for Legislative and Democratic Studies (National Assembly), Abuja, Nigeria. He holds a Ph.D. in Applied Economics from Xiamen University in 2017. Prior to that, he obtained a Bachelor's degree in Economics from the University of Ilorin and a Master's degree in Economics from the University of Lagos. Between February 2016 and July 2017, he was a Visiting Scholar at the Institute for Sustainable Economic Development of the University of Natural Resources and Life Sciences (BOKU) in Austria, and also a Guest Researcher at the EDEHN Laboratory of the Universite du Havre in France. His research interests include energy economics and policy, public financial management, development economics (with special reference to Africa) and policy impact evaluation using CGE modeling and micro-econometric analysis. He has received numerous academic awards and grants, including the 2014 CODESRIA-CLACSO-IDEAS South-South Collaborative Research Grant, EIB-GDN Applied Development Finance Fellowship and PEP PAGE II Research Grant. His research has been published in peer-reviewed journals including *African Insight*, *Renewable Energy*, *Energy Strategy Reviews*, *Journal of Cleaner Production*, *Energy and Environment*, and *Renewable and Sustainable Energy Reviews*.

List of Figures

List of Tables

CHAPTER 1

The Primer: Bracing Nigerian Trading Ecosystem for the Future

Gbadebo Odularu

1.1 Introduction, Rationale and the Context

In an era of big data, where every move is seemingly captured and recorded, traditional means of collecting data for official measures of the economy—from surveys to in-person price checks—appear increasingly outdated. Additionally, as the global economy changes with the spread of online shopping, 'free' internet sites and the gig economy, traditional methods of measurement may not adequately capture economic activity and variations in living standards. Privately collected big data has the potential to supplement or, in some cases, even supplant standard government indicators used to accurately capture changes in prices, quantities and quality. Further, harnessing the strengths of data sciences, AI and related financial instruments will generate inclusive development via

G. Odularu (✉)
Department of Economics and Finance, Bay Atlantic University,
Washington, D.C., USA
e-mail: g.odularu@ahusc.net

G. Odularu (ed.), *Strategic Policy Options for Bracing Nigeria for the Future of Trade*,
https://doi.org/10.1007/978-3-030-34552-5_1

improved efficiency and equity. However, difficulties relating to interpretation and access remain significant barriers to properly utilizing such data.

A strikingly emerging challenge is that the regulatory environment for digital trade is increasingly being tightened, particularly with regard to measures affecting data movement, infrastructure and connectivity (OECD 2019a). The Organisation for Economic Co-operation and Development (OECD) created a Digital Services Trade Restrictiveness Index (DSTRI), which identifies, catalogues and quantifies cross-cutting barriers that affect trade in digitally enabled services across 44 countries, covering the period from 2014 to 2018 with data available for every year (OECD 2019b). In other words, this requires governments to continually update data-related regulations and increasingly transfer data across borders or requiring that data be stored locally.

According to the Social Sciences and Humanities Research Council (SSHRC) of Canada, eight innovative technologies that are transforming and will continue to transform the global business infrastructure landscape in the next decades are artificial intelligence (AI), data analytics, sensors, blockchain, robotics, telepresence, 3D printing and synthetic biology. This will result immediately in unbundling traditional jobs into discrete tasks from an increasingly global labour pool, rising digitization of value chain eliminated the middlemen or human intermediaries, as well as reduction in transaction costs (shift from physical retail to online shopping). Further, the Horizon Canada notes that eight digital technologies which will combine to transform the global economy are:

- The Internet of Things will collect vast amounts of data and brings it to bear on the physical world.
- Artificial Intelligence (AI) and automated cognitive tasks will introduce new economic actors.
- Robotics will perform physical labour and provide an embodied platform for AI.
- Advanced telepresence will allow us to project ourselves and our expertise anywhere in the world that is connected to networks.
- Virtual reality will offer immersive non-physical worlds, while mixed reality will combine physical and virtual worlds, creating a third space distinct from both.

- Advanced materials are enabling the production of micro and nanoscale devices that can bring digitization to many new areas of low power.
- Decentralization production technologies such as 3D printing could use locally available inputs, including new biomaterials, to manufacture countless products on demand for local markets.
- Blockchain technologies create unique, non-copyable digital assets. This enables secure, low-cost transactions between parties who do not know each other. Further, AI and blockchain will replace human intermediaries in the sense that as they learn from data in the digital economy, AIs take over many roles currently played by humans. Blockchain reduces demand for trusted middle players in transactions. Depending on how fierce competition is and based on their data protection regimes, a small number of large firms could capture much of the information and profits in a networked economy.

Digital technologies are creating a global digital infrastructure in which traditional jobs are being unbundled into tasks and allocated to qualified, low-cost bidders across the planet, invariably eliminating middlemen and reducing costs. However, this has pervasive implications for income insecurity, inequality, mental health issues, ineffective nation state instruments, protectionism, etc.

In view of the digitalization of the global economy, rapid expansion of electronic commerce and the rising importance of digital trade in commodities, especially services, there is a need for an enhanced understanding of the functioning of e-commerce in Africa, and its implications for markets and competition. With Blockchain technology, artificial intelligence (AI) and similar innovations fast becoming an exciting new frontier for commerce in particular and socio-economic transformation in general, the future of digital trade seems promising in Africa. Five critical trends that describe the potential trajectory of the use of digital technology in Africa include inter alia: customer support in banking, inclusive development, financial services, insurance space and in product discovery in the e-tailing space. At present, e-commerce continues to be dominated by a few big players—China's Alibaba and JD.com and US firms Amazon, eBay and Walmart, where Amazon captures almost half of all virtual transactions in the United States. According to figures from Digital Commerce 360, e-commerce is growing year by year and in 2018, exceeded $2.86 trillion in sales around the globe, an 18% jump from 2017 figures.

In the face of increasing trade tariffs battles at the global level, trade facilitation remains a substantial area of policy research in which changes in markets, processes, products, firms and countries occur rapidly. Coincidently, in the last decade, e-commerce, technological advances and the rise of big data have changed the practice and landscape of trade facilitation. However due to its complexity and the need to improve the efficiency of trade flows, as well as their practical need to support decision making in trade operations, and the growing availability of data, more comprehensive approaches are becoming relevant in facilitating trade.

Based on this background, this book provides a good understanding of Nigeria's business opportunities, capacities, issues, challenges and lessons, with a special interest in sustainably enhancing the nation's business ecosystem in the digital age. It examines the contributions of trade facilitation-related policies, programmes, tools and initiatives towards fostering trade and business opportunities in the face of increasing non-tariff barriers, asymmetries and opacity that highly characterizes Nigeria's business landscape. The publication also comprises a selection of well-research articles that has the potential to better illuminate trade facilitation challenges in Nigeria. It also purports to improve the quality of trade facilitation policy making processes and programming in Nigeria.

This book provides different perspectives and roadmaps on these issues and argues that the future of African trade will need to reinvent itself not only to address these challenges, but also to cope with mass individualization on the one hand while exploiting business applications of digitization on the other hand. However, one of the essential challenges will be to find a compromise between these two developments—in alignment with the known triple bottom line of sustainability.

Invariably, these discussions are of importance because they draw attention to the contribution that Science, Technology and Innovation (STI) discoveries make to the wider Nigerian economy. The analysis focuses on how improvements in the border processes result in a significant increase in observed trade and commerce. The issues examined in the book are both relevant and timely. As a matter of fact, the issues bordering on doing business in Nigeria, regional integration and trade facilitation have taken a front burner in both sustainable business development policy and intellectual discourse in Nigeria. Since the launch of the African Continental Free Trade Area (AfCFTA) in March 2018, as well as its signing in July 2019, there have been academic and political processes towards deploying digital trade as an potent tool for domesticating the continental initiative in Nigeria.

1.2 Bracing for the Future of Trade and Unlocking Its Opportunities

Data and innovation, being the lifeblood of digital trade, digitizing commerce is an effective and innovative approach to unlocking Nigeria's full potential, thereby making Nigerian companies more competitive in the deployment of e-solutions, in alignment with international standards. Though framework adaptation is still being discussed, it is relevant to note that existing WTO rules and agreements cover digital trade (OECD 2019a).

The digital economy is driving the patterns and expansion of commerce, employment and economic transformation. According to the OECD, digitalization has reduced cost of global trade, connected a greater number of businesses, diffused innovations, and facilitated the co-ordination of global value chains. This has resulted in new challenges for trade policy makers beyond managing digital disruption and ensuring that the opportunities and benefits from digital trade can be realized and shared more inclusively. More specifically, digital trade encompasses digitally enabled transactions in trade in goods and services that can be digitally or physically delivered such as software, e-books, data, hotel booking, etc. it also encompasses business-to-business transactions within global value chains, as well as transactions between consumers or businesses purchasing from each other through online platforms. The opportunities and challenges arising from the future of trade can be addressed through digitization, and innovative development strategies that focus on technology-aided industrialization, trade and investment facilitation, creating an enabling business ecosystem and investment in human capital.

This is timely and relevant to Nigeria's socio-economic and political trajectory as well as those of other African countries as they brace up for the AfCFTA implementation. It is on record that the Central Bank of Nigeria (CBN) and Nigeria's National Assembly have 'shielded away' from crafting policy statements/acts that should govern the operational modality of blockchain. Their reason is not far-fetched, as there are limited information to the understanding of the multifaceted dynamics of modern technological tools like blockchain. Hence, this proposed study will be one of such attempts to provide such information and research-based evidence that can be leveraged upon to come up with policies to govern the operations of digital trade, based on its potential growth and attendant risks.

With the increasing digitization of the global value chains, low hanging sustainable development milestones could be achieved in Nigeria if it could leverage digitalization for unlocking the opportunities for the future of trade. As a result of globalization, technological developments, logistics and supply chains are increasingly being confronted by the unprecedented challenges of advancement in internet technologies, climate change, which all require radical solutions, while also offering huge opportunities.

Over the last decade, Nigeria has experienced significant economic changes partly due to the gradual digitization of its economic services. It is crucial to note that the global digital economy will revolutionize value chains and introduce different models for the production and consumption of goods and services. The digital trade is very crucial in the service sector in the sense that many of the technologies that will shape a digital economy apply directly to service delivery. This sector, therefore requires policy and capacity attention in order for it to maximally benefit from the ongoing global digitization within the AfCFTA window. In view of this, Artificial Intelligence (AI) solutions may provide inexpensive customized services in fields such as accounting, commerce, maritime, exports, imports, insurance, law, finance, health diagnostics and retail. For instance, the role of purpose-built robots in automating the fields of delivery, construction, cleaning and personal care. In other words, telepresence and mixed reality could allow off-site experts to guide low-skill on-site workers through complex tasks. Digital trade within the African marketplace will offer many opportunities and challenges for the Nigerian Government depending on how the Government recognizes, rethinks and responds proactively based on its current policy and programme planning assumptions. In other words, much more socio-economic and political activities may become digitally intermediated, customized, and globally distributed. Rapidly changing attitudes, business adoption, consumer acceptance and global applicability have informed the conversation about blockchain technology from stereotypical perspectives to an entirely new world of national e-commerce and digital strategies.

In spite of its four decades leadership role in enhancing regional integration in West Africa via the Economic Community of West Africa States

(ECOWAS), as well as other related African regional transformation matters, the global community found it difficult to understand why Nigeria was reluctant to sign the CFTA, alongside its neighbour Benin. One of the part-reasons is the dire need to embark on a country-wide consultations on the potential impacts of CFTA on the Nigerian economy, with particular reference on the fact that the Nigeran market will be flooded by goods from other African and non-African countries, thereby undermining domestic manufacturing and agribusiness capacities, many of which are currently producing below their potentials. However, Nigeria became signatory to the CFTA in July 2019.

At this pivotal time towards its economic trajectory, and from a data-driven policy perspective, Nigeria was reluctant to participate in the CFTA largely because of its businesses' low level of preparedness for the future of trade, economics and technology. Thus, the CFTA will further require Nigerian businesses and Government to brace themselves towards paving the way for a more digitalized trade, thereby creating a sustainable economy. For instance, there is a growing wave of businesses which adopt block chain (BC) technology in tracking something of value across the respective supply chains, therefore instilling consumer confidence. Nigerian could leverage on BC technology across all its economic sectors, including tracking and connecting buyers and sellers of millions of crude oil barrels. Having being signatory to the AfCFTA, the role of digital trade cannot be overemphasized as Nigeria prepares itself for the new ways of thinking, disruptive ways of life, overturning powerful institutions, and transforming business environments.

The window of opportunity towards brace Nigeria for the future of digital trade requires stronger, more urgent and more effective management actions at global, regional and national scales. As a signator to the AfCFTA, increasing national priority focus should be on the adoption of digital tools in accelerating trade and investment facilitation, that is, a trade and investment agreement that deals with these challenges, while building a multilateral-based international digital economy regime.

Its virile services sector, which has overtaken both agriculture and manufacturing sectors to become the biggest sector in the Nigerian economy, and representing about 58% in 2017. With some of the least developed digital tools in the world, the effective adoption of digitization and related blockchain technologies is still relatively new among most businesses in Nigeria. This provides both huge opportunities and challenges towards shaping the market and creating an enabling ecosystem for digitization to positively transform and flourish Nigerian businesses.

The trends reveal that an increasing number of SMEs are prepared to evolve rapidly towards contributing and benefiting from digital trade. The digital revolution era is becoming increasingly competitive as Nigerian MSMEs braces themselves to become more agile and responsive to market opportunities generated by digitization. This digital transformation is being driven by mass adoption of cutting-edge technologies and an upsurge in the use of smart mobile phones by a huge percentage of the population. Across the breadth of the sectors, from manufacturing, banking, agriculture and government, leveraging on digitization via the adoption of apps, platforms, smartphones, etc. towards complementing existing trade facilitation options requires rapidly increasing adoption of digital tools and technologies, hence transforming the way businesses are conducted in Nigeria, and bracing up for the future of trade on the continent.

1.3 Setting the Stage

The first two chapters portray Nigeria's readiness for digitization and explore what it means to develop a digital economy. These chapters discuss digitization from national, regional and global perspectives in order to set the tone for the subsequent issues in the book. In Chapter 2, Ndah Abu Ali and Gbadebo Odularu review Nigeria's experience in unlocking digital trade opportunities via e-commerce platforms. They argue that digital trade along the lines taken by the United States and China may offer a workable policy space where new wealth can be generated and sustainable jobs created, especially for the teeming youth population. In fact, a digitalized Nigerian economy would rapidly strengthen its institutional and regulatory framework which will be required to open economic space to MSMEs for a high, sustained and inclusive growth. In other words, bracing for the future of trade requires enacting reforms that break with the past towards opening globally digital economic space for job creation and wealth generation.

The trade facilitation and logistics performance of the Kingdom of Saudi Arabia (KSA) were discussed by Munaya A. Asiri and Gbadebo Odularu in Chapter 3. This chapter presents how Nigeria could take lessons from KSA's policy attempts at simplifying and harmonizing formalities, procedures and the related exchange of information and documents between the various partners in the supply chain in the digital age. Thus, upgrading the business ecosystem to become digitally enabling is the single most important policy choice for accelerating inclusive growth. In Chapter 4, Ndah Abu Ali reviews in details, the specific sectoral measures for facilitating trade under Nigeria's WTO Obligations. The selected sectors for discussion are fish, oil, gas and foreign exchange.

Abiola Abidemi Akinsanya, in Chapter 5, examines the need for innovative strategies for optimizing aid-for trade towards enhancing transport infrastructure and intra-regional trade facilitation in Nigeria and West Africa. It argues that AfT is a powerful policy instrument for minimizing trade costs, and facilitating digital trade in Nigeria, as well as within its West African regional neighbours.

In Chapter 6, Olusola Omoju provides evidence-based recommendations to the Nigerian Government on harnessing AfCFTA for economic diversification and expansion. Its policy recommendations fall under the umbrella of ensuring that trade logistics and infrastructure are efficient in order to enhance competitiveness of the Nigerian economy in the digital age and within the AfCFTA space.

In Chapter 7, Jonathan Adeyemi Aremu chronicles the evolution of Nigeria's regional and international trade agreements from a historical perspective. It provides strategies for negotiating Nigeria's trade agreements and forging a modern industrialized economy that capitalizes on unlocking the nation's digital trade potentials in alignment with the National Trade Policy and the National Economic Recovery Growth Plan (NERGP).

In response to the objective of this book which is to understand of how Nigeria is bracing itself for the future of trade, Chapter 8 presents selected digitization-enable trade facilitation tools for business problem-solving and trade decision-making options in Nigeria.

References

OECD. (2019a), 'Trade in the Digital Era'. OECD Going Digital Policy Note, OECD, Paris. Available online at: http://www.oecd.org/going-digital/trade-in-the-digitalera.pdf.

OECD. (2019b), 'Meeting of the OECD Council at Ministerial Level'. Paris, 22–23, May 2019. Available online at: http://www.oecd.org/mcm/documents/KIP%20-%20CMIN(2019)2%20-%20EN%20.pdf.

CHAPTER 2

Preparing Nigeria for Digital Trade Within the WTO E-commerce Negotiations: Issues and Policy Directions

Ndah Abu Ali and Gbadebo Odularu

2.1 Introduction

Digitalization has become a strong driver for inclusive growth and development. It supports trade creation, efficiency, and access to market.[1] Digital solutions are used to sell and deliver products and services while

[1] Legborsi Nuka Nwiabu, concept Note on Public–Private Dialogue (PPD) on Existing and Emerging Issues related to E-commerce and Digital Economy in Nigeria, submitted to Federal Ministry of Industry, Trade and Investment, 2019.

N. A. Ali (✉)
Federal Ministry of Industry, Trade and Investment, Abuja, Nigeria

G. Odularu
Department of Economics and Finance, Bay Atlantic
University, Washington, D.C., USA
e-mail: g.odularu@ahusc.net

G. Odularu (ed.), *Strategic Policy Options for Bracing Nigeria for the Future of Trade*,
https://doi.org/10.1007/978-3-030-34552-5_2

businesses move data across borders as an intrinsic part of their daily operations.[2]

The evolution in telecommunications capability across the world has made trade possible through electronic means (cross-border e-commerce). Hope and Sauli (2019), noted that research from eMarketer designated e-commerce global website sales in 2016 to be above US$22 trillion with increased projection annually. In today's discussion, the inclusion of digital issues in some bilateral and regional trade agreements signals the importance of trade in digital goods and services, as well as cross-border data flows, for trading system.

E-commerce today is a defining feature of the new economy and would continue to transform both international and domestic markets given its importance to trade. However, this transformation truly required a new framework as well as trade rules to govern its activities/operations. It is against this background that, some developed parties[3] within the WTO seeks to develop rules to regulate its operations.

76 partners[4] including the European Union and 48 other members of the World Trade Organization (WTO) on 25 January 2019 at the World Economic Forum in Davos, decided to start negotiations to put in place global rules on electronic commerce. Nigeria did not only endorse the launch but also confirm intention to commence WTO negotiations on trade-related aspects of electronic commerce. In the Joint Statement, the members seek to achieve a high standard outcome that would build on existing WTO Agreements and framework. This declaration came exactly

[2] Ibid.

[3] EU as block, Canada and Australia became the early proponent that seeks to develop rules in the WTO to regulate e-commerce operations.

[4] Albania; Argentina; Australia; Bahrain, Kingdom of; Brazil; Brunei Darussalam; Canada; Chile; China; Colombia; Costa Rica; El Salvador; European Union; Georgia; Honduras; Hong Kong, China; Iceland; Israel; Japan; Kazakhstan; Korea, Republic of; Kuwait, the State of; Lao PDR; Liechtenstein; Malaysia; Mexico; Moldova, Republic of; Mongolia; Montenegro; Myanmar; New Zealand; Nicaragua; Nigeria; Norway; Panama; Paraguay; Peru; Qatar; Russian Federation; Singapore; Switzerland; Chinese Taipei; Thailand; the former Yugoslav Republic of Macedonia; Turkey; Ukraine; United Arab Emirates; United States; and Uruguay issued a joint statement on the need to regulate e-commerce. The members recognized and agreed to take into account the unique opportunities and challenges faced by Members, including developing countries and LDCs, as well as by micro, small and medium-sized enterprises, in relation to electronic commerce.

one year after the successful exploratory talks that took place in the context of the e-commerce Joint Statement[5] initiative launched during the 11th WTO Ministerial Conference held in Buenos Aires, Argentina in December 2017.

Members that ascribed to the e-commerce discussions agreed to negotiate new rules to deal with trade issues including liberalization, consumer protection measures, efficiency measures, security-enhancing measures, and the development dimension of e-commerce.[6] The supporter on the subject matter believes that it's an important element for the global digital economy growth and it would further ensure that cross-border e-commerce is all-inclusive. In addition, it is further assured that e-commerce will promote development and benefit Micro Small and Medium Enterprises (MSMEs). However, Members standing against the negotiations particularly from the developing countries and least developing countries (LDCs) cited issue of regulatory capacity and infrastructure gaps thus posing a serious threat to development. In their view, developmental issues covered by the WTO Doha Round should take precedence over a new set of negotiations on e-commerce matter.[7]

Digital economy is fast evolving even as global internet traffic was 66 times higher in 2019 than in 2005 (UNCTAD 2019). The rapid growth of the Internet could aid the expansion of the digital landscape, impacted business operations, commercial transactions, and professional interactions and general life being. Back home in Nigeria, the Nigerian Communication Commission (NCC) reported that internet penetration has grown to about 102.8 million in June 2018 from 91.6 million in the previous year.[8]

[5] Nigeria and Benin Republic became the only two African countries that signed onto the Joint Statement in Argentina during the WTO 11th MC with a view to starting a formal negotiation on e-commerce rules.

[6] Africa and the WTO's E-commerce Agenda, Ashly Hope and Puseletso Sauli, 19th January 2018 cited from www.tralac.org on 30th May 2019.

[7] King & Spalding LLP, 2019, 'WTO Members Agree to Negotiate Rules on Global E-commerce' cited from https://www.lexology.com/library/detail.aspx?g on 8 June, 2019.

[8] 2018 NCC annual report cited from the Ernst & Young Research work on Digital Economy and value chain study.

Very good recognition of the digitalization of the economy is the fact that Nigeria had 92.3 million internet users in 2018 alone[9] with a projection to grow to 187.8 million internet users by 2023. The internet penetration amounted to 47.1% of the population in 2018 and is set to reach 84.5% in 2023.[10] Three countries Nigeria, Kenya, and South Africa dominate e-commerce sales in Africa. Nigeria, with a population of over 200 million people, is the most populous country in Africa and is the largest economy in terms of gross domestic product. The country also has the most e-commerce sites 40% of Africa's e-commerce ventures have headquarters in Nigeria.[11] Nevertheless, it has an internet penetration of about 48% compared to South Africa with a population of 55.5 million and a 54% internet penetration. Kenya with a population of 48.5 million and an impressive 79% internet penetration. Most of these problems persist but technology advances notably smartphones have given millions more Nigerians and Africans access to the Internet and mobile payment systems. Consequently, the continent may be the next emerging market to make significant strides in online shopping with estimates that the e-commerce sector in Africa generated $16.5 billion in revenue in 2017 and forecasts revenue of $29 billion by 2022.

Furthermore, Nigeria's e-commerce platform is growing faster as most Nigerians are embracing e-commerce as their preferred platform for buying and selling of goods and services. As a result of its rapid growth, e-commerce has started contributing to the growth of the Nigerian economy.[12] The National Bureau of Statistics (NBS) reported that ICT contribution to Nigeria's GDP has averaged 11.4% over the last 3 years (2015–2017). However, agriculture and the oil sector are still the major contributors to GDP.

E-commerce discussion has become a hot and sensitive topic globally but the key questions begging for answers include:

[9] NCC 2018.

[10] 2018 NCC Annual Report cited from Enrst and Young Research work on Digital Economy and Value Chain study.

[11] Ibid

[12] Update on Facilitating Broadband penetration to the National Industrial Policy and Competitiveness Advisory Council, Danbatta U.G 2018.

- How ready is Nigeria for this evolution despite the growth been witnessed?
- Does Nigeria have the right policies and institutional support for e-commerce activities? and
- What can be done at the international level to support Nigeria's current efforts and initiatives especially the legal framework of e-commerce in Nigeria?

This paper attempt to document/situate Nigeria's e-commerce ecosystem and her level of readiness to embraces the evolution of digital technology in international trade. In addition, how is the country preparing a pathway for an effective digital-led strategy on WTO e-commerce negotiations towards the global growth and development of SMEs.

2.2 A Brief Background on Digital Economy and E-commerce

A digital economy is made up of various components which include:

- **Platform Economy**: represents economic output generated largely from technological platforms. In general terms, the platform serves as a connector between interdependent people and the product or service they seek. Such platforms include Amazon, Google, and all e-commerce activities/transactions.
- **Gig Economy**: involves the exchange of labour for money between individuals or companies through digital platforms that facilitate matching between providers and consumers on a short-term and payment-by-task basis. It includes Outsourcing.
- **Industry 4.0**: also referred to as the fourth industrial revolution. It is the automation of manufacturing processes using customized and flexible mass production technologies.
- **Digital Services**: refers to automated services delivered through the Internet or electronic network that requires little to no human intervention. Such services include e-learning, music streaming, data analytics, robotics and artificial intelligence, machine learning and 3-D printing.

Table 2.1 Top 10 global tech companies

Rank	*Company*	*Revenue ($ b)*	*Countries*	*Employees (000)*	*Market cap ($ b)*
1.	Apple Inc.	229	USA	123	913
2.	Samsung Electronics	224	S/Korea	308	342
3.	Amazon	177	USA	541	801
4.	Foxconn	158	Taiwan	726	66
5.	Alphabet Inc.	111	USA	80	796
6.	Huawei	93	China	180	N/A
7.	Microsoft	90	USA	124	700
8.	Hitachi	85	Japan	303	32
9.	IBM	80	USA	386	145
10.	Sony	77	Japan	128	51

Source Fortune Global 500, 2017

The digital economy also encompasses government policy and regulation, electricity infrastructure, telecommunication industry, information and knowledge management systems, and intellectual property rights. Although, digital economy goes beyond the ICT industry considering that it is the foundation on which the digital economy relies. The size of the global digital economy was estimated as $11.5trillion about 15.5% of the global GDP in 2016.[13] The growth of the digital economy has been attributed majorly to the development of consumer-driven Internet.

Table 2.1 indicates that the top 10 ICT countries are USA, China, South Korea, and China with huge employment figures. Further, the ICT Development Index (IDI) is an index published annually by the International Telecommunication Union, an agency of the United Nations, which measures and compares developments in ICT between countries.

According to the IDI (see Fig. 2.1), the countries that have had the most developments in ICT in the last 3 years (2015–2017) include Iceland, South Korea, Switzerland, Denmark, and the United Kingdom. The Figure also shows relatively low IDI index for Nigeria, reflecting its current low level of digitalization, and the capacity for expansion.

[13] EY report 2018 submitted to Growth and Employment (GEM) Project.

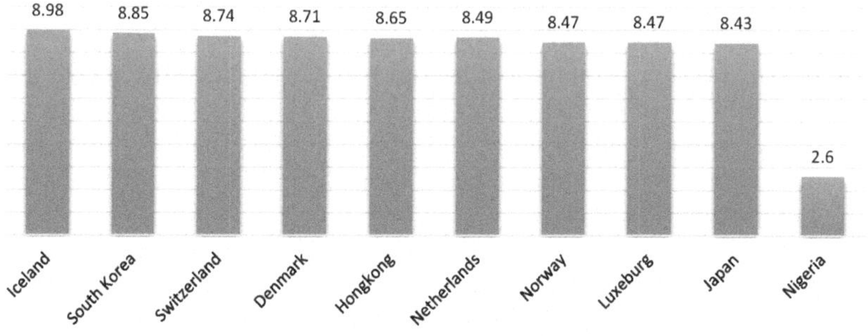

Fig. 2.1 Top 10 digital countries based on 2017 IDI index (*Source* International Telecommunication Union, 2018)

Table 2.2 shows the top 10 online trading firms in the World with Amazon in the United States having the largest revenue amounting to US$177 billion.

Table 2.2 Top 10 digital countries based on 2017 IDI index

S/N	*Company*	*Country*	*Revenue ($ b)*
1.	Amazon	USA	177
2.	Alibaba	China	15.6
3.	Walmart	USA	13
4.	Otto	Germany	12.1
5.	JD	China	11.6
6.	Priceline	USA	10.7
7.	eBay	USA	8.9
8.	Rakuten	Japan	7
9.	Zalando	Germany	4.1
10.	GroupOn	USA	3.1

Source MBASkool.com; Forbes

2.2.1 *Developed Member Countries Proposals on E-commerce*

- As part of EU's commitment to transparency and inclusiveness in the development of its trade policy, the EU in May 2019 made public its text proposal as endorsed by its Trade Ministers that new rules and obligations on e-commerce being part of the WTO negotiations on e-commerce.[14]
- The US proposals[15] posited that, the agreement applies to measures adopted or maintained by a party that affects trade by electronic means but does not apply to government procurement; to a service supplied in the exercise of Governmental authority or except for Article 14 (Open Government Data), to information held or processed by or on behalf of a party or measure related to information, including measures related to its collection.
- Brazil[16] via its communication dated 30 April 2019 presented a text-based proposal on e-commerce discussed under the Joint Statement process. Suggestions although not exhaustive and may be further revised, without prejudice to contributions or positions that Brazil may submit at a later stage.

2.2.2 *African Group Proposals on E-commerce Evolution*

In 2017 the Africa Group (AG) circulated a communication on e-commerce at the WTO with content that suggested a WTO multilateral framework on e-commerce could pose a serious threat for developing countries. The African Group posited that there seems to be a negative view of liberal trade principles with respect to e-commerce. Although, the

[14]The EU via its communication agreed in a JOINT STATEMENT ON ELECTRONIC COMMERCE EU PROPOSAL FOR WTO DISCIPLINES AND COMMITMENTS RELATING TO ELECTRONIC COMMERCE. The EU proposed to negotiate a series of WTO disciplines and commitments relating to electronic commerce and telecommunications services, aiming to enhance regulatory predictability, and improve market access conditions, to be incorporated in the schedules of the individual Members. The EU and its Member States maintain the possibility to define and implement cultural and audio-visual policies for the purposes of preserving their cultural diversity, including by not taking commitments on audio-visual services.

[15]USA recognize that economic growth and opportunities provided by digital trade and the importance of frameworks that promote consumer confidence in digital trade and of avoiding unnecessary barriers to its use and development.

[16]Brazilian proposal is attached as annexure III.

Group did not outrightly reject e-commerce but is not convinced that the benefits of e-commerce cannot be fully realized by African countries given the infrastructural and capacity gaps within its region. AG's presentation thus identified regulatory capacity as an issue for discussion with the submission seeking to discuss how member countries include mandatory disclosure of data, the disclosure of source codes and access to, and transfer of technology. Martin L. M. (2019)[17] noted that most African countries are simply not ready to effectively compete on e-commerce considering the low internet penetration in Africa.

2.3 Policy Issues on the WTO Work Programme on E-commerce

Under the current trading system of the WTO covered agreement, it is evident that there are no provisions which accommodate rules on e-commerce considering the evolution of digital technologies in international and domestic trade. During the second WTO Ministerial conference held in September 25, 1998, resistance from developing countries blocked the call by some members to review the existing WTO agreements with a view to starting negotiations new issues such as Government Procurement, Competition Policy, and electronic commerce. The resistance exists to date, but the question is whether if this is the best approach on negotiations that would help simplify existing realism on digital technology and commerce. Thus, the WTO Work Programme on Electronic Commerce was launched by the Geneva Ministerial Session in 1998, and this called for a comprehensive work programme trade-related aspect of global e-commerce. Figure 2.2 provides the analytical scheme on the setup of the WTO Work Programme on Electronic Commerce.

The 1998 WTO Ministerial Conference decisions on e-commerce were to be implemented by the three main councils of the WTO (Goods, Services, and TRIPS) with a promising launch on all the issues as depicted in Fig. 2.2 but have not gained any momentum. For instance, the work programme on moratorium for the application of Customs Duties on electronic transmission, WTO members are yet to come to an agreement on how to better address any of the many relevant trade-related aspects

[17] Martin Luther Munu, 2019, 'eCommerce and MSMEs: What Trade Rules Could Improve the Business Climate in Africa?'

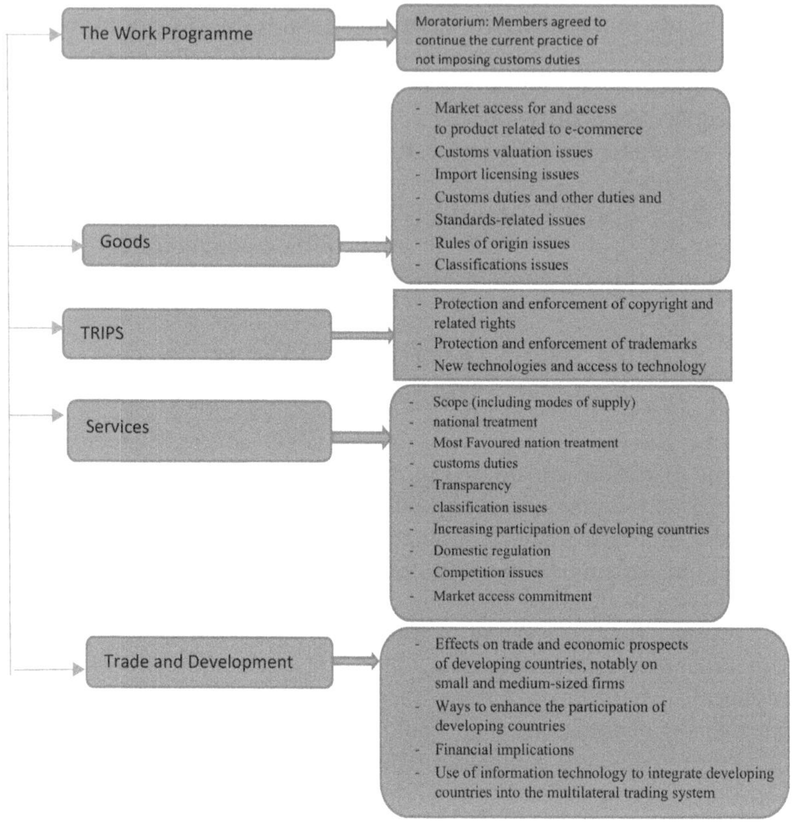

Fig. 2.2 Setup of the WTO work programme on electronic commerce (*Source* WTO: PATHS FORWARD ICTSD.ORG)

of global electronic commerce.[18] In addition, ICTSD 2018 Policy brief noted that:

> discussion over whether e-commerce falls within the scope of the General Agreement on Trade-in-services (GATS) mode 1 of services supply (cross border) or mode 2 (consumption abroad) or the debate over the interpretation of pertinent market access commitment made by individual members, and the exemptions established under GATS in a digital context.

[18] Updating the Multilateral Rule Book on E-Commerce: WTO Paths Forward, ICTSD Policy Brief, 2018.

The key questions include what are the customs, taxation, consumer protection, cross-border data management, other policy, systemic and commercial implications on business models such as services provided over the Internet or commitments on digitally delivered services?

Members agreed on the timeline of action with little or no significant progress to date (2019). According to the 2017 Joint statement on e-commerce to be operationalized and "initiate exploratory work toward future of WTO negotiations on trade-related aspects of electronic commerce"[19] a series of options must be considered (ICSTD 2018).

- The first option may be a trade in service approach, focusing on the GATS as the substantive blueprint in view of the fact that, technic discussions on e-commerce falls within the sub-sectoral scope of the GATS (e.g. telecommunications, distribution, transport, computer, and related, financial, etc.). Thus, developing a GATS disciplines on e-commerce would be the simplest approach towards any negotiations on e-commerce.
- A second option may be to follow a comprehensive approach covering e-commerce—related elements through disciplines in trade in services, goods, and trade-related intellectual property rights. This approach would encompass the various aspects of e-commerce business models and affected value chains by integrating them under a single initiative and thus providing further coherence.
- A third option may be to embrace a GATS and Goods approach with services at the core, plus a goods component. This approach would be complementary to the first option and would allow a more extensive coverage of e-commerce business models and affected value chains, but it would add complexity to a service only initiative.[20]

From Table 2.3, there are currently 29 Developing Countries, 3 LDCs[21] (**Benin, Lao PDR & Myanmar**)[22] that indicated interest to join the discussions on e-commerce. The African region is perceived as

[19] Updating the Multilateral Rule Book on E-Commerce: WTO Paths Forward, ICTSD Policy Brief, 2018.

[20] Ibid.

[21] This information is valid only as at time of writing the paper.

[22] This is at the date of writing the paper—26th June 2019.

Table 2.3 WTO members with interests in e-commerce

S/N	*Asia*	*Africa*	*Central America and Mexico*	*South America*	*G-20*	*Developed countries*	*Economies in transition not present in joint statement*
1.	Bahrain	Benin Rep.	Costa Rica	Argentina	Argentina	Canada	Armenia
2.	Brunei Darussalam	Nigeria	El Salvador	Brazil	Brazil	USA	Kyrgyzstan
3.	China		Honduras	Chile	China	European Union	Rep. of Moldova
4.	Hong Kong		Mexico	Colombia	Mexico	Japan	Tajikistan
5.	U.A.E.		Nicaragua	Paraguay	Turkey	New Zealand	
6.	Israel		Panama	Peru			
7.	Kuwait			Uruguay			
8.	Lao People's Democratic Republic						
9.	Malaysia						
10.	Mongolia						
11.	Myanmar						
12.	Qatar						
13.	Rep. of Korea						
14.	Singapore						
15.	Taiwan						
16.	Thailand						
17.	Turkey						

Source Author's analysis

the least represented with only Nigeria & Benin endorsing the joint statement. China, El Salvador, Georgia, Honduras, Mongolia, Nicaragua, Thailand, and the U.A.E joined the group to make it 76 members.

On one hand, despite developed countries robust consumer protection and data security regulations, many are still working on taxation-related issues, while on the other hand, several developing countries, the growth of e-commerce has led to significant legal and regulatory challenges, and where there are laws, it may be outdated, and they are undergoing review of new regulations to support new technologies such as cloud computing. The US submission on the WTO work programme on e-commerce addressed cross-border data flows and localization requirements, their trade implications, privacy concerns, as well as cloud computing (see Table 2.4).

The US communication on 17 December 2014, clearly specified what governments should do or should not do regarding cross-border information flows, localization requirements, privacy protection, and cloud computing. It also mentioned that cloud computing is covered under computer and related services (CPC 84). Furthermore, the United States put forward a non-paper, without any specific negotiating proposal but concentrated on new, comprehensive rules to liberalize e-commerce to enable the country to contribute positively to a flourishing digital economy. It included the prohibition of customs duties on digital products such as music, video, and software; securing national treatment and MFN for digital products; removal of barriers to free flow of information and data; promotion of free and open Internet; removal of localization requirements; and removal of requirements of forced technology transfer. It also mentioned faster and more transparent customs procedures, thus linking it to the provisions of the WTO Trade Facilitation Agreement, and how it can contribute to digital trade.

The Submission from Costa Rica, Hong Kong (China), Nigeria, Switzerland, Japan, and the separate customs territory of Taiwan, Penghu, Kinmen, and Matsu (6 members) proposed the establishment of a working group on electronic commerce. This working group could assess whether the clarification or strengthening of existing WTO rules is necessary, assess the priority needs of developing countries (particularly least developed countries) relating to the development of infrastructure for e-commerce, enable technical assistance and capacity building, etc. The Russian Federation also proposed the establishment of a working group on electronic commerce under the General Council, which will provide a forum for discussions on e-commerce issues and its development, including the possibility of developing international rules.

The submission from China and Pakistan dated November 16, 2016, listed measures that can be adapted to create a sound trade policy environment to facilitate cross-border e-commerce. It referred to exchange of information on regulatory measures, procedures such as those related to supplying services directly supporting cross-border e-commerce transactions, and other policies relevant to cross-border e-commerce such as consumer protection and privacy, publication of laws, regulations, and administrative measures, and inform the WTO of such publication sites,

Table 2.4 Elements of submissions on work programme for WTO e-commerce

United States	*Japan, Russia, Hong Kong and Pakistan*	*China*	*Africa group (including Nigeria)*	*Brunei, Darussalam; Colombia; Costa Rica; China, Pakistan and including Nigeria*	*MIKTA group*	*ASEAN group*
• Prohibiting digital custom duty • Promoting free and open market • Promoting transparency and stakeholder participation in the development of regulations and standards • Ensuring faster, more transparent custom procedures • Barring forced technology transfer • Preventing localization barrier • Recognizing conformity assessment procedure • Enabling cross-border data flows	• Barriers to e-commerce faced by stakeholders. Do the existing WTO framework and initiatives address these barriers? • Engaged in addressing identified specific issues with concrete suggestions and proposals in the appropriate for a summary of recent report is attached to the submission	• Moratorium on customs duties on electronic transmission • Facilitating cross-border e-commerce • Promoting paperless trading • Electronic signature, electronic authentication, and electronic contracts • Transparency • Develop and cooperation	• Challenges facing developing countries and the digital divide • Attempts to identify the type of national measures that some have employed to build national capabilities	• Trade facilitation and e-commerce • Infrastructure gaps to enable e commerce • Access to payment solutions • Online security	Consisting of Mexico, Indonesia, Korea, Turkey, and Australia maintained that the WTO should focus more attention on digital data, need to reflect on which aspects could be pursued in the immediate term under the existing WTO e-commerce work program and which aspects will be delivered in the long term after further analysis, discussion and cooperation	MEMBERS focus on how e-commerce can help MSMEs from developing countries. Developing facilitative trade rules may support MSMEs foray into e-commerce by reducing exposure to regulatory uncertainty

Source Author's design

make available and update regularly the procedures for import and export of goods under cross-border e-commerce, and set up enquiry points.

Some developing countries made written submissions to the work programme, but overall, the participation of developing countries in terms of written submissions was moderate and of least developed countries, almost non-existent. The core concern of many developing countries was that they should have the policy space to promote national digital industrial development, give subsidies, offer tax benefits, protect infant industry, and have the right to use local content requirements.

Developing countries have expressed concerns about their capabilities to implement new regulations at a pace fast enough to keep up with technological changes. Several new services have evolved in the context of e-commerce, and there are differences among countries on whether electronically traded services should be classified under Mode 1 or Mode 2. Due to such differences in views across countries, there was a consensus that e-commerce falls under the scope of the existing WTO agreements and no new trade rules should be created for e-commerce.[23]

Currently, there are two sections of this e-commerce negotiation which include the on-going negotiations group and other group undergoing studies and research towards development. Overall, if one examines the communication from WTO members between July and November 2016 till date, it is clear that a number of developed countries and many developing countries opined that e-commerce will support development; members were keen on more dedicated discussions on e-commerce, and they would like to engage in a more structured manner.

2.4 Benefits of E-commerce

Although the benefits from e-commerce does not occur automatically, it is widely acknowledged that it presents greater opportunities for small companies to enter global markets and penetrate global value chains. Hope and Sauli (2019) noted that using the Internet, small and medium enterprises could export and import goods and services with little infrastructure. E-commerce advocates argued that it is cheaper to maintain a website and compete on a larger scale than to maintain large business premises thus e-commerce could lower production and trading costs and

[23] Wunsch-Vincent and McIntosh (2005).

saves time.[24] In addition, for businesses, e-commerce helps to lower the cost of advertisement and low barriers to entries.

According to the proponents, the WTO rules on e-commerce targets at enhancing opportunities and addressing challenges of e-commerce in both developed and developing countries. The negotiations are expected to improve the multilateral legal framework that consumers and businesses, especially smaller ones could rely on to make it easier and safer to buy, sell, and do business online. The expected outcome would include but not limited to:

i. Improve consumers' trust in the online environment and combat cybercrime
ii. Tackle barriers that prevent cross-border sales
iii. Guarantee validity of e-contract and e-signatures
iv. Permanently ban customs duties on electronic transmissions
v. Address forced data localization requirements and forced disclosure of source code
vi. E-commerce platforms are indispensable in enabling MSMES to gain access to markets. E-commerce provides opportunities to mainstream the informal economy into the formal economy.

During an interactive session organized by the Federal Ministry of Industry, Trade and Investment with relevant stakeholders on e-commerce and digital trade, participants noted that other accrued benefits of e-commerce for Nigeria may include:

i. Support for economic development;
ii. Improve business communication and coordination thereby facilitating globalization;
iii. Facilitate Trade,
iv. Reduce cost of business operation, transaction, procurement, and material cost;
v. Reduce cost of production and marketing;
vi. It can be a driver of economic growth, inclusive trade, and job-creation

[24] Africa and the WTO's E-commerce Agenda, Ashly Hope and Puseletso Sauli, 19th January 2018 cited from www.tralac.org on 30th May 2019.

vii. It can also be a catalyst for the transition of trade transactions involving micro, small, and medium-sized enterprises (MSMEs) from the informal to the formal sector and from domestic to international markets.
viii. Improve ICT and transport connectivity, better legal and regulatory frameworks and new e-commerce and payment solutions are enabling more countries to take advantage of opportunities offered by online commerce, and
ix. Better customer service such as quicker response.

Ahmed and Richard (2015)[25] noted that the benefits of e-commerce can be identified by tangible and intangible benefits. Tangible on one hand includes business efficiency, the transformation of traditional market, retained and expanded customer base and acquisition of niche market. While on the other hand, intangible consist of consumer loyalty and convenient shopping.

2.5 The Nigerian ICT Economy and the Regulatory Framework

Nigeria is principally an oil-based economy with revenue from the sale of crude oil constituting about 75% of its consolidated budgetary revenues and close to 90% of its exports. The country remains the largest economy in Africa ahead of the likes of South Africa, Angola, Kenya, and others. According to the NBS report 2017, ICT contribution to Nigeria's GDP has averaged 11.4% over the last 3 years (2015–2017). However, agriculture and the oil sector remain the major contributors to GDP (Nigerian Bureau of Statistics Report, 2017).

In Nigeria, as depicted in Fig. 2.3, the primary regulatory for ICT and all digital matters is the Federal Ministry of Communication Technology (FMCT). The Ministry coordinates and monitors the implementation of the government's ICT policies and promotes the use and development of technology in Nigeria. The FMCT is supported by several regulatory bodies including the Nigerian Communications Commission, the

[25] *International Journal of Scientific Engineering and Applied Science (IJSEAS)* Volume 1, issue 3, E-commerce, Problems and Prospect in Nigeria, Ahmed Lawal and Richard Chukwu Ogbu, June 2015.

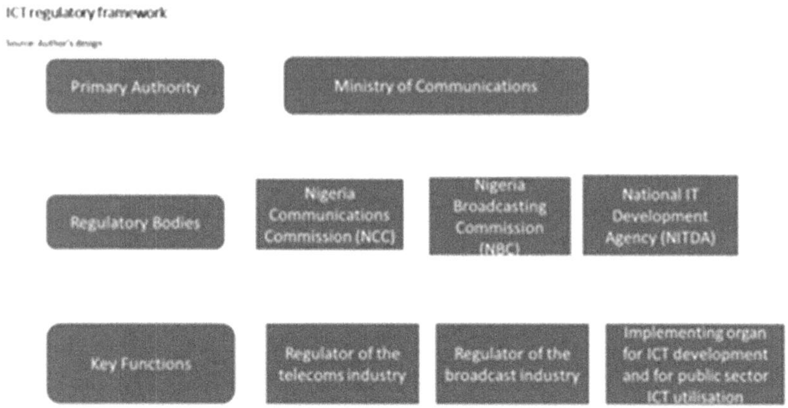

Fig. 2.3 A diagram showing the components of the Nigerian ICT regulatory framework (*Source* NITDA, 2018)

National Broadcasting Commission and the National Information Technology Development Agency (NITDA).

The Nigerian Communications Commission (NCC) regulates the telecommunications sector. Its functions include licensing of operators, monitoring of tariffs and service quality and customer protection. The National Broadcasting Commission (NBC) regulates the broadcasting industry. It issues licenses, assigns broadcast frequencies, and monitors compliance. The National Information Technology Development Agency (NITDA) implements the government's National IT policy. It was established by the NITDA Act 2007 which empowers it to plan, promote, and develop IT penetration. Figure 2.3 presents a schema of the Nigerian ICT regulatory framework.

2.6 Business Factors Impacting the Nigerian Digital Economy

Business factors impacting the digital economy in Nigeria can be classified into both internal and external factors. Basically, the internal factors include issues of skills storage, creativity and innovation, and availability of ICT equipment. While external factors consist of poor or lack of digital infrastructure, lack of funding support, High cost of data vs value (the

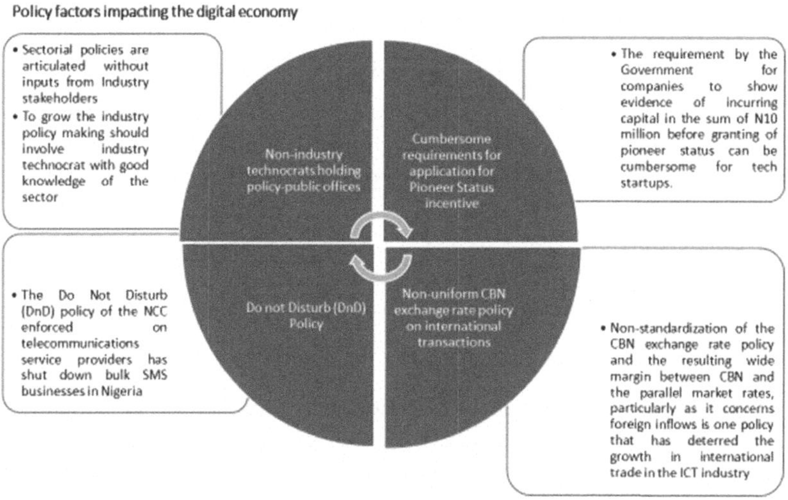

Fig. 2.4 Policy factors impacting the digital economy in Nigeria (*Source* EY Research work on Digital Economy 2018)

price of data in Nigeria is still relatively high compared to other developed countries. The telecommunications market is dominated by four key players MTN, 9mobile, Airtel, and GLO. Price plays a significant role in the consumption of data in Nigeria. Nigeria's internet data speed at 3.9 megabits per second (mbps) remains relatively slow compared to global standard of 7.2mbps (Akmai Technologies report 2018). Cybersecurity has been a major deterrent to participation in the digital economy, with various cases of cybercrime attacks in Nigeria. Some individuals still decide not to participate in the digital economy in order to eliminate this risk. The federal government estimated the annual cost of cybercrime in Nigeria to be about 0.08% of the country's GDP, which was about N75 billion in 2015.[26] The Cybercrime Act 2015 provides the legal, institutional, and regulatory framework for the prohibition, detection, and prevention of cybercrimes in Nigeria (Fig. 2.4).

[26] EY report 2018 submitted to Growth and Employment (GEM) Project.

2.7 A Glance at Nigeria's Situation and Its Readiness for Digitalization

Nigeria has set up a three-year ICT Roadmap (2017–2020) to facilitate the development of the ICT industry and increase its contribution to the nation's GDP. The Road map focuses on four pillars namely:

- Governance,
- Policy, Legal and Regulatory Framework
- Industry and Infrastructure
- Capacity Building

The country has also identified strategies to address some cross-cutting issues which are expected to create 2.5 million jobs and ensure broadband penetration to all parts of Nigeria by 2020. Some of the strategic steps being implemented by Nigeria in order to achieve the digitalization of its economy, include *inter alia*:

- **Establishment of a National Committee on E-commerce**: Taking note of e-commerce as an important driver of innovation, competitiveness and growth, with huge potentials for entrepreneurs and small and medium-sized enterprises (SMEs) development in Nigeria, the Federal Ministry of Industry, Trade and Investment convened the 1st Enlarged National Focal Point (ENFP) meeting in April 2019 with a view to assessing Nigeria's e-commerce ecosystem and readiness. Arising from that meeting it was agreed and resolved to establish a National Standing Committee on e-commerce.
- The National Committee on e-commerce primary task is to update all national, regional and global commitments, identifying new challenges and priorities, and affording particular attention to the effects resulting from the ubiquity of the Internet, technological convergence, high-speed networks, the digital economy, open government, and e-government, and the data revolution, without ignoring the need to continue expanding ICT access and use and close existing gaps.

The Objective of the National Committee on e-commerce is to advice, develop, and put forward recommendations towards formalizing and legalizing e-commerce including legislation for protection of consumers rights and data and the adoption of the relevant regulatory frameworks on e-commerce and digital economy with a view to supporting evidence-based policymaking. Specifically, the committee would help to:

- Harmonize existing legal and institutional framework for e-commerce and develop a national policy and strategy on e-commerce
- Identify areas/sectors in e-commerce value chain and support its development for access to the global e-commerce market space
- Provide backstopping and technical support to the Nigeria Trade negotiation on e-commerce
- Develop a scheme with a monitoring and evaluation framework built into ensure sustainability
- Identify areas of gaps and need for capacity building
- Suggest ways and means of mobilizing and raising funds for e-commerce policy advocacy.

The membership of the Committee[27] which is Chaired by the Permanent Secretary of Federal Ministry of Industry, Trade and Investment has members drawn from the Ministries Departments and Agencies (MDAs), Organized Private Sector (OPS), Civil Society, Media and Academia/Research Institutes/Universities as well as Donor Agencies/Development Partners.

2.7.1 Movers and Shakers of the Nigerian Digital and E-commerce Space

In addition to the Nigerian Government which provides the enabling ecosystem and regulatory framework for the realization of the country's digitalization potentials, selected private sector entities play significant roles in shaping the future of the digital economy. Some of these include:

Jumia

- Jumia in Nigeria was launched by the Africa Internet Group (AIG) in 2012. Two years later, Jumia introduced Black Friday in Nigeria, and

[27] List of the membership and the Terms of Reference is enclosed as annexure 1.

Jumia Force, an independent sales consultant program catering to populations that did not have access to the Internet. In 2017, Jumia was ranked for the second year in a row, in the MIT 50 Smartest Companies globally.

Konga

- Konga.com is a Nigerian electronic commerce company founded in July 2012 with headquarters in Lagos. The company serves a retail customer base that continues to grow exponentially, its range of services are designed to ensure optimum levels of convenience and customer satisfaction with the retail process; these services include its lowest price guarantee. In May 2018, Konga and Yudala merged to leverage the combined strengths of both companies to become the leading online and offline trading platform.

DealDey

- DealDey was launched in March 2011, as an online platform that features trade discounts being offered by merchants across Nigeria. Its philosophy is based in connecting buyers with sellers offering trade discounts. DealDey supports local businesses and in return, they support consumers with good savings, to create an opportunity for local merchants who want to attract new customers and consumers who want to save money and take advantage of services and activities.

Gloo Ng

- Gloo.ng is an electronic retailing service and corporate procurement engine, delivering a wide variety of high-quality brands of supermarket goods. Gloo.ng provides its clients with convenient, efficient, and affordable means of shopping for supermarket goods, saving them time and money.

Jiji

- Jiji.ng is an online marketplace that provides solutions to sell and buy products displayed on the platform. Sellers can post advertisements on the platforms, and buyers can purchase products by contacting the seller directly through the platform. The company is highly focused on its security and endeavours to resolve issues in a timely manner.

Cheki.com

- Cheki is an online marketplace for a wide range of quality vehicles. They offer a state-of-the-art advertising medium for users to buy and sell their cars, vans, bikes, trucks, and other vehicles.

Mall for Africa

- Mall for Africa is an African e-commerce solution provider. They provide a platform that allows buyers to purchase items from international stores. They also have a patented app, platform, and payment system to give users access to hundreds of US and UK e-commerce retailers and more than 8.5 billion products combined.

Cars45

- Cars45 is a Nigerian car buying service that allows sellers and buyers of Nigerian used cars to exchange value quickly, cheaply and with unhindered access to independent relevant information required for decision-making. They also have inspection centres for the cars at strategic locations.

Webmall

- WebMall, launched in 2013, is one of Nigeria's leading e-commerce platforms. They provide online and offline tools to promote the businesses of merchants as well as affordable merchant plans. Customers have access to an extensive range of high-quality products and an excellent logistics service.

Payporte

- Payporte is an online retail store with operational offices across the United States of America, the United Kingdom, and China.

Table 2.5 Top 10 e-commerce companies

S/N	*Name*	*Ownership*	*Revenue (N million)*	*Market share (%)*
1.	Jumia	Local	225,920	5.6
2.	Konga	Local	141,658	3.5
3.	DealDey	Local	93,494	2.3
4.	Payporter	Local	83,578	2.1
5.	Cheki.com	Local	77,912	1.9
6.	Mall for Africa	Local	65,163	1.6
7.	Cars45	Local	45,331	1.1
8.	Gloo Ng	Local	36,831	0.9
9.	Jiji	Local	26,915	0.7
10.	Webmall	Local	9916	0.2
	Top 10 prayers		806,718	20.1
	Others		3,203,282	79.9
	Total		4,010,000	100.0

Source Ernst & Young Research (2018)

Launched on the 25th day of September 2014, Payporte has an online and offline presence to meet customers in order to offer an extensive array of products on one platform, at the best prices.

Table 2.5 presents Nigeria's top 10 e-commerce companies that are currently driving and shaping the sector.

2.8 Selected Challenges of E-commerce Implementation in Nigeria

Digital infrastructure including the high cost of internet connectivity in Nigeria remains a major issue requiring government intervention. Nigeria's internet penetration remains very low and it is one of the major threats to e-commerce implementation in the country. Below are succinct challenges of e-commerce in Nigeria:

- **Trust**: Nigeria is currently fighting corruption, and the issue of online scams remains a big factor, hence, trading online becomes a misrepresentation. A place where phishing is regular, individuals are distrustful about listing their private information online. Some customers are yet to figure out how they can trade online, while others are concerned about being scammed, and the lack of trust from Nigerian consumers is a huge hindrance for e-commerce business in Nigeria.

- **Payment Solutions**: issues on creating an enabling regulatory environment, increase interoperability among e-payment platforms, access to competitive payment solutions is a critical facilitator and promote mobile payments and other cashless solutions.
- **ICT Infrastructure and Services**: Affordable and reliable ICT infrastructure is fundamental to achieve an inclusive digital economy. Foster cooperation among all stakeholders in support of the digital transformation and bridge the digital divide through digital skills and provision of access to fast and reliable Internet for all.
- **Trade Logistics: Transport and Trade Facilitation**: Streamline customs clearance to limit obstacle for the growth of e-commerce, Regional Trade Facilitation programmes aimed at promoting regional integration. Foster monitoring and simplification system for trade procedures, facilitate the integration of trade and logistics services, government to support the development of e-commerce delivery solutions across the packaging-shipping-delivery chain of e-commerce.
- **E-commerce Skill Development**: Educate consumers and merchants on the costs and benefits of cashless transactions, e-commerce courses should be included in the curriculum of tertiary education and Provision of access to finance by creating a robust financial architecture that funds innovation and entrepreneurship at all points across the e-commerce value chain.

2.9 Policy Recommendations on Tapping the Full Potentials of Digital Trade

Nigeria believes that e-commerce is an economic reality that is unlocking the potentials of economies by triggering growth and creating wealth and jobs. However, Nigeria is mindful of the supply side constraints. When an initiative seeks to engage many countries with diverse levels of economic development, a systemic approach would be needed to effectively enable universal participation. If e-commerce is to deliver shared benefits to the WTO membership at large proper attention must be paid to the digital divide. The necessary infrastructure and accompanying access must be assured for communities in developing countries that will otherwise be even more marginalized as the rest of the world benefits from e-commerce. In order to effectively benefit from e-commerce operations, authors key recommendations for Nigeria and other developing members of the WTO includes the need to:

- Regulate digital platform and develop national marketing platform with a view to gaining from e-commerce.
- Develop domestic digital capacity and digital infrastructure. Increased infrastructure investments will improve the competitive environment in the ICT industry by providing access to previously unexplored markets in the country. Improved power supply would significantly reduce the high operating cost incurred in this sector.
- Strengthen ICT and broadband infrastructure, enhance national e-commerce platforms' capacities and regulate increasingly powerful digital platforms through the implementation of applicable competition laws.
- Harness digital start-ups through Digital Innovations Hubs. NITDA has created an ICT innovation hub, which has the capacity to produce e-literate groups from low skilled or low paid workers, unemployed people, and those with disabilities who do not have access to these ICT facilities.
- Extract technical assistance, support, e-commerce Ecosystem and experiences from more advanced economies.
- Ensure proper regulatory settings enabler and support digital development, especially, digital development clarity on laws around digital documents, signatures, payments, and contracts. It should be noted that a robust competition enforcement and consumer protection measures should be in place to ensure consumers are getting the best prices and services and can seek redress as well as frameworks to ensure consumers information is kept safe.

References

Ahmed Lawal and Richard Chukwu Ogbu, (2015), 'E-commerce, Problems and Prospect in Nigeria', *International Journal of Scientific Engineering and Applied Science (IJSEAS)* Volume 1, issue 3, 2015.

Ashly Hope and Puseletso Sauli, (2019), 'Africa and the WTO's E-commerce Agenda', 19th January 2018 cited from www.tralac.org on 30th May 2019.

Ernst & Young, (2018), Report on Digital Economy Commissioned by World Bank Growth and Employment (GEM) Project.

ICTSD, (2018), 'Updating the Multilateral Rule Book on E-Commerce: WTO Paths Forward', ICTSD Policy Brief, 2018.

King & Spalding LLP, (2019), 'WTO Members Agree to Negotiate Rules on Global E-commerce' cited from https://www.lexology.com/library/detail.aspx?g on 8 June, 2019.

Legborsi Nuka Nwiabu, (2019), 'Existing and Emerging Issues related to E-commerce and Digital Economy in Nigeria', submitted to Federal Ministry of Industry, Trade and Investment, 2019.

Martin Luther Munu, (2019), 'eCommerce and MSMEs: What Trade Rules Could Improve the Business Climate in Africa?'

Sacha Wunsch-Vincent and Joanna McIntosh, (2005), 'WTO, E-commerce and Information Technologies: From the Uruguay Round Through the Doha Development Agenda: A Report to the UN ICT Task Force'.

UNCTAD's, (2019), 'eCommerce Week: From Digitalization to Development took place from 1–5 April at the Palais des Nations', Geneva.

CHAPTER 3

Trade Facilitation and Logistics Performance in Saudi Arabia: Lessons and Policy Directions for Nigeria in the Digital Age

Munaya A. Asiri and Gbadebo Odularu

3.1 An Overview of the Global Trade Patterns

International trade is the physical movement and electronic transfer of goods and services across national borders and it has been a major engine for economic growth and development in the world. However, overall trade costs remain excessively high in many developing countries of the region. Policies and factors affecting international trade costs are identified. National, regional, and international trade facilitation and logistics costs play a key role in the world economy. But there is one particular characteristic that distinguishes international logistics from Domestic

M. A. Asiri (✉)
General Authority for Statistics, Riyadh, Saudi Arabia
e-mail: mnoo311@hotmail.com

G. Odularu
Department of Economics and Finance, Bay Atlantic University, Washington, D.C., USA
e-mail: g.odularu@ahusc.net

G. Odularu (ed.), *Strategic Policy Options for Bracing Nigeria for the Future of Trade*,
https://doi.org/10.1007/978-3-030-34552-5_3

logistics and its impact on the global economy. One particular characteristic is the crossing of borders between two or more countries besides the complexity consisting of a mix of cultural, political, technological, and economic issues.

According to Fig. 3.1, the world had a total export of 17,814,095,058.78 in thousands of US$ and total imports of 16,125,913,021.13 in thousands of US$ leading to a positive trade balance of 1,688,182,037.66 in thousands of US$ The Effectively Applied Tariff Weighted Average (customs duty) for World is 4.57% and the Most Favored Nation (MFN) Weighted Average tariff is 7.74%. The trade growth is 1.50% compared to a world growth of 1.50%. GDP of World is 80,737,576,004,679.91 in current US$. World services export is 5,416,463,868,315.51 in Bop, current US$ and services import is 5,103,526,748,962.05 in Bop, current US$. World exports of goods and services as percentage of GDP is 36.95% and imports of goods and services as percentage of GDP is 34.75% (WITS).

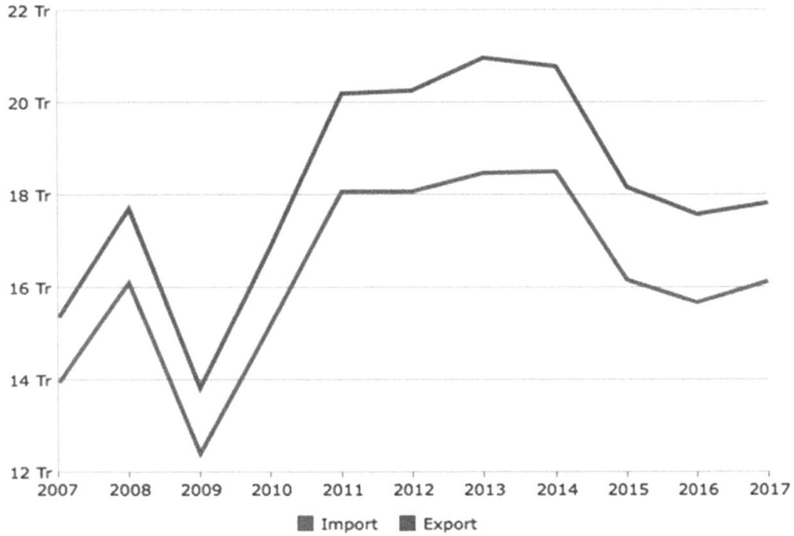

Fig. 3.1 Global export and import data (*Source* Authors' calculation and WITS)

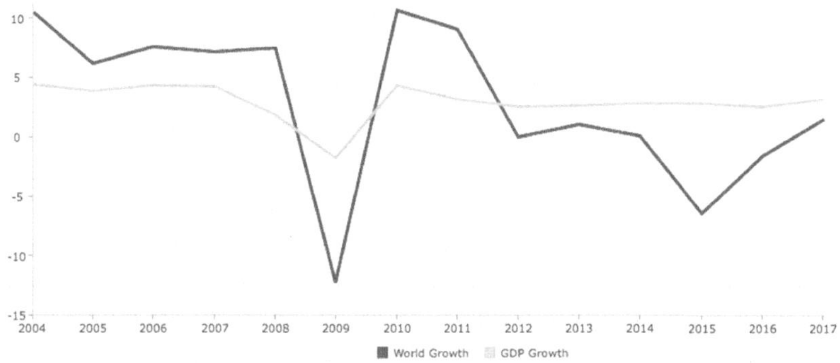

Fig. 3.2 Global growth and GDP increases (*Source* Authors' calculation and WITS)

The most important indicators that measure the trade performance are exports, imports, products, tariffs, GDP, and related envelopment Indicator such as customs. Thus, Fig. 3.2 explains world growth and GDP growth from 2004 to 2017. The GDP growth remained stable over the years except the period of 2007–2010 when the economic crisis happened. Most of the world countries have made a major effort to reduce barriers to trade and to make their economies more open and they have made significant progress in lowering trade tariffs and dismantling quota systems. International trade has increased and manufacturing has become more global, with developing, emerging and transition economies connecting with international supply and value chains in terms of both their exports and imports. The most important indicators that measure the trade performance are exports, imports, products, tariffs, GDP, and related envelopment Indicator.

Based on this background, this study aims to leverage on the lessons that Nigeria can learn in the trade facilitation and logistic performance and experience of Saudi Arabia and its place in the region. It will explore the strength and weaknesses of the different dimensions of its trade facilitation and logistics performance, as a basis for optimizing the trade facilitation space in Nigeria.

3.2 A Brief Review of Existing Literature

Trade-related complementary policies on transport and telecommunications services, customs procedures, port efficiency, standards and technical regulations, and flexibility of factor markets are increasingly seen as a key to enhancing a country's trade performance. Tariff reforms alone are insufficient. Much attention has been given to reforming soft and hard infrastructure for trade. The trade facilitation agenda comes as a complementary measure to vast trade liberalization efforts around the world over the past half-century, which have lowered tariff barriers significantly but left considerable non-tariff barriers in place. The main goal of trade facilitation is to help make trade across borders "imports and exports" easier, faster, and cheaper, and more predictable it is about simplifying and harmonizing formalities, procedures, and the related exchange of information and documents between the various partners in the supply chain. It also encompasses all governmental agencies that intervene in the transit of goods and the various commercial entities that conduct business and move the goods.

Arvis et al. suggest that trade facilitation policy should pay special attention to improving transport and logistics performance, particularly in low-income countries and in sub-Saharan Africa, where these could have highly significant impacts on trade costs.

Felipe and Kumar, Fink et al., Hammar, Moïsé, Otsuki, and Wilson et al. examine the relationship between trade facilitation and trade flows in various countries. They provide evidence that applying trade facilitation measures will result in substantial benefits that outweigh their costs. Furthermore, Hertel and Mirza used the World Bank's Logistics Performance Index (LPI) to apply thorough analysis to various trade facilitation dimensions. Overall, using several trade facilitation measures, previous studies have revealed that trade facilitation is expected to enhance trade flows and result in many benefits.

3.2.1 Logistics and Trade

Logistics is the one important function in business today. No marketing, manufacturing or project execution can succeed without logistics support. Logistics is the process of planning, implementing, and controlling procedures for the efficient and effective transportation and storage of goods, including services and related information, from the point of origin to the point of consumption. The goal of the logistics is to successfully meet customer satisfaction. This definition includes inbound, outbound, internal, and external movements. Logistics is defined by Bowersox as: "... a term which denotes a total approach to the management of the distribution process including all of those activities involved in physically moving raw materials, in process inventory and finished goods inventory from point of origin to point of use or consumption." In other words, logistics combines the traditionally defined areas of materials management and physical distribution. Every business establishment is aimed at providing quality, timely, and effective products or services to their customers as a means of retaining them and opening more customer doors. Logistics is very important in business for it actually leads to the ultimate consummation of the sales contract. Logistical support enables the actual movement, delivery, and transportation of goods or services from a seller to a buyer.

3.2.2 Importance of Logistics Performance

The World Bank's LPI uses as a starting point for the assessment of logistics performance. All these indicators are measured on a scale of 1 (low) to 5 (high). All the data used in the study are for the period of 2007–2016.

According to the World Bank, the six LPI dimensions to two main categories. The first category relates to main inputs to the supply chain (customs, infrastructure, and quality of logistics services). The second category involves service delivery performance outcomes, namely timeliness, ease of arranging international shipments, and tracking, and tracing. Logistics systems usually involve complex combinations of sequential activities. Poor performance in one dimension might be related to inconsistency among policy actions targeting other dimensions. For example, government restrictions on logistics services may enhance logistics quality but might increase shipment costs. Therefore, a policy program encompassing overall logistics performance improvement has a greater chance of yielding effective and sustainable results than partial reforms.

The World Bank provides source "international logistics" for supply chain and countries and it is a tool to help them to identify the challenges and opportunities they face in their performance on trade logistics and what they can do to improve their performance. The components analyzed in the international LPI were chosen by the World Bank based on recent theoretical and empirical research and on the practical experience of logistics professionals involved in international freight forwarding.

Also, World Bank has a section called "domestics logistics" Domestic logistics is the distribution of goods within a country. Managing logistics domestically is very different from managing logistics internationally because of the much narrower geographic scope in a domestic operation. Domestics use four major determinants of overall logistics performance to measure performance and they are Infrastructure, Services, Border procedures and time, and Supply chain reliability.

Domestic logistics can utilize a variety of transportation options for moving goods, out of which road transport is the most common preference. Domestically, road transport in itself also provides a variety of options while international logistics have limited transportation options and some would require only rail while others would require only flight or sea transport. International logistics may also involve using multiple transportation alternatives for a single transaction. There are some additional costs to be considered with regard to international logistics which include tariffs, government taxes, fees, and currency exchange fluctuations while in the domestics logistics, the costs involved include just store facilities, transportation, workers, and technology. In order to build relationships between businesses or between a business and the customers, trust is the most important factor, which decides on the nature of the relationship. It gets easier to build trustworthy relationships domestically but, in international cases, different country regulations, geography, and economic roadblocks present more challenges in building reliable relationship.

The levels of importance of logistics performance are measured by the five-point, in which 1 means very unimportant and 5 means very important. As for the level of satisfaction of logistics policy, 1 refers to very low and 5 refers to very high.

Faria et al. (2015), have found that the greatest obstacles are bureaucratic issues such as customs clearance time with physical inspection, a high number of agencies to import and export and a high number of documents required to allow the import and export. The quality and efficiency of logistics services can matter for international trade as a weak logistics infrastructure and operational processes can be a major obstacle to global trade integration. In countries with poor governance and where institutions governing trade transactions and procedures are weak, traders can face significant difficulties in dealing with public sector employees such as customs officials (Gani, 2017).

One of the major obstacles is additional costs such as time delays in shipping that can take several forms but ultimately, they increase the cost to firms that are then passed on to consumers.

There are gaps in logistics performance between the high-income group countries and the low and middle-income group of countries (Arvis et al., 2012). With regard to the "logistics gap" between the high-income countries, it is argued that the transport and logistics in the developing countries, including the supporting for integration into other global value chain "GVCs", still face very significant obstacles (Gani, 2017).

Several studies have suggested that investments in infrastructure may be associated with export growth and business development. One key issue in the literature is the condition of infrastructure. The difference in the condition of infrastructure (communication and transportation) among countries affects export performance more than the traditional trade barriers in developing countries.

Langley and Holcomb stated that integrated global logistics service is crucial for creating customer value. Richardson also suggested that the key factor for the development of international companies relies on their logistics and supply chain management ability. If an enterprise can make effective logistics plan and management, it will be able to obtain optimal integration of overall production processes and the global market demand, which would deal with the problems of production output and capital.

Existing studies on logistics and trade generally tend to show consistent outcomes and point to a general direction that there is a positive correlation between improved logistics and more trade. For example, Arvis et al. (2007, 2010) presented descriptive statistics suggesting a positive association between logistics performance and important outcome indicators such as trade openness. Other studies have shown that inefficiencies within the transportation infrastructure can have adverse effects on trade. For example, Dettmer et al., in their study on air cargo in South Africa, have concluded that a more liberal market for air cargo services could reduce transport costs and promote further integration.

Transport and logistics service (air and maritime connectivity and logistics performance) includes the whole range of transportation infrastructure (high speed roads, terminal facilities, storage warehouses, and runway length) and services from seaports, land-based transportation systems, as well as air transport. Transport is the most expensive component of trade logistics and an adequate infrastructure is required to facilitate transportation. High prices, poor service, and a lack of certainty in transport and logistics cannot engage any country in the world markets (Gani, 2017). Infrastructure, though still a constraint in developing countries, seems to be improving. While satisfaction with rail infrastructure is again low in all regions, satisfaction with infrastructure quality varies by infrastructure type (World Bank, 2014).

3.3 An Analysis of the Nigerian Economic Diversification and Trade Facilitation Landscape

Nigeria has one of the largest economies in Africa and, according to Goldman Sachs, one of the next 11 countries with a high potential of becoming among the world's largest economies in the twenty-first century. Nigeria with a population close to 200 million people is the most populous nation in Africa and is projected to be 480 million by 2050. Nigeria has a youthful population with over 36% between 15 and 35 years. It is advantageously located in the Gulf of Guinea with direct freight access to North America, South America, Europe, and Asia. Nigeria can be the production hub to access the developed markets of North America and Europe, which have a combined GDP of over US$43 trillion.

Nigeria's economy is the 26th largest in the world and the biggest in Africa where it is the leading oil exporter, with the largest natural gas reserves. As a result of its 2014 rebasing exercise, Nigeria's GDP almost doubled from US$270 billion in 2013 to US$510 billion in 2014, and its economy has become more services-driven (about 61% of GDP in 2016). This GDP increase by about 90% resulted from, inter alia, re-estimation of the contributions of certain sectors of the economy such as telecommunications, entertainment, and retail, which were previously not captured or underreported; the informal sector was re-estimated to account for about 44% of GDP.

Nigeria's economy recorded a strong growth of about 7% per year in the decade leading up to 2015, thanks to high world prices of oil and natural gas. However, the sharp fall in oil prices since the third quarter of 2014 has posed major challenges to the economy, which significantly slowed down to 2.7% in 2015 and further went into recession in 2016 with a growth rate of −1.5%. Exports declined by 45%, led by a sharp fall in revenue from oil from 23.4% of GDP in 2011 to 3.7% in 2015. Low export receipts (mainly from oil) subsequently induced lower domestic demand that has impacted the non-oil sector. Weaknesses in the business environment (e.g., unreliable and expensive electricity supply, and governance issues, including in the oil sector) have also played their part.

Nigeria is an original Member of the WTO and actively participates in the activities of the organization. However, despite its efforts to ensure compliance with its WTO obligations, Nigeria still lags behind with some 20 notifications. Nigeria is also a founding member of the Economic Community of West African States (ECOWAS) and is fully engaged in negotiations to establish a continental free trade area (CFTA) under the African Union by 2017. Negotiations between the EU and the West African States on an Economic Partnership Agreement (EPA) were concluded on June 30, 2014; Nigeria has not yet signed this agreement. Under the African Growth and Opportunity Act (AGOA), Nigeria benefits from preferential access for its petroleum to the US market.

3.4 Nigeria's Trade Facilitation and Diversification Challenge

The major factors accounting for the relative decline of the country's economic fortunes are easily identifiable as political instability, lack of focused and visionary leadership, economic mismanagement, and corruption. A prolonged period of military rule stifled economic and social progress, particularly in the three decades of 1970s–1990s. During these years, resources were plundered, social values were debased, and unemployment rose astronomically with concomitant increase in crime rate.

However, since 1999 economic growth in Nigeria has risen substantially, with an annual average of 7.4% in the last decade. But the growth has not been inclusive, broad-based and transformational. The implication of this trend is that economic growth in Nigeria has not resulted in the desired structural changes that would make manufacturing the engine of growth, create employment, promote technological development, and induce poverty alleviation. Available data has put the national poverty level at 54.4%. Similarly, there has been rising unemployment with the current level put at 19.7% by the National Bureau of Statistics (NBS).

The Nigerian economy is import-dependent with very little non-oil exports. It relies heavily on crude oil and gas exports with other sectors trailing far behind. For example, crude oil accounts for about 90% of foreign exchange earned by the country while non-oil exports account for the balance. The economy is, therefore, susceptible to shocks in the oil industry. In recent times, these shocks have been caused by either development in the international crude oil market or the restiveness in the Niger Delta region of the country. Agriculture and other mining (besides oil and gas) have been abandoned to the rural poor. Economic and social infrastructure, especially power is grossly dilapidated. The power sector is generally recognized as a binding constraint on Nigerian economy. Poor corporate governance, both in the public and private sectors have led to high incidence of corruption and inequity in income distribution. Although corruption is a global scourge, Nigeria appears to suffer particularly from it. Everyone appears to believe that the nation has a "culture of corruption." Over the years, Nigeria has earned huge sums of money from crude oil, which appears to have largely gone down the sinkhole created by corruption. The prospects for the Nigerian Economy depend on the policies articulated for the medium-to-long term and the seriousness with which they are implemented.

In 2017, as the Nigerian economy emerges from recession, economic recovery has been very slow. The Nigeria Biannual Economic Update of April 30, 2018, says "economic gains were largely driven by an expansion in oil output and continued steady growth in agriculture. However, the report notes, labor-intensive sectors remained weak, which contributed to an increase in the rate of unemployment and underemployment in 2017. Poverty is also believed to have increased slightly. Gross domestic product (GDP) growth, which reached 0.8% in 2017, is expected to hover just over 2% in 2018, according to the report." It further says the Nigerian government's Economic Recovery and Growth Plan (ERGP) will achieve macroeconomic growth if it is properly implemented. In recent times, the government's focus on business regulations has paid off; Nigeria has moved up in the World Bank Ease of Doing Business 2018 report; however, the report says more intensive effort needs to be made to get the private sector energized. The report says that most of the structural reforms outlined in the ERGP need to go beyond the preliminary stages to ensure the economic growth targets envisaged. The Nigerian government has identified the power sector as a critical focus, as is evidenced in the Power Sector Recovery Plan, with a focus to support implementation of power sector reform. The economic update qualifies these achievements, noting that Nigeria's performance is still insufficient, particularly in the social sector.

The economic recession and the subsequent devaluation/depreciation of the Nigerian naira (pegged to the US dollar until June 2016) somehow contained imports dominated by manufactured products. In June 2015, restrictions were introduced on access to foreign exchange from the Central Bank of Nigeria (CBN) for 41 categories of imports (ranging from rice, soap, and private jets to personal travel for education and healthcare), with a view to containing outflows of international reserves and "resuscitating" domestic industries. The current account shifted from a surplus of US$10.8 billion in 2011 to a deficit of US$15.4 billion in 2015, and international reserves significantly dropped from a peak of US$43.8 billion in 2013 to US$28.3 billion in 2015.

Generally, the economic crisis and the various measures taken to address it have more significantly reduced exports than imports, and the importance of trade for Nigeria has decreased, with a trade (in goods and services) to GDP ratio of 21.1% in 2015, down from 52.8% in 2011. The United States has been replaced by the European Union (EU) as the largest market for Nigeria's exports, while the EU remains the primary source of its imports. Nigeria is a net importer of services.

Despite its current modest contribution to GDP (10% in 2015), oil still accounts for about 90% of export earnings and 70% of government revenue. Therefore, in line with its Vision 20:2020 and its ERGP 2017–2020 aiming to make the country one of the top 20 leading global economies by 2020, Nigeria identified four priority sectors for its economic diversification efforts: agriculture, solid mineral mining, construction materials, and manufacturing.

Nigeria intends to diversify its economy away from oil by building a competitive manufacturing sector, which should facilitate integration into global value chains (GVCs) and boost productivity; as well as a strong services sector to be supported by an enabling environment for private-sector-led growth, industrial competitiveness and sustainable development. The recent merging of trade, industry and investment under the ambit of the Federal Ministry of Industry, Trade and Investment (FMITI) reflects Nigeria's intention to effectively coordinate between these three key areas to improve its trading and investment environment.

Nigeria's investment regime is largely liberal, with 100% foreign ownership allowed in all but the petroleum sector where investment is limited to joint-ventures or production-sharing agreements and a minimum share of 55% must be owned by the Government. It is compulsory for foreign investors to be locally incorporated as limited liability companies. As part of the Government's efforts to improve Nigeria's competitiveness, the registration fee for setting up a company was reduced from ₦50,000 to ₦15,000 in 2013. As a member of ECOWAS, Nigeria has applied the five-band (zero, 5%, 10%, 20%, and 35%) Common External Tariff (CET) since April 2015, albeit with a certain flexibility. In 2017, Nigeria's average applied MFN tariff rate is 12.7%, up from 11.9% in 2011. Its final bound tariff rates average 117.3% and the tariff binding coverage remains low at 19.2% of total lines. Low binding coverage and high average bound rates leave ample margins for tariff changes, thus rendering the tariff regime less predictable.

Under ECOWAS, Nigeria also applies the Import Adjustment Tax (IAT) available to member States that consider flexible application of the CET (higher or lower protection of selected products) to be necessary during the five-year transition period; and a 0.5% community fee. The IAT applied by Nigeria ranges from 5 to 60%, with the highest rate charged on cereals (60%). A Supplementary Protection Tax is also available under ECOWAS as a safeguard measure; Nigeria has not used it. Moreover, a myriad of additional taxes and levies are unilaterally collected by Nigeria on imports and exports.

Nigeria's economic aspirations have remained that of altering the structure of production and consumption patterns, diversifying the economic base and reducing dependence on oil, with the aim of putting the economy on a part of sustainable, all-inclusive and non-inflationary growth. The implication of this is that while rapid growth in output, as measured by the real GDP is important, the transformation of the various sectors of the economy is even more critical. This is consistent with the growth aspirations of most developing countries, as the structure of the economy is expected to change as growth progresses.

Successive governments in Nigeria have since independence in 1960, pursued the goal of structural changes without much success. The growth dynamics have been propelled by the existence and exploitation of natural resources and primary products. Initially, the agricultural sector, driven by the demand for food and cash crops production was at the center of the growth process, contributing 54.7% to the GDP during the 1960s. The second decade of independence saw the emergence of the oil industry as the main driver of growth. Since then, the economy has mainly gyrated with the boom-burst cycles of the oil industry. Government expenditure outlays that are dependent on oil revenues have more or less dictated the pace of growth of the economy. Looking back, it is clear that the economy has not actually performed to its full potential, particularly in the face of its rising population.

3.5 A Brief Discussion on Saudi Arabia Trade Flows and Experience

Saudi Arabia had a total export of 207,572,139.90 in thousands of US$ and total imports of 129,795,970.53 in thousands of US$ leading to a positive trade balance of 77,776,169.37 in thousands of US$. The trade growth is −5.41% compared to a world growth of −1.59%. GDP of Saudi Arabia is 686,738,400,000 in current US$. Saudi Arabia services export is 18,020,787,306.67 in Bop, current US$ and services import is 76,817,869,330.63 in Bop, current US$. Saudi Arabia exports of goods and services as percentage of GDP is 34.84% and imports of goods and services as percentage of GDP is 28.56% (Fig. 3.3).

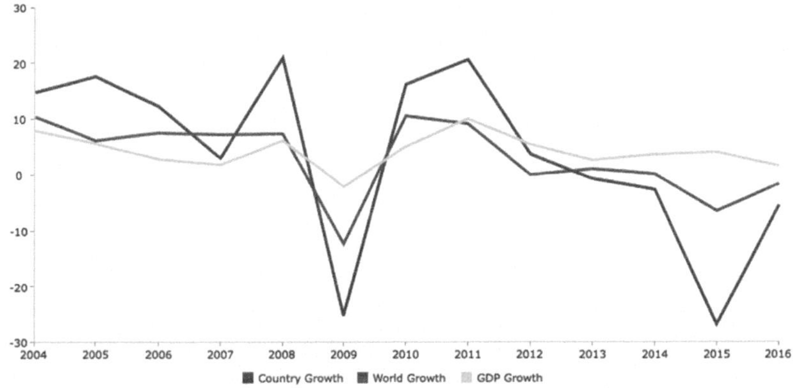

Fig. 3.3 Saudi Arabia country growth, world growth and GDP growth (*Source* Authors' calculation and WITS)

3.6 Overview of Trade Facilitation and Logistics in Saudi Arabia

Saudi Arabia is the largest economy in the Middle East and the richest Arab country. The policy of large-scale public works undertaken by the Government, as well as foreign direct investment and the soundness of the banking and financial system, have enabled the country to become the number one regional economy and one of the largest in the world. However, the economy of Saudi Arabia is almost entirely based on oil. GDP growth has been gradually declining since 2015 to a point where the economy moved into a recession in 2017 (−0.5%). Saudi Arabia has been ranked as the 20th most economically competitive country in the world. It is the world's largest producer and exporter of petroleum products, and also, the largest oil producer. Saudi Arabia's trade remains heavily dependent on the oil and petroleum-related industries, including petrochemicals and petroleum refining (Table 3.1).

Saudi Arabia has made a remarkable progress in both sectors export and import. As can be seen from the Fig. 3.4, there were different trends for export and import. Imports increased steadily between 2007 and 2014 and started to decline in 2015. Imports reached their highest level in 2015 to $655,033 million and its lowest level in 2016. Exports on the other hand followed a fluctuating trend and reached its highest level in 2012 to $1,456,502 million and its lowest level in 2016. The growth rate of the import sector during the years is 55.47% while the rate of the

Table 3.1 Saudi Arabia export and import

Year	*RSA/million*	
	Export	*Import*
2007	874,403	338,088
2008	1,175,482	431,753
2009	721,109	358,290
2010	941,785	400,736
2011	1,367,620	493,449
2012	1,456,502	583,473
2013	1,409,523	630,582
2014	1,284,122	651,876
2015	763,313	655,033
2016	688,423	525,636

Source Saudi Statistics

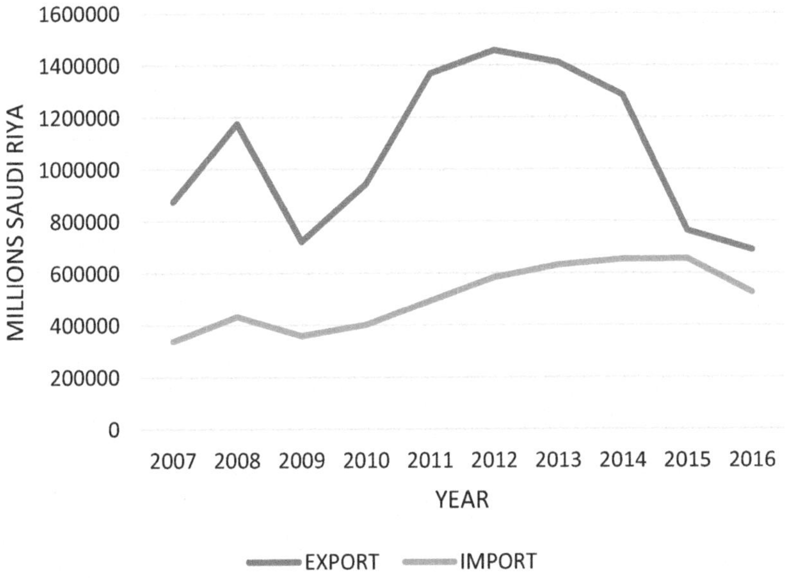

Fig. 3.4 Saudi Arabia import and export: 2007–2016 (*Source* International Trade Center)

export sector is −21.26%. Supporting all these trade activities is logistics and supply chain operations. Logistics performance is strongly associated with the reliability of supply chains and the predictability of service availability.

3.6.1 Logistic in Saudi Arabia

The Kingdom of Saudi Arabia is located strategically between three continents Asia, Africa, and Europe. The transport and logistics sector in Saudi Arabia is supporting a population of 32.28 million (2016) and plays a crucial role as enabler and prerequisite for growth in the country as well as for the "economic cities" (EC's). As a result of the economic growth and development, annual cargo volumes will triple from 300 million tons in 2005 to around 900 million tons in 2020. The two most important ports for imports are Jeddah Islamic Port and King Abdul Aziz Port Dammam. Jubail Industrial Port is the biggest port for export, Yanbu Industrial Port follows as the second biggest port for exports. This implies that hinterland connections are as important as maritime transport and ports. The existing infrastructure, however, has not yet kept pace with the industrial development of Saudi Arabia and is still inadequate with limited inland road, rail and sea connectivity. For this reason, numerous projects for the development of ports, roads and railway transportation have been planned. With the right incentives and also by leveraging the country's strategic location to attract traffic to its seaports, airports, logistics network; Saudi Arabian Government aims to strategically privatize operation and management of components of the transport and logistics sector (Andreas, 2013).

3.6.2 Customs Procedures

Saudi Customs succeeded in completing the customs procedures for more than 1,373,000 customs declarations during the first half of 2018. Saudi Customs pointed out that the volume of exports and imports during the mentioned period exceeded 66 million tons with a value of SR365,715,910,000 (Faisal Saad Albedah, Deputy Governor for Trade Facilitation). More than 80% of Saudi Customs declarations are cleared within an average of 24 hours, and many shipments receive direct clearance before they reach the Customs ports. Also, the ongoing transformation has contributed in achieving the objectives of the 24 hour clearance program launched by the Saudi Customs late last year. By reducing the number of documents needed for import and export, and activating the pre-arrival electronic submission, the Customs procedures and mechanisms have been greatly enhanced.

The most prominent achievement during the last period was the issuance of the new customs clearance practice guide, which authorized companies to issue customs clearance license. The guide also included many amendments that aim to contribute to monitoring customs imports and exports clearance activities, reducing customs violations, and addressing possible operational disputes.

The electronic national system for import and export "Fasah" in achieving positive outcomes in the clearance procedure, through enabling companies to track and complete their clearance procedures electronically. The system that was launched as a joint effort of 25 government entities, mostly aims to automate cross-border trade procedures, build a unified integrated electronic data interchange portal, and increase customs clearance transparency within import and export operations.

More work is underway on several projects that include improving exemptions and restrictions procedures, developing logistics services, and automating additional customs procedures. Stressed that developing import and export mechanisms will support and enhance the Kingdom's positioning within the "cross-border trade" axis is one of the most significant topics in the World Bank Group's Business Practice Report.

In 2016, Saudi Arabia by scoring 3.22 (out of a maximum of 5) in the LPI scale of the World Bank and was ranked 52 out of 160 countries. If we breakdown its logistics performance of 2016 into the six dimensions (Graph 5) we see that the weakest points are the efficiency in the clearance process and uncompetitive shipment prices.

According to the World Bank's analysis on Saudi Arabia LPI overall score for the period of 2007–2016, the highest rate was around 3.23 in 2010 and went down to 3.15 in 2014. By 2016 it has increased to 3.17. In conclusion, the rate of logistic performances has made highly significant progress from 2007 to 2010 but in recent years it is fluctuating between 3.15 and 3.20.

The trends in the six dimensions of logistic performance index such as customs, shipments, tracking & tracing, infrastructure, logistics competence, and timeliness from 2007 to 2016. The trends for each of these indicators include:

Customs: Efficiency of customs clearance process in Saudi Arabia was reported as 2.6914 in 2016, according to the World Bank collection of development indicators, compiled from officially recognized sources. In 2007, it started to grow and reached the highest point 2.91 while in 2010 the performance had decreased. Customs is the weakest dimension compared to other dimensions.

Infrastructure: Global production networks depend on transport operations. Trade and transport facilitation are at the core of stimulating economic development. Transport infrastructure has a significant impact on the productivity and the cost structure of private firms. Saudi Arabia has allocated $43.8 billion for transport, telecommunications, water, agriculture, and other related infrastructure. Additionally, it has several railway projects in the pipeline. The country's construction sector contributes around 8% of Saudi Arabia's total GDP, making it the largest construction market in the Middle East. Around 67% of construction investment is direct from the government with large-scale projects in the sector for the coming years set to reach $800 billion (Nicole Dsouze). During 2007 and 2014 there was a sharp increase in the infrastructure from 2.90 to 3.35 and then the percentage gradually went down to 3.23 in 2016.

Timeliness: The timeliness of shipments in reaching destination measures the reliability of shipment delivery times. In 2010, it was around 3.77 then it has decreased to reach 3.53 by 2016.

Tracking and tracing: Traceability is a product of the logistics sector. Tracking and Tracing is a process during logistics or distribution of goods, where the goods which are being transported are monitored as per their locations, i.e., previous, current, and next location. At the beginning of this period this indicator has increased from 2007 to 2010 from 3.2 to 3.33 then in 2014 went down to reach 3.15 and by the year 2016 it was about 3.25.

International shipment: This dimension gives an estimate of the country's performance in arranging shipments at competitive prices. In 2007 was around 2.9 then it has made an improvement to reach 3.2 by 2016.

Logistics competence: The LPI's indicator relating to competence and quality of logistics services measures the overall competence of the logistics services provided by parties within the logistics system. Achieving logistics excellence requires continuous improvement in reliability, responsiveness and well-functioning support services. In 2010, the quality of logistics service was around 3.3 and it was the best performance during the years then it has decreased by 2016.

3.6.2.1 Saudi Arabia Domestic Logistics Performance

The number of border agencies: The number of export agencies was 2 in 2007, after a little bit of fluctuation it remained at 2 in 2016 as well so we do not see much improvement in the number of export agency. On the other hand, the number of import agencies was 1.8 in 2007 but it increased to 2 in 2016 therefore, there was an improvement in import border agencies. Percentage of physical inspection; in 2007 it was 32%, but it has improved much faster and now in 2016 it is 61.99%. This represents a major improvement in this indicator. Table 3.2 compares the domestic logistics performance of Saudi Arabia for 2007–2016 period.

Table 3.2 Saudi Arabia during the years 2007, 2010, 2012, 2014, 2016

Saudi Arabia	*2016*	*2014*	*2012*	*2010*	*2007*
Export time and cost/Port or airport supply chain					
Distance (kilometers)	47	300	132		
Lead time (days)	3	8	5	2.29	
Cost (US$)	N/A	1000	506		
Export time and cost/Land supply chain					
Distance (kilometers)	108	300	186		
Lead time (days)	2	8	3		
Cost (US$)	N/A	1000	932		
Import time and cost/Port or airport supply chain					
Distance (kilometers)	104	300	145		
Lead time (days)	7	9	6	6.32	
Cost (US$)	N/A	1000	1225		
Import time and cost/Land supply chain					
Distance (kilometers)	595				
Lead time (days)	13				
Cost (US$)	N/A				
Shipments meeting quality criteria (%)	64.65	40	78.67		
Number of agencies—exports	2	3	2	3.5	2
Number of agencies—imports	2	3	2	3	1.8
Number of documents—exports	3	5	3		
Number of documents—imports	2	5	2		
Clearance time without physical inspection (days)	2	5	3	3.98	3.9
Clearance time with physical inspection (days)	4	5	4	7.61	
Physical inspection (%)	61.99	35	36.23	65.52	32
Multiple inspection (%)	5.72	35	3.2	3.39	50
Declarations submitted and processed electronically and on-line (%)	25				
Importers use a licensed Customs Broker (%)	100				
Able to choose the location of the final clearance (%)	N/A				
Goods released pending customs clearance (%)	66.67				

Source World Bank

Possibility of a review procedure: In 2007, the possibility of a review procedure was 50%. This indicates also Custom Clearance: In 2007 custom clearance was 3.9 days, it also improved over time and now the clearance is made in 2 days. Multiple inspections (%): In 2010 multiple inspections were 3.39% and it improved now toward 5.72%. So the country has also improved in this sector. Clearance time with physical inspection (days): In 2010 clearance time was 3.98 days, now in 2016 it is 4 days, so the country does not show much improvement in the clearance time with physical inspection. Cost: The cost has decreased significantly from 2007 to 2016. Trade logistics are playing a better role for the country now. It had introduced different cost criteria according to the number of days. Shipments meeting quality criteria (%): The quality criteria shipments have reduced over time from 78.67 in 2012 to 64.65% in 2016. So the country should focus on this and try to improve this percentage.

Number of documents: Number of documents for the import and export has not shown much variation over time. This relates to the fact that the biggest problem is customs clearance procedures and delays. According to the World Bank, the average number of container clearance days in 2014 is nine days, while in Dubai two days. The second problem there is no train to transport goods between the port of Jeddah and the port of Dammam and the port of Jubail and the dry port in Riyadh. The third problem is the need to develop ports and the speed of download and loading of ships and increase the depth of water to enable ports to receive large ships and provide free zones for re-exports. The fourth problem there is no land for logistics areas for logistics companies at reasonable prices in or near the ports. The last problem is that the system does not allow the establishment of logistics services companies that provide all logistic services to the customer, like other developed countries logistically. In other words, companies in the Kingdom are carriers, stockers, trustees, or importers. They do not have the right to combine some of these activities, which means that it is impossible to develop this sector in Saudi Arabia without changing these old systems decades ago. However, Saudi Arabia has launched many programs to enhance LPI and has planned for transformation strategies.

Since 2016, Saudi Arabia has made progress in improving its logistics services. infrastructure and traceability to meet world-class standards. Import and export processes are more organized and governance structures and regulations are being reformed and they open a path to markets and private sector involved. KSA is also pushing public–private partnerships both to finance its infrastructure and to acquire capabilities from other top logistics markets. The good news is that investment money is beginning to roll in. In a report by Al-Masha Capital, Saudi Arabia and the United Arab Emirates (UAE) are deemed the most attractive targets for logistics investments in the region and among the easiest markets to operate in.

3.6.3 Saudi Arabia Compared to Its Region

According to the data, in 2016 it seems likely that Saudi Arabia LPI score was 3.16 and none OECD was about 3.15 compare them with their region 2.89. There was no difference between Saudi and non-OECD high-income countries but Saudi was in better position compared to the average of Middle East and North Africa region. Saudi was better in terms with the exception of customs and logistics competence compared to its region and income group.

3.6.4 Saudi Arabia's Nine-Point Logistics Transformation Strategy

Recognizing the growth potential that its logistics sector can have on non-oil trade and investment—a key objective of its Vision 2030—the Kingdom puts a nine-point logistics transformation strategy. The strategy will be a significant enabler for the country's logistics success.

- **Enhance and reengineer the import/export process**: Becoming an international logistics hub begins with reducing the time, cost, and variability of importing and exporting goods. KSA already has some nice wins in this area thanks to automation and progress efforts to reengineer the import/export methods. For example, average declaration clearance times at seaports have been cut in half to just 2.2 days and at airports to just 1.2 days, and the amount of import–export paperwork is down by 75%.
- **Digital transformation**: Digital technology has significantly improved KSA's security, transparency, and control over the import–export process. Today, importers track the status and progress of their shipments in real-time. Customs brokers receive automated status notifications on their mobiles and are prompted to create their declarations as soon as the shipping manifest is available online, i.e., prior to ship arrival. KSA recently launched two new digital initiatives: a port community system to guarantee secure and efficient exchange of information, and a digital payment platform to accelerate the payment process.
- **Develop a transport infrastructure**: The Kingdom aims to improve the quality, safety, and efficiency of the country's transport infrastructure. The plan calls for development of several major assets, including the Saudi Landbridge railway to connect the east and west

coasts of Saudi, and two new rail corridors, Ras-Al Khair-Dammam in the east and Yanbu-Jazan in the west. Next on the agenda could be construction of new multimodal logistics terminals to fill the increasing need for sea-to-air and rail-to-road connectivity.

- **Eliminate air cargo bottlenecks**: Saudi Arabia works to improve airports and expand air cargo facilities to eliminate infrastructure bottlenecks. According to vision 2030, the objective is to increase total air cargo capacity in the Kingdom from 0.8 million tons/year today to 6.8 million tons/year by 2030.
- **Meet international regulatory standards**: Saudi Arabia wants to attract more competition and private-sector participants, then its regulatory environment must be in line with international standards. It will help logistics players to move the logistics performance in the area. The government works to give licenses to warehouse operators and makes remarkable effort to improve efficiency and safety standards.
- **Improve seaport quality and efficiency**: Efforts are underway to identify and repair the inefficiencies of seaports. The initial focus is on growing port specialization, reforming governance and oversight, and updating concession frameworks. Also, Saudi Arabia wants to create a more level playing field by separating port regulations from port ownership and assigning a dedicated regulating entity. Concession frameworks are revised to become more transparent, fair, and attractive to international terminal operators.
- **Reform the rail sector**: The rail sector is going through similar reforms. Recently, railway regulation was separated from railway ownership and assigned to an independent regulator and is called (the Public Transport Authority). The government is consolidating and restructuring all railway operations, and planning to award operations and maintenance contracts for passenger and freight services to reputable international operators.
- **Engage the private sector**: The Kingdom takes a great step to engage private sectors in the markets. Recently, awarded a 20-year contract to Singapore's Changi Airport Group to handle operations at the new King Abdul-Aziz International Airport (KAIA) in Jeddah. Similarly, SATS, Singapore's biggest ground handler, has agreed to develop and operate a new cargo terminal at King Fahd International Airport (KFIA) in Dammam (supply chain brain). Similar schemes

to increase private sector participation are being considered for the King Khalid International Airport in Riyadh.

- **Develop special economic zones**: The kingdom works to reduce the costs and barriers to setting up new businesses, signing trade agreements, and attracting foreign direct investment. There are many plans underway to develop several new special economic areas.

3.7 Conclusion and Policy Recommendation: Optimizing the Policy Space Toward Strengthening Trade Facilitation and Logistics Performance in Nigeria in the Digital Age

The Nigerian economy has grossly underperformed relative to her enormous resource endowment and her peer nations. It has the 6th largest gas reserves and the 8th largest crude oil reserves in the world. It is endowed in commercial quantities with about 37 solid mineral types and has a population of over 170 million people. Yet economic performance has been rather weak and does not reflect these endowments. Compared with the emerging Asian countries, notably, Thailand, Malaysia, China, India, and Indonesia that were far behind Nigeria in terms of GDP per capita in 1970, these countries have transformed their economies and are not only miles ahead of Nigeria but are also major players on the global economic arena.

Improving trade facilitation and logistic performance are very crucial for Nigeria to attain its competitiveness as stated in its economic diversification plan. Improvement in logistics activities leads to less loss of goods in transit, so it leads to low trading costs, due to less damage to goods, the company has not borne extra production costs, which are beneficial for the development of country. Improving the trade facilitation and logistics performance will help Nigerian companies and start-ups effectively fight its bottlenecks and reduce any types of inefficiency. This will help it improve its productivity, production, and thus output. Improving logistics performance will give an advantage to the company over other firms who are still fighting logistics issues and high trading costs.

In Nigeria, the role of trade and the implementation of trade facilitation programs have evolved over the years. For example, infrastructure, tracking and ease of arranging shipment have improved slightly, while the customs is still complicated, and this continually remains one the main obstacle that faces supply chain and the quality of trade facilitation and logistics services. Though the Nigerian Government has announced that some programs toward achieving its trade facilitation and logistics target, the country has a lot of lessons to learn from Saudi Arabia, which embarked on comprehensive programs toward enhancing its transportation capacities. Further, digital technology will be a key enabler and driver of the numerous changes envisaged by Vision 2030, with the goal of developing the nation's digital infrastructure and stimulating the related economic sectors, industries, and private sector entities. The digital transformation is the most important component that the government should be concentrating on. Nigeria should have a digital strategy.

With the highly unstable global oil prices, the Nigerian Government is charting a new direction toward developing an economy that is non-oil dependent by announcing a bold reform in line with its Vision 2030. The reform would have long-term effects on the economic structure but also enhancing the diversification milestones and fostering increasing private sector engagement. In addition to the fact that integrated private sector participation will enhance the ecosystem that allows logistics to thrive, creating successful partnerships between private sector investors and the government will be a critical factor in shaping the Nigerian economy over the coming years. Considering the 2030 vision, the diversification will rely less on government financing and increase investment by the private sector. Creating successful partnerships between private sector investors and the government will be a critical factor in shaping the economy over the coming years. Vision 2030 will stimulate the economic growth of non-oil economic sectors and open new services and products fulfilling the pursuit of Nigeria to become a global trade facilitation and logistics hub.

References

Andreas, H. (2013). Logistics in Saudi Arabia.

Arvis, J.-F., Mustra, A. M., Panzer, J., Ojala, L., Naula, T. (2007). *Connecting to Compete 2007: Trade Logistics in the Global Economy—The Logistics Performance Index and Its Indicators.* Washington, DC: World Bank.

Arvis, J.-F., Mustra, A. M., Ojala, L., Shepherd, B., Saslavsky, D. (2010). *Connecting to Compete 2010: Trade Logistics in the Global Economy—The Logistics Performance Index and Its Indicators*. Washington, DC: World Bank.

Faria, R. N. D., Souza, C. S. D., Vieira, J. G. V. (2015). Evaluation of Logistic Performance Indexes of Brazil in the International Trade. *RAM: Revista de Administração Mackenzie*, *16*(1), 213–235.

Gani, A. (2017). The Logistics Performance Effect in International Trade. *The Asian Journal of Shipping and Logistics*, *33*(4), 279–288.

The International Bank for Reconstruction and Development/The World Bank. (2014). Turku School of Economics, Logistic Performance Index Surveys.

CHAPTER 4

Understanding the Role of Selected Measures in Facilitating Trade Under Nigeria's WTO Obligations: Lessons and Policy Agenda for Selected Sectors—Oil and Gas, Fish, and Foreign Exchange

Ndah Abu Ali

4.1 Introduction

This chapter analyzes the consistency of certain measures introduced by Nigeria in light of its obligations under the World Trade Organization ("WTO"). Broadly, these measures relate to the oil and gas industry, the importation of fish and fish products, and foreign exchange. It provides an overview of each measure, analyzes it in light of Nigeria's WTO obligations, provides potential justifications, and presents recommendations on possible strategies that Nigeria could pursue with regard to the measure to ensure the continuance of their broader policy objectives in a WTO-consistent manner (Sections 4.2, 4.3, 4.4).

N. A. Ali (✉)
Federal Ministry of Industry, Trade and Investment, Abuja, Nigeria

G. Odularu (ed.), *Strategic Policy Options for Bracing Nigeria for the Future of Trade*,
https://doi.org/10.1007/978-3-030-34552-5_4

4.2 Certain Measures Regarding the Oil and Gas Industry

This section analyzes the Nigerian Oil and Gas Industry Content Development Act, 2010 ("Act") in light of Nigeria's WTO obligations.

4.2.1 Overview of the Measures

In 2010, Nigeria introduced the Nigerian Oil and Gas Industry Content Development Act ("Act"). An analysis of the sections of the Act described below reveals three measures that may raise potential concerns with respect to Nigeria's national treatment obligations under the WTO:

- Measure 1: The Act mandates that operators and contractors comply with minimum *content requirements* and give *first consideration* to goods and services listed in the Schedule to the Act.
  - Section 7 requires that all operators, "submit a Nigerian Content Plan ("the [Content] Plan") to the Board demonstrating compliance with the Nigerian content requirements of this Act."
  - Section 10 provides that the Content Plan "shall contain provisions intended to ensure that first consideration shall be given to services provided from within Nigeria and to goods manufactured in Nigeria."
  - Section 11 provides that "the minimum Nigerian content in any project to be executed in the Nigerian oil and gas industry shall be consistent with the level set in Schedule to this Act."
  - Section 12 provides that the Content Plan must set out "how the operator and their contractors will give first consideration to Nigerian goods and services."
  - Section 13 provides that the Content Plan sets out how the operator or alliance partner "intend to ensure the use of locally manufactured goods where such goods meet the specifications of the industry."
- Measure 2: The Act mandates that the Nigerian government give *first consideration* to "Nigerian independent operators" with respect to certain activities in the oil and gas industry.

  - Section 3(1) provides that "Nigerian independent operators shall be given first consideration in the award of oil blocks, oil field licences, oil lifting licences and in all projects for which contract is to be awarded in the Nigerian oil and gas industry subject to the fulfilment of such conditions as may be specified by the Minister."[1]

- Measure 3: The Act mandates that the Nigerian government, operators, and contractors give *exclusive consideration* to indigenous Nigerian service companies in respect of activities that concern contracts and services listed in the Schedule to the Act.
  - Section 3(2) provides that "there shall be exclusive consideration to Nigerian indigenous service companies which demonstrate ownership of equipment, Nigerian personnel and capacity to execute such work to bid on land and swamp operating areas of the Nigerian oil and gas industry for contracts and services contained in the Schedule to this Act."[2]
- Measure 4: The Act mandates that operators and contractors give *first consideration* to Nigerians for employment and training.
  - Section 28 provides that "Nigerians shall be given the first consideration for employment and training in any project executed by any operator or project promoter in the Nigerian oil and gas industry."

4.2.2 Analysis of the Measures

This section analyzes these Measures in light of Nigeria's WTO obligations relating to trade in goods.

[1] Nigerian Oil and Gas Industry Content Development Act (2010) Cap. (2), §3(1), http://www.eisourcebook.org/cms/January%202016/Nigerian%20Oil%20and%20Gas%20Industry%20Content%20Development%20Act%202010.pdf [hereinafter NOGID].

[2] *Id.* §3(1).

4.2.2.1 *Measures 2, 3, and 4 Are Outside the Scope of the GATT and TRIMS*

The GATT is applicable to goods.[3] In contrast the GATS applies to "measures by members affecting trade in services."[4] Additionally, TRIMs applies to "investment measures related to trade in goods only ...."[5] Measures 2, 3, and 4 are likely outside the scope of GATT and TRIMs because they related to trade in services and not goods and therefore do not violate Nigeria's commitments under the WTO.

Measure 2. It may be submitted that Section 3(1) applies exclusively to the segment of the business which entails the extraction of oil and gas. It refers to projects related to the award of oil contracts that result in oil blocks, oil licenses, and oil lifting, as well as all other projects in which there results the awarding of contract in the oil and gas industry. Therefore, the line of business for which this section applies likely concerns only operators that supply services and does not extend to companies that supply goods.

This interpretation is supported by a reading of Section 44(3) of the Nigerian Constitution. Under the current 1999 Nigerian Constitution, the Federal Government has proprietorship and "control of all minerals, mineral oils and natural gas in" Nigeria.[6] Hence, operators in the oil and gas business cannot own minerals in Nigeria, and their business is instead to provide services for the extraction of all oil and gas. In this regard, Section 3(1) is likely outside the scope of GATT as it mandates first consideration in relation to the supply of services.

As regards the analysis of this section under Nigeria's GATS commitments, it is pertinent to note that the national treatment obligation

[3] General Agreement on Tariffs and Trade 1994, Apr. 15, 1994, Marrakesh Agreement Establishing the World Trade Organization, Annex 1A, The Legal Texts: The Results of the Uruguay Round of Multilateral Trade Negotiations 17 (1999), 1867 U.N.T.S. 187, 33 I.L.M. 1153 (1994) [hereinafter GATT].

[4] General Agreement on Trade in Services, Apr. 15, 1994, Marrakesh Agreement Establishing the World Trade Organization, Annex 1B, The Legal Texts: The Results of the Uruguay round of Multilateral Trade Negotiations 284 (1999), 1869 U.N.T.S. 183, 33 I.L.M. 1167 (1994) [hereinafter GATS].

[5] Agreement on Trade-Related Investment Measures, Annex 1A, Apr. 15, 1994, Marrakesh Agreement Establishing the World Trade Organization, Annex 1A, The legal Texts: The Results of the Uruguay Round of Multilateral Trade Negotiations 143 (1999), 1868 U.N.T.S. 186 [hereinafter TRIMS Agreement].

[6] Nigerian Constitution, Art. 44(3).

applies only for sectors for which a member has made specific commitments. Nigeria's Schedule of Specific Commitments does not contain any commitments on oil and gas services. Accordingly, Section 3(1) also does not likely violate Nigeria's commitments under GATS.[7]

Measure 3. Nigeria could claim that Section 3(2) does not create any preference for locally manufactured goods, and therefore, it is outside the scope of GATT. This Section mandates exclusive consideration solely for "service companies" and only for the award of "contracts and services contained in the Schedule to th[e] Act." Accordingly, on its face, Section 3(2) applies to services and service suppliers and does not apply to goods. Hence, the provision is likely outside the purview of GATT.

Furthermore, even though Section 3(2) would be analyzed under the GATS, Nigeria has not made any national treatment commitments related to oil and gas services in its schedule of specific commitments.[8] Hence, it is likely that this provision does not violate Nigeria's obligations under GATS.

Measure 4. Section 28 expressly provides first consideration only to Nigerians for employment and training in projects in the Nigerian oil and gas industry. Accordingly, this Section applies only to services and service suppliers and does not apply to goods. Hence, the provision is likely outside the purview of GATT.

Section 28 would be analyzed under the GATS. However, as Nigeria has not made any national treatment commitments related to oil and gas services in its Schedule of Specific Commitments, it is likely that this provision does not violate Nigeria's obligations under GATS.[9]

4.2.2.2 Measure 1 Is Not Likely in Violation of GATT Art. III:4 and TRIMs Art. 2.1

GATT Art. III:4 provides that "[t]he product of the territory of any [member] ... shall be accorded treatment no less favorable than that

[7] Nigeria has made commitments with regard to financial services and transportation services in its Schedule of Specific Commitments and some aspects of such commitments may overlap with services in the oil and gas sector. However, the examination of GATS specific issues are presently beyond the mandate of this Memorandum and will be examined only upon further instructions. *See* GATS, Schedule of Specific Commitments.

[8] *Id.*

[9] *Id.*

accorded to like [national] products ...."[10] TRIMs Art. 2.1 provides that Trade-Related Investment Measures that are inconsistent with GATT Art. III while TRIMs Art. 2.2 refers to Annex A which provides examples of measures that are inconsistent with GATT Art. III:4. This includes, pursuant to 1(a) of the Annex to the TRIMs, measures that are:

> mandatory or enforceable under domestic law or under administrative rulings[] ... and which require: "domestic laws or under administrative rulings ... and which require the purchase or use by an enterprise of products of domestic origin or from any domestic source, whether specified in terms of particular products, in terms of volume or value of products, or in terms of a proportion of volume or value of its local production[] ...[11]

Thus, a measure that falls within 1(a) of the Annex to the TRIMs is a violation of the TRIMs Art. 2.1 and GATT Art. III:4.[12] In *Canada-Feed* the Appellate Body ("AB") held that local content requirements, imposed by the Canadian government on private companies, to procure locally manufactured goods, violated GATT Art. III:4 and Art. 2 of TRIMs.[13]

Measure 1 may appear to establish local content requirements in respect of goods manufactured in Nigeria. As noted above, Measure 1 prescribes minimum Nigerian content requirements for operators and contractors. Section 11 states that companies "shall comply with the minimum Nigerian content for [a] particular project item ... set out in the Schedule of the Act."[14] The Schedule to the Act contains a list of goods and services and the corresponding percentage of minimum Nigerian content required for each. For instance, the minimum Nigerian content of

[10] GATT Art. III:4.

[11] TRIMS Art. 2.1.

[12] GATT Art. III:8 provides an exemption to the national treatment obligation. The Article states that "[t]he provisions [of GATT Art. III] shall not apply to laws ... governing the procurement by governmental agencies of products purchased for governmental purposes and not with a view to commercial resale or with a view to use in the production of goods for commercial sale." It is unlikely that Nigeria rely on this exemption, because the Act governs an industry in relation to which products, namely those listed in the Schedule to the Act, are purchased with a view to use in the production oil and gas for commercial resale.

[13] Appellate Body Report, *Canada—Measures Relating to the Feed-In Tariff Program*, ¶172, WT/DS412/AB/R, WT/DS426/AB/R (May 13, 2013).

[14] NOGID, *supra* note 1, §11(3).

"Pressure Vessels" is set at 80% in units of tonnage.[15] This may be taken to mean that operators and contractors in the oil and gas industry are required to satisfy their needs of pressure vessels by procuring 80% of their needs of pressure vessels measured by tonnage from locally manufactured goods.

However, Nigeria may contend Measure 1 is consistent with its national treatment obligations as the measure does not *specifically* mandate operators and contractors to procure locally manufactured goods. It only mandates that in procuring the goods listed in the Schedule, operators and contractors comply with the minimum prescribed "*Nigerian Content*." The Act defines "Nigerian content" as "the quantum of composite value added to or created in the Nigerian economy by a systematic development of capacity and capabilities through the deliberate utilization of Nigerian human, material resources and services in the Nigerian oil and gas industry."[16] It may be submitted that, in order to satisfy the "minimum Nigerian Content" requirements, "value" must be added or created in the Nigerian economy. Nothing in the definition of Nigerian Content specifically mandates the procurement of locally manufactured goods. Thus, in the example above, an operator or contractor can satisfy the 80% minimum content requirement for pressure vessel by using non-locally manufactured goods that are imported into Nigeria by a local importer and thereby creating "value in the Nigerian economy."

Further, it can be discerned that the Content Plan requirements under the Act are discretionary and ambiguous, and the Board, charged with implementing the provisions of the Act, will exercise its discretion consistent with Nigeria's WTO obligations. In the Content Plan, the operator must "set[ ] out how the operator and their contractors will give first consideration to Nigerian goods and services, ..."[17] The Act also states that the Content Plan "shall contain [a]detailed plan on how the operator ... intend[s] to ensure the use of locally manufactured goods where such goods meet the specifications of the industry."[18] Thereafter, the Board, charged with implementing the provisions of the Act, will "review and assess the plan and, if satisfied that the plan complies with the provisions

[15] *See, e.g. Id.* Schedule.

[16] *Id.* §109.

[17] *Id.* §12.

[18] *Id.* §13.

of this Act, issue a Certificate of Authorization ('the Certificate') to the operator for that project."[19] These provisions indicate that the role of the Board is to observe if value is being added to the Nigerian economy as stated in the Content Plan and not giving preference to locally manufactured goods.

According to the AB, if the text is not clear,[20] the claimant will have to meet a "***high threshold***, and put[ ] forward sufficient evidence with respect to each [element of the measure], that a panel would be in a position to find that the ... [measure] may be challenged, as such."[21] In making such argument, Nigeria would primarily rely on "[t]he presumption that WTO Members act in good faith in the implementation of their WTO commitments is particularly apt in the context of measures challenged 'as such'."[22]

In conclusion, Nigeria could contend that the ambiguity in the text makes it difficult for a claimant to challenge the Act because there is no *specific* interpretation of the Act that mandates compulsory procurement of Nigerian goods and that the Board will exercise its discretion in a WTO-consistent manner.

4.2.3 Possible Justifications

4.2.3.1 The Measures May Be Justified as Necessary for Nigeria's Essential Security Interests

Article XXI allows a WTO member to take "any action which it considers necessary for the protection of its essential security interests ... taken in time of war or other emergency in international relations ...."[23] Further, nothing under the GATT can be construed "to prevent any contracting

[19] *Id.* §8.

[20] The party asserting a violation has the burden to show that the measure is inconsistent by relying primarily on the text "which may be supported, as appropriate, by evidence of the consistent application of such laws, the pronouncements of domestic courts on the meaning of such laws, the opinions of legal experts and the writings of recognized scholars." Appellate Body Report, *United States—Countervailing Duties on Certain Corrosion-Resistant Carbon Steel Flat Products from Germany*, ¶157, WT/DS213/AB/R (Nov. 28, 2002).

[21] Appellate Body Report, *United States—Laws, Regulations and Methodology for Calculating Dumping Margins ("Zeroing")*, ¶198, WT/DS294/AB/R (Apr. 18, 2006).

[22] *Id.*

[23] GATT Art. XXI.

party from taking any action in pursuance of its obligations under the United Nations Charter for the maintenance of international peace and security."[24]

In order to rely on Article XXI (b)(iii), a Member would need to demonstrate that: (i) it considers the measure necessary for its essential security interest and that the (iii) measure is taken in a time of war or other emergency in international relations. Additionally, in order to rely on Article XXI(c), a member would need to demonstrate "that the measure is in pursuance of its obligations under the United Nations Charter for the maintenance of international peace and security."[25]

A plain reading of the GATT Art.XXI(b)(iii) probably indicates that a Member is the sole judge of what is "necessary for its essential security interest." Indeed, this has been the assertion of every Member that has previously invoked GATT Art.XXI. For instance, in 1961, at the time of the accession of Portugal, Ghana had a boycott on Portuguese goods. Ghana asserted that "under ... Article[XXI] each contracting party was the sole judge of what was necessary in its essential security interest ...."[26]

Nigeria may be able to demonstrate that its essential security interests are substantially served by adopting the Measures under the Act. There is evidence suggesting that the lack of indigenous communities' participation in the oil and gas industry is directly related to the violence in the Niger Delta, where most of Nigeria's oil resources are located. In this regard, the Act enables indigenous communities to become important stakeholders in the oil and gas industry, curbing violence, vandalism and the sabotage of oil facilities in the Niger Delta.[27]

Nigeria could demonstrate that the violence in the Niger Delta is a reaction to the lack of indigenous communities' participation in the wealth generated by oil and gas production in the region. Oil production in the Niger Delta led to worsening living standards for inhabitants of the Niger Delta as the income from the agriculture sector was not

[24] *Id.*

[25] *Id.*

[26] GATT/CP.3/SR.22, Corr. 1.

[27] International Crisis Group, Curbing Violence in Nigeria (III): Revisiting the Niger Delta (2015), http://www.crisisgroup.org/~/media/Files/africa/west-africa/nigeria/231-curbing-violence-in-nigeria-iii-re-visiting-the-niger-delta.pdf.

replaced with service opportunities in the oil and gas industry.[28] Consequently, the indigenous people who heavily populate the Delta were confronted with poverty and lost livelihood. Such factors were critical elements in the rise of terrorism and violent criminal activities in the Delta. In turn, the oil industry became the direct target of terrorist acts, kidnapping and other violent outbreaks with many Delta communities aiming to completely destabilize it.[29] Moreover, "[m]uch of the rhetoric of militant Niger Delta groups is echoed by regional politicians, who have demanded a greater share of Nigerian oil wealth and the right to pick the ruling party candidate for elections in 2007."[30] The militant groups in the area continue to "demand local control of oil wealth" and threaten International Oil Companies ("IOC") to withdraw immediately from the world's eighth-largest oil exporter.[31]

It is important to note that there is evidence suggesting that the promotion of local service suppliers and local employment under the Act are directly related to curbing violence. Nigeria's several IOCs have already undertaken steps toward participation of local communities to ensure the safety and security of their personnel and operations and "reach out directly to the community to assess needs and develop creative solutions to the Delta's dire situation."[32]

Therefore, Nigeria may contend that it considers the Act necessary to "increase the regions security apparatus while also directly addressing community needs, the ability of militants to find recruits, mobilize, and carry out attacks may be greatly reduced over time."[33]

The security threat in the Niger Delta has a global impact. The situation creates an international terrorism threat. The spokesperson for the Movement of the Emancipation of Nigerian Delta ("MEND"), the umbrella group for militant groups in Niger Delta, brags that their attacks will create "an economic tsunami that will sweep the entire oil industry"

[28] *Id.* 1.

[29] Jennifer Giroux, Turmoil in the Delta: Trends and Implications, 2 Prospective of Terrorism, no. 2, 2008, http://www.terrorismanalysts.com/pt/index.php/pot/article/view/45/html.

[30] Daniel Howden, Nigeria: Shell May Pull Out of Niger Delta After 17 Die in Boat Raid, CorpWatch (Jan. 17, 2009), http://www.corpwatch.org/article.php?id=13121.

[31] *Id.*

[32] Giroux, *supra* note 27.

[33] *Id.*

noting that their attacks will be on dates "that will never be forgotten, like 9/11." "Not only is such a development dangerous as it would cause greater volatility in the market but it might also inspire militant groups living in *other* oil-rich countries to mimic such a model."[34] "In December 2005, MEND carried out its first attack when it bombed a pipeline and demanded for the evacuation of all foreign oil companies by 12 February 2006."[35] On 16 February 2006, the militant groups attacked Shell's facilities, damaging pipelines and killing at least 17 workers.[36]

In addition to MEND, Boko Haram, a religious extremist group pledging allegiance to the Islamic State in Iraq and Levant ("ISIL"), has been declared by the US Department of State as a Foreign Terrorist Organization.[37] "[A] Nigerian analyst with the International Crisis Group (ICG) asserts that the move will encourage [Boko Haram] to aggressively target U.S. interests in Nigeria ...." Hence, "Nigeria's security and stability has added importance to the U.S.. ..."[38]

The campaign of violence did not only include foreign corporations but also involved threats to foreign governments. In an email to the media, the group issued the following statement: "We wish to warn the ***Chinese government*** and its oil companies to steer well clear of the Niger Delta. The Chinese government by investing in stolen crude places its citizens in our line of fire."[39]

Furthermore, the attacks not only drastically affect—and in some cases, cripple—oil production, but they also affected the price of oil at the global level. For example, "in January 2008, an attack on oil facilities in Port Harcourt killed 13 people and sent crude oil futures soaring as

[34] *Id.*

[35] *Id.*

[36] Howden, *supra* note 28.

[37] Giroux, *supra* note 27.

[38] *Id.*

[39] Craig Timberg, Militants Warn China Over Oil in Niger Delta, Wash. Post (May 1, 2006), http://www.washingtonpost.com/wp-dyn/content/article/2006/04/30/AR2006043001022.html.

market analysts speculated that Nigerian supply would face further disruptions."[40] This indicates that scale of violence in the Delta region translated "not only into local disruption, but also into regional and international shocks in the form of higher oil and gas costs."[41]

In light of the war against terrorism and related emergency in international relations, Nigeria may contend that the measures under the Act are necessary to protect its essential security interest and invoke GATT Art. XXI(b)(iii).

Further, in relation to GATT Art. XXI(c), it may be contended that as the terrorist activity and violence in the Delta have a global impact, it is a threat to international peace and security. Nigeria could also argue that the Act seeks to promote involvement of local communities as an effort to maintain international peace, security, and stability. Nigeria could rely on some EU trade agreements which, in relevant parts, at measures that are "related to the maintenance of international peace and security" include the protection of human rights.[42] Thus, Nigeria may also rely upon GATT Art. XXI(c) to justify the Act.

4.2.3.2 The Measures May Be Justified as Necessary for the Protection of Human and Plant Life

In order for a measure to be justified under Art. XX(b), it is necessary to satisfy the following elements: (i) the policy objective of a measure is the protection of human and plant life, (ii) the measure is necessary to achieve the said objective, and (iii) the measure satisfies the requirements of the introductory chapeau, that it is not applied in a manner which would constitute "a means of arbitrary or unjustifiable discrimination between countries where the same conditions prevail," and is not "a disguised restriction on international trade."[43]

In determining whether the policy objective of a measure is the protection of human life and health, the measure's "design and structure"

[40] Giroux, *supra* note 27.

[41] *Id.*

[42] Comprehensive Economic and Trade Agreement, EU-CA, *concluded* Sept. 29, 2014, ANNEX 8-E, http://trade.ec.europa.eu/doclib/docs/2014/september/tradoc_152806.pdf.

[43] Appellate Body Report, *EC—Tarrif Preference*, ¶7.201–7.202, WT/DS246/AB/R (Dec. 1, 2003).

must reveal a link between the policy and preferential treatment,[44] or such a link must be determined through extrinsic evidence.[45] Therefore, in determining whether the policy objective of a measure is the protection of human life and health, Nigeria would have to provide evidence suggesting that stimulating the oil and gas services sector is aimed at protecting the life and health of humans and plants.[46] Nigeria Delta region has decades of endemic violence that has caused loss of human life in the region.[47] Moreover, there is also evidence that establishes that the violence in the region has led to severe environmental damage through the continuous attacks on oil pipelines and facilities. Consequently, Nigeria may be able to establish that its measures are designed to halt the violence and prevent environmental damage in the Delta region.

Nigeria may also be able to show that the measure is necessary to achieve its objective. This element requires, among other things, that the measure "produce[s] a material contribution to the achievement of its objective ...."[48] Nigeria could show that increasing the participation of the local communities through stimulating employment in the oil and gas sector may materially contribute to decreasing violence, as it ensures that local communities are stakeholders in the industry. Indeed, this is an approach that OICs have adopted to ensure the safety of their operations. For instance, "Shell [the Dutch oil operator] has taken one interesting step by hiring 'community liaison officers' to begin direct dialogues with the Delta communities ...."[49]

Finally, GATT Art. XX's chapeau requires that the application of the measure must not constitute a "means of arbitrary or unjustifiable discrimination" or a "disguised restriction on international trade."[50] Under the WTO jurisprudence, a measure is arbitrary—and a disguised restriction on trade—if it "bear[s] no rational connection to the objective falling

[44] *Id.*

[45] *Id.* ¶7.206–7.207.

[46] *Id.* ¶7.206–7.207.

[47] Giroux, *supra* note 28.

[48] Appellate Body Report, *Brazil—Retreaded Tyres*, ¶151, WT/DS332/AB/R (Dec. 3, 2007) [hereinafter *Brazil—Retreaded Tyres*].

[49] Giroux, *supra* note 28.

[50] *Brazil—Retreaded Tyres*, *supra* note 43, ¶226–228.

within the purview of a paragraph of Article XX ...."[51] Moreover, the assessment "should be made in the light of the objective of the measure."[52] To the extent that Nigeria could prove that there is a connection between, on the one hand, stimulation of labor and employment under the Act and the betterment of the Nigerian economy, and on the other hand, the betterment of the Nigerian economy and the prevention of loss to human and plant life, the measures may surpass the requirement of the chapeau.

4.2.3.3 The Measures May Be Justified as an Action Required to Promote the Establishment of an Industry

Article XVIII:C allows WTO members to "deviate from [the GATT] ... where governmental assistance [is] required to promote the establishment of an industry with a view to raising the general standard of living of the country concerned."[53] In order for GATT Art. XVIII:C to apply, three considerations must be satisfied. These considerations involve (i) the scope of the exception (Members and measures covered), (ii) its requirements, and (iii) the procedures applicable for the review of a Member's measures.[54]

Article XVIII:C applies to members "the economy of which can only support low standards of living and is in the early stages of development."[55] This element arises from GATT Art. XVIII:4(a) and is common to multiple sections of Article XVIII as to Members covered. Ad Article XVIII clarifies that the phrase "can only support low standards of living," is to be read in consideration of the: "normal position of that economy and shall not base their determination on exceptional circumstances such as those which may result from the temporary existence of exceptionally favourable conditions for the staple export product or products of such contracting party."[56]

Ad Article XVIII also confirms that the phrase "in the early stages of development" is: "not meant to apply only to contracting parties which

[51] *Id.*

[52] *Id.*

[53] Article XVIII, *in* WTO, WTO Analytical Index 456 (3rd ed. 2012).

[54] GATT Art. XVIII:4(a).

[55] *Id.*

[56] GATT Ad Art. XVIII.

have just started their economic development, but also to contracting parties the economies of which are undergoing a process of industrialization to correct an excessive dependence on primary production."[57]

Nigeria can be considered as a Member that falls within the purview of the aforementioned descriptions, as its economy is undergoing a process of industrialization and several sectors are in the nascent stages of development. The World Bank in its Nigeria Economic Report (NER), 2014 indicated that the per capita national poverty rate based on the official poverty line may now be as low as 33.1% and a large share of the Nigerian population is still not far above the poverty line, indicating vulnerability.[58] The unemployment rate in Nigeria according to a usual (ILO) definition is likely lower than 10%. In *India – Quantitative Restrictions* the conditions were held to apply to India, despite being ranked above Nigeria both in terms of GDP per capita (with purchasing power parity) and in indicators such as the Human Development Index.[59]

Moreover, Article XVIII:C requires that the measure must be applied (i) "with a view to raising the general standard of living of its people" and (ii) "no measure consistent with the other provisions of this Agreement is practicable to achieve that objective."[60] With regard to raising standard of living, the Decision on Safeguard Action for Development Purposes adopted on 28 November 1979,[61] states that WTO members agreed that programmers and policies of economic development aimed at raising the standard of living of the people:

> may involve in addition to the establishment of particular industries the development of new or the modification or extension of existing production structures with a view to achieving fuller and more efficient use

[57] *Id.*

[58] Nigeria Economic Report: Improved Economic Outlook in 2014, and Prospects for Continued Growth Look Good, World Bank (July 22, 2014), http://www.worldbank.org/en/country/nigeria/publication/nigeria-economic-report-improved-economic-outlook-in-2014-and-prospects-for-continued-growth-look-good.

[59] Panel Report, *India—Quantitative Restrictions on Imports of Agricultural, Textile and Industrial Products*, ¶3.224–3.249, WT/DS90/R (Apr. 6, 1999).

[60] GATT Art. XVIII:13.

[61] Decision of 28 November 1979, "Safeguard Action for Development Purposes", L/4897, BISD 26S/209–210.

of resources in accordance with the priorities of their economic development.[62]

Hence, despite the fact that the oil industry is established in Nigeria, the Act could reasonably be viewed as a transformation of an existing industry to achieve better economic outcomes for Nigeria.[63]

With regard to the feasibility of other alternatives, Nigeria would have to examine the difficulties that "alternative measures, such as tariffs (or tariff quotas) and subsidies … might create for the achievement of the objectives proposed by the [Nigerian Government]."[64] It is reasonable to conclude that tariff quotas and subsidies are not feasible alternatives to tackle violence and lack of local participation in the oil and gas industry. Indeed, for the industry to prosper, indigenous people would need to be stakeholders in the future development of the industry.[65]

Lastly, in relation to the procedural requirements of GATT Art. XVIII:C, Nigeria must comply with the procedure set out in GATT Art. XVIII:13 which imposes notification and consultation obligation on the Member taking the measure. The Members must notify other members of the measure. If within 30 days other members do not request a consultation, the Member will be free to deviate from its GATT obligation. In this case, Nigeria did not comply with the notification requirement. It is very likely however that Nigeria is not foreclosed from relying on Article XVIII. For instance, a panel on Art. XVIII considered certain measures by the Government of Ceylon. "which had not been notified to the CONTRACTING PARTIES before they were put into force[.]" The panel merely "[expressed] the hope that if the need for similar temporary measures should arise in the future, the Ceylon Government would inform the CONTRACTING PARTIES before putting such measures into force."[66] Consequently, the position of the panel seems to indicate that failure to notify other members may not be fatal to a party's reliance on Article XVIII.

[62] *Id.*

[63] *See also* L/751, adopted on November 28, 1957, 6S/112, 114–115, ¶ 6–9.

[64] *Id.*

[65] Giroux, *supra* note 28.

[66] L/932, "Notifications by Ceylon," adopted on November 22, 1958, L/932, 56S/75, 78, ¶8.

4.2.4 Action Plan

Based on the above analysis of the Measures, their compliance with GATT Art. III:4 and TRIMs Art. 2.1 and possible justifications that Nigeria may pursue in their support, the following action plan is suggested for the path ahead in continuing to achieve the broader policy objectives of the Measures and the Act in a WTO-consistent manner.

- The concerns raised against the Act primarily relate to Nigeria's national treatment obligations under GATT and TRIMs. It is likely that upon challenge, these concerns may not be adequately defended in the event of a WTO Dispute. Therefore, in order to mitigate the concerns raised by WTO Members, Nigeria could consider amending the Sections and the Schedule of the Act by eliminating references to goods. By eliminating local content requirements on goods and limiting the Schedule of the Act to services, Nigeria would be eliminating the aspect of the Act which is most likely in conflict with national treatment obligations of the GATT and TRIMs. As Nigeria has not made any commitments under its Schedule of Specific Commitments of the GATS for oil and gas services, creating preferences for services and service suppliers may face weaker opposition from WTO members. Appendix-B contains suggested modifications to the Sections of the Act.
- In parallel, Nigeria should begin to communicate its intention to rely upon GATT Art. XXI, the security exception, to justify the Act. Nigeria must in all possible fora assert that the Act is necessary for maintaining peace and security in the Niger Delta and that Nigeria is the sole judge to determine what *it considers* necessary to protect its essential security interest.
- Finally, Nigeria must begin the consultation process with the relevant Committee required for proceeding with obligations under GATT Art. XVIII:C in order to ease the concerns raised by other WTO members.

4.3 Certain Measures Regarding the Importation of Fish

4.3.1 Overview of the Measures

The Federal Department of Fisheries ("FDF") of Nigeria's Federal Ministry of Agriculture is the department responsible for supervising and regulating the production, importation, and distribution of fish and fish products. The Government of Nigeria, through the FDF, has introduced several measures to regulate imports of fish into Nigeria, allocate quantity permitted to be imported, and lay down the procedures for obtaining licenses to import fish into Nigeria titled "Proposed Guidelines."[67] Primarily, the Proposed Guidelines introduce a procedure for obtaining an import license for import of an "allocated quantity" of fish as per the Letter of Clearances that are issued by the FDF. The Proposed Guidelines, also specify the types of fish that are permitted to be imported.

The FDF issues a Letter of Clearance to importers indicating, among other things, the quantities and values of fish to be imported on a bi-annual basis.[68] The Proposed Guidelines are silent on the quantity allowed per importer, however, there is evidence that Nigeria aims at "a 25% reduction of fish importation annually" to be achieved through the Letter of Clearance system. Fish importers apply to the Central Bank of Nigeria ("CBN") to obtain the foreign exchange required to pay for their fish imports by completing a "Form M" document. The "Form M" applications are made to the CBN by attaching the Letters of Clearance for the importation of fish issued by the FDF. Subsequently, the importers seek an import license for the consignment as provided under the Proposed Guidelines per import purchase or shipment.

The Proposed Guidelines require the importer to submit the application for the import license at least 7 working days prior to the expected date of arrival of the vessel with cargo. The application is required to be submitted with other information and documents such as the Completed Vessel data, Proforma Invoice containing the type, quantity, and price of the fish, Radiation and Toxic-Free certificate, Health Certificate,

[67] Federal Department of Fisheries, Proposed New Guidelines on Fish Importation (on file with author) (Hereinafter Proposed Guidelines). The Beneficiary has communicated that the "Proposed Guidelines" are actually in effect.

[68] *Id.* ¶ 1.11.

Approved (Exchange Control) Form M, Bill of Lading, labeling denoting the quantity, type of species, and destination of the fish, and other criteria.[69]

The following provisions of the Proposed Guidelines may operate as restrictions or prohibitions on fish imports into Nigeria and are grouped into two measures, collectively referred to as the "Fisheries Measures":

- *Measure 1:* The Proposed Guidelines prohibit the importation of fish other than certain permitted pelagic fish. The prohibition covers farmed fish, either frozen or smoked, and products of farmed fish into Nigeria.
  - Para. 1.3 provides that: "Importation shall be limited to pelagic fish (Mackerel, Sardine, Horse Mackerel, Herring, Blue Whiting, Hake, Stockfish/ Stockfish Head and Croacker). The intention is to promote or stimulate local fish production and avoid Nigeria being used as a dumping ground. This list of species is to be reviewed periodically."
  - Para. 1.5 provides that: "Any imported farmed fish (frozen, smoked or products) shall be destroyed at the expense of the importer and fines would be paid at N1 per KG to Federal Government, subject to review."[70]
- *Measure 2:* The Proposed Guidelines limit the importation of certain pelagic fish per importer up to the "allocated quantity" decided by the FDF in the Letter of Clearance issued to that importer.
  - Para. 1.2 provides that: "Each fish importing company shall not exceed her allocated quantity. Any company that exceeds her allocated quantity should not be issued with another letter of clearance while her license will be revoked."

4.3.2 *Analysis of the Measures*

The Measures limit the quantities and the types of fish and fish products that can be imported into Nigeria. These Measures raise some concerns

[69] *Id.* ¶3.1–3.15.

[70] Proposed Guideline, *supra* note 59.

with respect to GATT Art. XI.[71] With certain limited exceptions, GATT Art. XI:1 provides that "[n]o prohibitions or restrictions ... made effective through quotas, import or export licenses or other measures, shall be instituted or maintained by [a member] ... on the importation of any product of [other member] ...."[72] In order to determine whether a measure violates GATT Art. XI, it is necessary to ascertain if the measure (a) falls within the purview of type of measures covered by the Article and (b) constitutes a "prohibition" or a "restriction" on the importation of a product from a member.

It is a well-settled position that an import licensing system that makes effective a prohibition or restriction on imports and a total ban on imports are covered by the provisions of GATT Art. XI:1. Moreover, a measure which "limits" or has a "limiting effect" on the importation of goods is understood to be a "restriction," while one that operates as a complete ban on importation is understood to be a "prohibition."[73] The Fisheries Measures effectuates an import licensing system and a total ban, operating both as total import prohibition on certain fish and also as an import restriction on other types of fish, and hence, is likely to be in violation of GATT Art. XI.

Measure 1 limits the importation of fish in Nigeria to certain pelagic fish, viz; Mackerel, Sardine, Horse Mackerel, Herring, Blue Whiting, Hake, Stockfish/ Stockfish Head, and Croacker. Hence, it imposes a total prohibition on the importation of any type of fish other than said pelagic fish. An absolute prohibition on the importation of the other types of fish is carried out. Measure 1 also prescribes that any imported farmed fish, frozen or smoked, or products of imported farmed fish are to be destroyed, imposing an absolute prohibition on the import of farmed fish into Nigeria. Hence, Measure 1 imposes a de facto zero quota on imports of any type of fish other than the said pelagic fish and farmed fish.

Measure 2 mandates that each pelagic fish importing company shall not exceed the "allocated quantity" allotted to it by the FDF under the Letter

[71] The analysis will reference concerns raised at the Council for Trade in Goods and at the Committee for Import Licensing, as per the mandate provided the Beneficiary. Other possible violations shall be examined in detail upon further instructions from the Beneficiary.

[72] GATT Art. XI:1.

[73] Panel Report, *India—Autos*, ¶ 7.269–7.270, WT/DS146/R, WT/DS175/R (Dec. 21, 2001).

of Clearance. In case a company exceeds the allocated quantity, no additional Letter of Clearance shall be issued and the license to import shall also be revoked. The issuance of the import license is dependent on the Letter of Clearance being granted by the FDF.[74] The process of obtaining an "allocated quantity" under a Letter of Clearance is at non-automatic and at the discretion of the FDF insofar as the Proposed Guidelines do not provide any particular numerical "allocated quantity." The "allocated quantity" is decided on a case-by-case basis and the Authorities are not bound to mandatorily grant the application for a Letter of Clearance. The issuance of the Import License also appears to be discretionary, but, as it is subject to the grant of a Letter of Clearance and the "allocated quantity," it is also subjected to the same discretionary and non-automatic assessment as the Letter of Clearance. Through these requirements, the FDF applies an import restriction on the quantity of fish permitted to be imported into Nigeria.[75] Thus, Measure 2 operates as a restriction by having a limiting effect on the importation of fish into Nigeria through a license system and a *de facto* quota on the import of certain pelagic fish.

4.3.3 Possible Justifications

4.3.3.1 The Measures May Be Justified as Exceptions to Quantitative Restrictions

GATT Art. XI:2 provides exclusions to the general prohibition on quantitative restrictions. In particular, GATT Art. XI:1 does not apply to import or export prohibitions or restrictions (a) "necessary to the application of standards or regulations for the classification, grading or marketing of

[74] As delineated in the Responses By Nigeria To The Concerns Raised By Iceland, Norway And Uruguay On The Reported Restrictive Policy By Nigeria On Importation Of Fish And Fish Products, through the issuance of Letters of Clearance, the FDF seeks to effectuate a quota in furtherance of a proposed new Fish Policy that aims at stimulating domestic production and a 25% reduction of fish importation annually in order to grow the fish industry in Nigeria. Responses By Nigeria To The Concerns Raised By Iceland, Norway And Uruguay On The Reported Restrictive Policy By Nigeria On Importation Of Fish And Fish Products, Committee on Import Licensing, G/LIC/Q/NGA/1 dated Oct. 27, 2014.

[75] Import licensing systems that are discretionary and non-automatic have been found to operate as an import restriction and violate GATT Art. XI:1. *See* Panel Report, ***India—Quantitative Restrictions***, ¶5.130, WT/DS90/R (Apr. 6, 1999).

commodities in international trade[]" or (b) "necessary to the enforcement of governmental measures which operate: ... to restrict the quantities of the like domestic product permitted to be marketed or produced, ..."[76]

The Measures May Be Necessary to the Application of Standards or Regulations for Classification, Grading, or Marketing of Fish

Nigeria could argue that the Fisheries Measures are intended to regulate the marketing of imported fish in Nigeria and defense under may be claimed. In order for a measure to be justified under GATT Art. XI:2(b) the following conditions must be satisfied, (i) the measure is an import prohibition or restriction and (ii) the measure is necessary for the marketing, classification, or grading of fish.

Based on case law dealing with other provisions of the GATT, necessity is understood to entail an analysis of weighing and balancing of the importance of objectives pursued, of the contribution of the measure to the ends sought by it, and of the existence of other less trade-restrictive reasonably available alternatives. The drafting history indicates that this exception applies to governmental measures relating to the orderly marketing of agricultural commodities for which storage facilities in both the country of origin and destination were insufficient[.] ...."[77]

Nigeria has consistently reported significant and voluminous imports of fish and has indicated that it has insufficient cold storage facilities.[78] Moreover, adequate cold storage facilities are necessary to ensure safe and wholesome marketing of imported fish. Hence, Nigeria may be able to argue that the restrictions and prohibitions are necessary so that existing limited storage capacity is utilized for the safe storage of imported fish prior to its marketing. Over-importation, when combined with inadequate cold storage facilities, leads to marketing of unwholesome and unhealthy fish. The Fisheries Measures therefore contributes to the safe and wholesome marketing of imported fish by limiting over-importation.

[76] GATT Art. XI:2

[77] Article XI, *in* WTO, WTO Analytical Index 456 (3rd ed. 2012).

[78] Speech Delivered by Dr. Akinwumi Adeshina, The Honorable Minister of Agriculture and Rural Development, Re-Positioning the Fisheries Sector (Feb. 25, 2014), http://www.boldanagro.com/2014/02/re-positioning-fisheries-sector-speech.html.

Hence, Nigeria may rely on GATT Art. XI:2(b) in justifying the Fisheries Measures, but there would be a significant burden to establish that the Fisheries Measures are the "least trade restrictive" alternative for applying regulations or standards for the grading, classification or marketing of fish in Nigeria. It may be noted that as there is no established jurisprudence on the interpretation of "necessary" under GATT Art. XI:2(b), it may be the case that the standard is not as high as that of "necessary" under GATT Art. XX.

The Measures May Be Necessary to the Enforcement of Governmental Measures Which Operate to Restrict the Quantities of Like Domestic Fish Permitted to Be Marketed or Produced

GATT Art. XI:2(c)(i) allows WTO Members to impose import restrictions on fisheries, so long as they are necessary for the enforcement of governmental measures which restrict the quantities of the like domestic product permitted to be marketed or produced. This exception may be considered to require three elements: (i) an import restriction (ii) governmental measures which restrict the quantities of the like domestic product permitted to be marketed or produced, and that (iii) the measure be "necessary" for the enforcement of the said governmental measures.

Measure 1 operates as a total ban on the importation of farmed fish and fish other than certain pelagic fish. Hence, the exception under GATT Art. XI:2(c)(i) which applies only in relation to import "restrictions" may be allowed only with regard to Measure 2.

The Nigerian Sea Fisheries Act and of the Sea Fisheries Licensing Regulations may serve Nigeria in the context of justification under GATT Art. XI:2(c)(i) to the extent that both are governmental measures that appear to restrict the quantities of the domestic sea fish permitted to be marketed or produced in Nigeria. The Sea Fisheries Act and the Sea Fisheries Licensing Regulations have discretionary domestic licensing provisions which operate to restrict the total domestic sea fishing, including all pelagic and non-pelagic fish, by means of regulating and limiting the domestic licenses issued for domestic sea fishing.[79] Furthermore, the Inland Fisheries Act and the Inland Fisheries (Fish Quality Assurance)

[79] Sea Fisheries Act, Sections 3, 4, 6, http://faolex.fao.org/docs/pdf/nig18399.pdf; Sea Fisheries Licensing Regulations, Sections 1, 2, 4, 5, 6, 7, 8, 9, 10, 11, http://faolex.fao.org/docs/pdf/nig18399.

Regulations are also governmental measures that may be read to operate to restrict quantities of domestic sea fish, farmed fish and fish products insofar as it imposes restrictions on the manner of fishing, production processes permitted, types or species permitted, and quality of the fish itself.[80] These laws and regulations do not apply a numerical ceiling but are governmental measures that restrict the quantities of domestic fisheries through licensing requirements as well as other provisions regulating fishing, marketing, harvesting, and processing of domestic fish and fish products. Hence, these are identifiable as governmental measures which operate to restrict the quantities of all domestic fish permitted to be marketed or produced in Nigeria.

With respect to the "necessity" requirement, on the basis of case law relating to similar provisions it is likely to be interpreted as entailing that the defended measure be both designed/adopted to enforce the governmental measure restricting the like domestic product, and be necessary for such enforcement. Sea fishing is generally carried out for pelagic species. Nigeria has adopted a policy of promoting fish farming to reduce the reliance on sea fishing owing to a multitude of reasons, including the health and safety of fishing communities.[81]

It may be argued that Nigeria has imposed restrictions on sea fish through the Nigerian Sea Fisheries Act, the Sea Fisheries Licensing Regulations, the Inland Fisheries Act, and Inland Fisheries (Fish Quality Assurance) Regulations to promote the consumption of farmed fish and restriction on imports of certain pelagic sea fish is necessary to enforce the continued consumption of farmed fish and fish products. Thus, the governmental measures to restrict the quantities of the domestic sea fish would be rendered infructuous if indeed the import restriction was not applied to sea fish and farmed fish and fish products. Hence, it may be argued

[80] Inland Fisheries (Fish Quality Assurance) Regulations, Sections 1, 2, 5, 6, 7, 10, 11, http://faolex.fao.org/cgi-bin/faolex.exe?rec_id=120410&database=faolex&search_type=link&table=result&lang=eng&format_name=@ERALL.

[81] *See* Dr. Akinwumi Speech, *supra* note 80 ("The Nigerian marine waters are plagued with almost daily attacks by armed robbers on our shrimp trawling vessels, leading to killings and maiming of crew members, abduction of key officers and demand for huge ransom for their release, seizure of vessels for days leading to loss of fishing days, and the removal of fishing/communication equipment and catches.... These attacks have become an embarrassment to security agencies ... The socio-economic impact is huge ....").

that the Fisheries Measures in the Proposed Guidelines are import restrictions which are "necessary" for enforcing the governmental measures for restricting the total sea fish that are produced and marketed in Nigeria.

Finally, the proviso to GATT Art XI(2)(c)(i) mandates that public notice of the total quantity or value of the product permitted to be imported for a specified future period and any change in such quantity or value be provided. Hence, Nigeria may consider immediately issuing a public notice in this regard. Moreover, the restrictions applied under GATT Art.XI:2(c)(i) cannot be such as to reduce the total of imports relative to the total of domestic production, as compared with the proportion which might reasonably be expected to rule between the two in the absence of restrictions. The determination of this proportion is to be calculated with due regard to the proportion prevailing during a previous representative period and to any special factors which may have affected or may be affecting the trade in the product concerned. Hence, Nigeria would need to ensure that Measure 2 does not affect the total quantity of imports in a manner prohibited under this proviso. Further, a comparison of present imports of the permitted pelagic fish with the level of imports of the same types of fish before the introduction of the Measure 2 may reveal that no such reduction of the total of imports in relation to the domestic production has occurred. Hence, the said justification for Measure 2 under GATT Art. XI:2(c)(i) may be considered.

4.3.3.2 The Measures May Be Justified Under the General Exceptions Clause

Nigeria may be able to rely on Art. XX to defend its Fisheries Measures. Art. XX can be invoked as a justification for WTO-inconsistent measures, that, among other things are: (i) "necessary to protect human, animal or plant life or health[], (ii) "necessary to secure compliance with laws or regulations which are [themselves] not inconsistent with the provisions of" the GATT, or (iii) measures that, with certain conditions, relate "to the conservation of exhaustible natural resources."[82]

For an Art. XX defense to succeed, a two-tiered test must be met.[83] First the measure must fall under one of the exceptions listed in the various subparagraphs of Art. XX. Second, the measure must satisfy the

[82] GATT Art. XX.

[83] *Brazil—Retreaded Tyres*, *supra* note 43, ¶139.

requirements of the chapeau of Art. XX that the measure is not "applied in a manner which would constitute a means of arbitrary or unjustifiable discrimination between countries where the same conditions prevail or a disguised restriction on international trade."[84]

The Measures May Be Necessary to Protect Human Health

It could be argued that the Fisheries Measures aim to prevent the distribution of decaying and unfit fish in Nigeria which results from over-importation of fish stored in inadequate and unhealthy storage conditions, by prescribing prohibitions on the importation of non-pelagic and farmed fish and products, and by imposing quantitative restrictions on the importation of certain pelagic fish.

A justification under subparagraph (b) of GATT Art. XX requires that (i) the measure be designed to protect human health and (ii) be necessary for such protection. Necessity is understood to entail an analysis of the importance of the values and objectives pursued, of the contribution of the measure to the ends sought by it, and of the existence of other less trade-restrictive reasonably available alternatives.

The Fisheries Measures could be presented as designed to protect the health of the consumers from risks caused by the spread of consumption of decomposed and unwholesome imported farmed fish that does not conform to Nigeria's regulations.[85] Nigeria claims to not have adequate cold storage facilities to ensure that imports of sea fish are stored and marketed in wholesome, healthy and non-decomposed conditions.[86] The imported sea fish and farmed fish and fish products cannot be distinguished at the point of sale to the consumers between safely stored and unhealthily stored fish. Owing to the over-importation and insufficient cold storage capacity, decomposing imported fish is being marketed in Nigeria. This places consumers in Nigeria at risk from the consumption of imported fish. Thus, the Fisheries Measures under the Proposed Guidelines could be presented as designed to protect the health of the consumers.

[84] GATT Art. XX.

[85] See Proposed Guidelines, *supra* note 59, ¶1.2.

[86] Responses by Nigeria to the Concerns Raised By Iceland, Norway And Uruguay on the Reported Restrictive Policy by Nigeria on Importation of Fish and Fish Products, Committee on Import Licensing, G/LIC/Q/NGA/1 (Oct. 27, 2014).

Furthermore, the limitations on importation of fish contribute to protecting the health and safety of consumers by preventing over-importation and marketing of unsafe and unhealthy fish. It should be noted that there would be a significant burden to establish that the Fisheries Measures are the "least trade restrictive" alternative. Nigeria may submit that preventing over-importation and allowing importation commensurate to storage capacity are the "least trade restrictive"measures available as other methods may not be reasonably available to ensure the health and safety of the consumers. Hence, a justification under GATT Art. XX(b) may be pursued for the Fisheries Measures.

The Measures May Be Necessary to Secure Compliance with Laws Not Inconsistent with WTO Obligations

It could also be argued that the Fisheries Measure is justified under GATT Art. XX(d) as being necessary to secure compliance with a WTO-consistent law or regulation, such as the Nigerian Sea Fisheries Act and Regulations thereunder and the Inland Fisheries Act and Regulations thereunder. For a measure to be justified under subparagraph (d) of Article XX, the measure (i) must be designed to secure compliance with a national law or regulation which itself is not GATT-inconsistent, and (ii) must be necessary to ensure such compliance.

It can be argued that domestic statutes and regulations in Nigeria operate to ensure that fish and fish products marketed to consumers in Nigeria are wholesome, healthy and not in a decomposing condition. For instance, the Nigerian Sea Fisheries Act regulates the quantity of fish, the kind of fishing and the quality of the fish that is marketed in Nigeria. Similarly, the Inland Fisheries Act and the Regulations have specific standards and requirements applicable to the production of fish, processing of fish products, storage and place of sale, and the marketing of safe and wholesome domestic fish.[87] By restricting and prohibiting imported fish, the Fisheries Measures operate to ensure that the imported fish that is marketed to consumers in Nigeria is in line with the objectives pursued by these domestic laws. Stale and decaying fish and fish products that otherwise do not conform to the standards of processing, production, storage,

[87] The Inland Fisheries Regulations also provides for destruction of farmed fish that is not in conformity with the provisions of the Regulations. *See* Inland Fisheries Regulation, *supra* note 82.

and marketing applicable to domestic fisheries are not sold to consumers in Nigeria.

Assuming that these domestic laws and regulations are also not inconsistent with Nigeria's WTO obligations, Nigeria could argue that the Fisheries Measure is necessary to secure compliance with the abovementioned domestic regulations relating to marketing and sale of the wholesome and healthy fish.

As noted above in relation to GATT Art. XX(b), it would be a significant burden to establish that the Fisheries Measures are the "least trade restrictive" alternative. Nigeria may submit that the Fisheries Measures are the "least trade restrictive" measures as the domestic laws also operate to restrict and prohibit sale of unhealthy fish to consumers in Nigeria and without the limitations on importation of fish, the objectives of the domestic law may not be reasonably achieved. To that end, a justification under GATT Art. XX(d) may be pursued to defend the Fisheries Measures.

The Measures May Relate to the Conservation of Exhaustible Natural Resources

Nigeria may justify its measure by invoking Art. XX(g) which allows for a WTO-inconsistent measure if the measure (i) relates to the conservation of natural resources and (ii) if such measure is "made effective in conjunction with restrictions on domestic production or consumption[.]"[88] It is important to note that unlike GATT Art. XX(b) and (d) mentioned above, GATT Art. XX(g) does not entail a "necessity" requirement.

Nigeria could argue that sea fish are exhaustible natural resources. Being mindful of the conservation of its exhaustible natural resources, the Nigerian Sea Fisheries Act ensures that fishing activities are not likely to be prejudicial to the interests of the sea fishing industry in Nigeria and the promotion of farmed fish is to ensure that the dependence on sea fish is reduced and consumer demand can be sustainably met with farmed fish. Hence, the Fisheries Measures operate to increase reliance on farmed fish and conserve the sea fish which is treated as an exhaustible natural resource. Notably, *ex facie,* Measure 1 operates to create a prohibition on imports of farmed fish. Nigeria may submit that the prohibition

[88] GATT Art. XX(g).

on imports of farmed fish and fish products greatly stimulates the marketing of domestic farmed fish as a substitute for sea fish, thereby replacing the existing demand of sea fish. Thus, the Fisheries Measures operate to ensure the conservation of sea fish by decreasing the reliance on sea fish.

Further, for a measure to be justified under subparagraph (g) of Article XX it must be made effective in conjunction with restrictions on domestic production or consumption. As stated above in the context of defense under GATT Art. XI:2, Nigeria has imposed limits on the domestic production of sea fish. The Fisheries Measure may be considered to be rendered effective with domestic restrictions and may pass muster as a provisional justification under GATT Art. XX(g).

The Measures May Comply with the Requirement Under the Chapeau

As a final note, it is to be taken into account that a justification under GATT Arts. XX(b), XX(d), and XX(g) must also fulfill the requirements of the chapeau of GATT Art. XX which establishes that measures must not arbitrarily or unjustifiably discriminate between countries where the same conditions prevail, and must not tantamount to a disguised restriction on trade. A measure is arbitrary, when for example, the discrimination does not bear a rational relationship with the objectives it pursues.

An important distinction resulting from the Fisheries Measures is that, while Measure 2 only imposes a restriction, Measure 1 imposes a prohibition on imports of fish. A further distinction that results from the Fisheries Measures is that while they place limitations on imported fish, no such limitation is placed on domestic fish. These distinctions may be challenged as arbitrary if they bear no rational relationship with the several objectives that are used for justifying them under GATT Art. XX.

However, Nigeria may argue that the rationale for distinguishing between fish that are totally banned and those that are only restricted is based on consumer preferences and existing cold storage capacity. Consumers' preferences in Nigeria lead to a higher demand for the restricted fish than the prohibited fish. The Fisheries Measure draws a distinction that takes into account the consumer preference in Nigeria. Therefore, the distinction not only bears a rational relationship to the objective of ensuring risk to human life and health, securing compliance with domestic fisheries laws and regulations, and the conservation of sea fish, but also balances and preserves the consumer preferences in Nigeria.

As regards the absence of any express limitations on domestic fish, it can be argued that the domestic laws and regulations of Nigeria indeed operate to limit domestic fish, as those laws and regulations place conditions on the types of fish, the manner of fishing, size of the fish, and the method of production, among others, that have a limiting effect on domestic fish. Furthermore, Nigeria could argue that any differences regarding the limitations themselves arise from the different cold storage needs that arise in respect of domestic fish. The demand for the limited cold storage facilities arising from the supply of domestic fish is lower, and therefore the Fisheries Measures and the fisheries laws and regulations need not have the same limiting effect. Therefore, Nigeria may argue that the distinction drawn by Fisheries Measures is not arbitrary nor a disguised restriction on trade and satisfy the requirements *chapeau* of GATT Art. XX.

4.3.3.3 The Measures May Be Justified Under the Balance-of-Payments Exception

The GATT contains two sets of rules under which WTO Members may take measures to address balance-of-payments difficulties. These rules are set out in GATT Arts. XII and XVIII:B, and are further elaborated in the Understanding on Balance-of-Payments Provisions [hereinafter referred to as the "BoP Understanding"]. GATT Art. XVIII:B has been designed as an exception for developing countries, is more lenient than GATT Art. XII, and may be invoked not only to safeguard a Member's financial position and balance-of-payments (as GATT Art. XII), but also to ensure a level of reserves adequate for the implementation of its program of economic development. It would therefore be the preferred route for Nigeria to adopt.

GATT Art. XVIII:9 provides:

> In order to safeguard its external financial position and to ensure a level of reserves adequate for the implementation of its programme of economic development, a contracting party coming within the scope of paragraph 4 (a) of this Article may, subject to the provisions of paragraphs 10 to 12, control the general level of its imports by restricting the quantity or value of merchandise permitted to be imported[.][89]

[89] GATT Art. XVIII:9.

Three sets of considerations must be satisfied in order for GATT Art. XVIII:B to apply. These considerations involve (i) the scope of the exception (members and measures covered), (ii) its requirements, and (iii) the procedures applicable for the review of a Member's balance-of-payments restrictions.

As to Members covered, it is likely that Nigeria be considered falling within the purview of GATT Art. XVIII:B as discussed in the Section above.[90] As to the measures covered, Balance-of-payments measures can only be applied after several requirements are met. Firstly, GATT Art. XVIII:9(a) establishes that a WTO Member may take a balance-of-payments measure provided that it does not "exceed those necessary: (a) to forestall the threat of, or to stop, a serious decline in its monetary reserves." The BoP Understanding further explains that restrictive import measures taken for balance-of-payments purposes "may not exceed what is necessary to address the balance-of-payments situation."[91]

The nature of Nigeria's current balance-of-payments situation is likely to be of the type for which GATT Art. XVIII:B was specifically designed. For the last few years, the international price of crude oil has dramatically decreased. Rising to the overwhelming price of 123 dollars in 2012, the OPEC basket price of oil has now averaged below 28 dollars (February 2016). This represents a decrease of over 77% in the price of oil. The crash of oil prices was especially dramatic in 2014. That year alone the price of crude oil fell over 50%, starting at 106 dollars and falling to 52 dollars by the end of December (Fig. 4.1).[92]

Even though the petroleum sector represents only 14% of the Nigerian economy, oil is a critical commodity as it contributes to over 90% of exports and is the main source of foreign direct investment inflows.[93] This enormous dependency on oil means that oil export disruptions have the potential to significantly impact Nigeria's balance-of-payments. These disruptions have thus caused a considerable contraction in the supply of foreign exchange. Since the decline of the international price of crude oil, the Nigerian government has been under exceeding pressure to offset

[90] *See supra* Part II.C.3.

[91] GATT Art. XVIII:9(a).

[92] OPEC Basket Price, OPEC, http://www.opec.org/opec_web/en/data_graphs/40.htm (last visited Apr. 22, 2016).

[93] National Bureau of Statistics of Nigeria, http://www.nigerianstat.gov.ng/ (last visited Apr. 22, 2016).

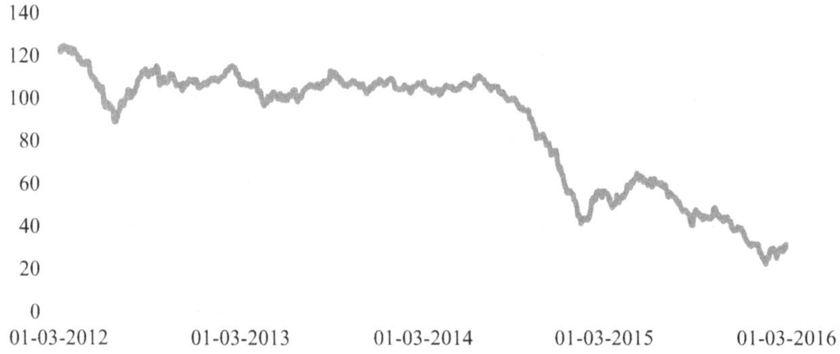

Fig. 4.1 Oil prices in USD (*Source* OPEC reference basket [2016])

balance-of-payments difficulties and to provide foreign exchange liquidity support for the naira. In particular, to ensure that demands of foreign exchange are met without affecting the naira price of the dollar, the CBN has placed a *de facto* peg on the naira and has as a result been forced to forgo much of its foreign exchange reserves. Nigeria's foreign exchange reserves, which rose to over $47.9 billion in 2013, have been on the decline, reaching $34.2 billion by the end of 2014, and further declining to $27.8 billion today (March 2016) (Fig. 4.2).[94]

It may be claimed that the fall of foreign exchange reserves in Nigeria can be described as a "serious decline," and it may be possible that the measures taken by Nigeria are considered as not exceeding what is necessary to address the balance-of-payments situation. However, the determination of the seriousness of Nigeria's monetary reserves decline, and of whether or not the Fisheries Measures exceeds what is "necessary to forestall the threat of, or to stop," this decline, is nevertheless, as established in GATT Art. XV, a matter that is reserved for the IMF. As provided by GATT Art. XV:2,

> In all cases in which the CONTRACTING PARTIES are called upon to consider or deal with problems concerning monetary reserves, balances of payments or foreign exchange arrangements, they shall consult fully

[94] Central Bank of Nigeria, https://www.cbn.gov.ng/ (last visited Apr. 22, 2016).

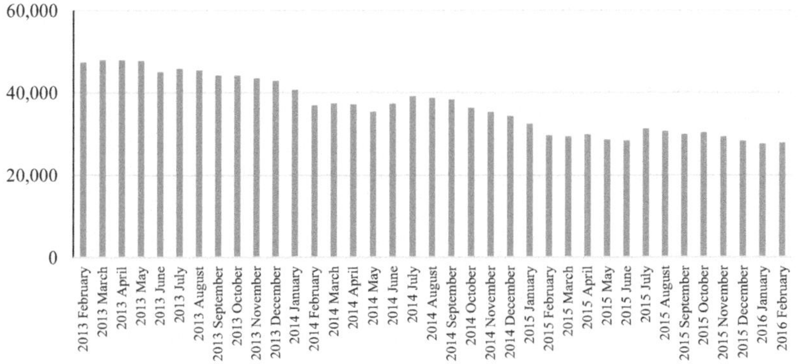

Fig. 4.2 Nigeria's foreign reserves in USD millions (*Source* Central Bank of Nigeria [2016])

> with the International Monetary Fund. In such consultations, the CONTRACTING PARTIES shall accept all findings of statistical and other facts presented by the Fund relating to foreign exchange, monetary reserves and balances of payments, and shall accept the determination of the Fund as to whether action by a contracting party in exchange matters is in accordance with the Articles of Agreement of the International Monetary Fund, or with the terms of a special exchange agreement between that contracting party and the CONTRACTING PARTIES. The CONTRACTING PARTIES in reaching their final decision in cases involving... paragraph 9 of Article XVIII, shall accept the determination of the Fund as to what constitutes a serious decline in the contracting party's monetary reserves, a very low level of its monetary reserves or a reasonable rate of increase in its monetary reserves, and as to the financial aspects of other matters covered in consultation in such cases.[95]

It will therefore be important for Nigeria to establish the severity and proportionality of its Fisheries Measure *vis-à-vis* the IMF, if a defense under GATT Art. XVIII:B is pursued. It is likely that, nevertheless, the Fisheries Measure will not exceed what is necessary to forestall the threat

[95] GATT Art. XV:2.

of, or to stop' the decline in monetary reserves because of the attenuated participation of fisheries imports in the current account of Nigeria.[96]

Secondly, GATT Art. XVIII:10 requires that measures taken for balance-of-payments reasons be temporary. It provides that as conditions improve, the measures be "progressively relaxed" and "eliminated" when conditions no longer justify their maintenance. As explained by para. 1 of the BoP Understanding, in applying balance-of-payments measures, Members are bound to publically announce as soon as practicable, time-schedules for their removal. Nigeria must therefore prepare and begin to design a time-limit of application for the application of its Fisheries Measures, and proceed to announce a schedule for fading it out if it is to have recourse to GATT Art. XVIII:B.

Nigeria should take into account that the temporal scope need not be definitive, as Members are given the possibility to modify the schedule to take into account changes in the balance-of-payments situation. Furthermore, the proviso of GATT Art. XVIII:11 imparts discretion for relaxation and elimination to the Member taking the measure of, so long as it is related to its development policy.

Thirdly, while GATT Art. XVIII:10 allows WTO Members to take measures, such as the Fisheries Measures, that discriminate with respect to different products, it also adds two provisos under this scenario such that the restrictions are so applied as to avoid unnecessary damage to the commercial or economic interests of any other member or unreasonably prevent the importation of any description of goods in "minimum commercial quantities" if such exclusion would impair regular channels of trade; and that the restrictions do not prevent the "importation of commercial samples" or "compliance with patent, trade mark, copyright or similar procedures."

Finally, in order to invoke GATT Art. XVIII:B as a justification for its Fisheries Measures, Nigeria must also comply with the procedure set out in GATT Art. XVIII:12. This procedure is set out to ensure that WTO Members observe the rules established for balance-of-payments restrictions, and it imposes a consultation obligation on the Member taking the measure. The starting point for consultations is the notification of

[96] Based on 2015 Trade data of Nigeria from the International Trade Centre. *See* Nigeria 2015 Data, International Trade Centre, http://www.intracen.org/layouts/CountryTemplate.aspx?pageid=47244645034&id=47244652394 Data, 2015 (last visited May 15, 2016).

the measure, which is required to take place no later than 30 days after its announcement. However, reverse notification is possible, as affirmed in para. 10 of the BoP Understanding. Consultations with the WTO's Committee on Balance-of-Payments Restrictions are, pursuant to GATT Art. XVIII:12(a), expected to follow immediately after the institution of the measure, and in any event within four months of its adoption as clarified in para. 6 of the BoP Understanding. Nigeria has not, as of yet, notified the General Council of the adoption of the Fisheries Measures and it has not initiated consultations within the Committee on Balance-of-Payments Restrictions. It should consider doing so as soon as possible in order to benefit from the provisions of GATT Art. XVIII:B.

In determining how to proceed in relation to the balance-of-payments exception, Nigeria should consider all the strict requirements that it imposes. Nigeria should also bear in mind that GATT Art. XVIII:B imposes consultation obligations which it is expected to observe, as it has done so in the past when taking other balance-of-payments measures before the turn of the century.

4.3.4 Action Plan

Based on the above analysis of the Fisheries Measures and possible justifications that Nigeria may pursue in their support under GATT Art.XI:2, XX, and XVIII:B the following action plan is suggested for the path ahead in continuing to achieve the broader policy objectives of the Fisheries Measures in a WTO-consistent manner.

- Nigeria may consider raising its MFN tariff on imports of fish up to the bound levels. Nigeria has binding tariff commitments on agricultural products including fish and fish products at 150%. Nigeria has notified only the ECOWAS[97] as a preferential trade agreement.[98] However, the majority of fish imports are from non-ECOWAS countries viz; China, United States, Netherlands, India, Belgium, United

[97] Economic Community of West African States (ECOWAS), Revised Treaty of the Economic Community of West African States (ECOWAS), July 24, 1993, http://www.refworld.org/docid/492182d92.html.

[98] ECOWAS Countries are: Benin, Burkina Faso, Cabo Verde, Côte d'Ivoire, Ghana, Guinea, Guinea-Bissau, Liberia, Republic of Mali, Niger, Nigeria, Senegal, Sierra Leone, The Gambia, Togo.

Kingdom, France, and Germany.[99] To that end, an increase in Nigeria's MFN tariff for fish imports up to the bound rate will impact all major fish import sources except the non-ECOWAS countries. The increase in import tariff will cause a significant increase in fish import costs and thereby, considerably reduce the imports of fish. This would also generate additional revenue for Nigeria.

- Nigeria may also rely on imposing Sanitary and Phytosanitary ("SPS") measures to restrict fish imports for the purpose of protecting human or animal life or health. These measures may include inspection or certification requirements. Nigeria may rely on scientific evidence and risk assessments already available from other WTO Members and could introduce immediate provisional measures. Technical Barriers to Trade ("TBT") measures may also be enacted to lay down mandatory guidelines and restrict fish imports using technical regulations, packaging, marking, or labeling requirements relating to the fish or fish products. If applied in conformity with the provisions of the SPS and TBT Agreements, Nigeria may be able to restrict fish imports without imposing quantitative restrictions.
- Anti-dumping or Countervailing duty proceedings against the large-scale imports of fisheries and fish products may provide an effective way to restrict fish imports. If imports are at lower prices than domestic prices in the exporting countries and causing "injury" to the domestic industry, or if exporters appear to be benefiting from subsidies from their own governments, an anti-dumping or countervailing duty can serve to apply additional duties to these imports for five years, with the possibility of continuing the duties through sunset reviews and have a restricting effect. However, in order to benefit from this solution, Nigeria should consider promulgating anti-dumping and countervailing duty laws as no such laws are currently in place.
- A safeguard proceeding may be initiated against the large-scale imports if it can be established that there has been a sudden, sharp and significant increase in imports, which was unforeseen and is causing injury to domestic producers. Successful proceedings can ensure that additional duties or a quota could be imposed up to a period

[99] Nigeria 2015 Data, *supra* note 98.

of 4 years, with gradual liberalization. This may immediately thwart the imports of fisheries and support the infant industry objective of the government of Nigeria. However, in order to benefit from this solution, Nigeria should consider promulgating safeguard laws as no such laws are currently in place.

- To introduce the Fisheries Measures as mandated by GATT Art. XVIII:B, Nigeria must seek to cooperate and fully consult with the IMF. The IMF is the organization entrusted with exchange questions, and it will therefore be the organization that makes the factual and statistical findings that are required to defend the Fisheries Measures in the WTO. Nigeria must also begin the consultation process with the Committee on Balance-of-Payments Restrictions and make any necessary amendments to the Fisheries Measures, in order to be able to avail itself of the defense enshrined in GATT Art. XVIII:B and to ease the concerns raised by other WTO Members.
- Finally, Nigeria may consider amending the provisions of the Proposed Guidelines so as to eliminate possible arbitrary statutory elements and discrimination between the restricted and prohibited fish. Nigeria should also endeavor to take internal measures in conjunction with the Proposed Guidelines such that comparable restrictions are made effective to domestic fish. These steps could improve the possibility of the Fisheries Measures being found in conformity with the requirements of the *chapeau* of GATT Art. XX.

4.4 The Measure Concerning Foreign Exchange

4.4.1 Overview of the Measure

On 23 June 2015, the CBN released a circular announcing that 40 categories of goods and 1 category of services would be excluded from the official Nigerian foreign exchange market ("Forex Measure"). The CBN's circular contains a list of "goods and services not valid for foreign exchange in the Nigerian foreign exchange markets."[100] The list includes items such as rice, cement, meat products, textiles, private airplanes,

[100] Central Bank of Nigeria, Inclusion of Some Imported Goods and Services on the List of Items Not Valid for Foreign Exchange in the Nigerian Foreign Exchange Market (June 23, 2015) (on file with author) (Hereinafter CNB Circular).

toothpicks, margarine, and certain foreign exchange services. Appendix contains the entire list of items in the circular. As a result of Forex Measure, the CBN's foreign exchange window is no longer accepting foreign exchange operations, the underlying transaction of which is the importation of any of the goods or services listed.[101]

The official foreign exchange market in Nigeria includes the inter-bank foreign exchange market and all operations with authorized dealers, banks and *bureaux-de-change* conducted *via* the CBN's foreign exchange window. The official foreign exchange market does not include the parallel market, which is also a legal market of foreign exchange in Nigeria.[102] As a result, on its face, the Measure does not completely restrict access to foreign exchange. Instead, the measure instructs importers requiring foreign exchange for the importation of any of the 40 goods and for the furnishing of the service therein described (i.e. requiring dollars for the

[101] We were originally told that the Beneficiary had either requested a roll-back of the Forex Measure or considering modifying the content of the list. Nevertheless, from our consultations it appears that the measure is currently enforced as such.

[102] Before February of 2015, foreign exchange trading in Nigeria took place in at least four different but interconnected foreign exchange market segments:

1. The official foreign exchange market managed by the CBN and operating under a Retail Dutch Auction System (RDAS) that consisted of a window available twice a week through which authorized dealers/banks would bid for foreign exchange on behalf of end users;
2. The inter-bank foreign exchange market in which banks sell foreign exchange independently sourced by them at a higher rate;
3. The market of the *bureaux-de-change*, comprised of operators that obtain foreign exchange from authorized dealers and sell it at a rate slightly higher than that of the CBN; and
4. The parallel market, which is the open market for the sale of foreign exchange, and which is usually sourced by smaller street retailers who conduct exchange transactions at the higher end of market rates.

On 18 February 2015, the CBN closed the RDAS segment of the foreign exchange market and announced that foreign exchange needs would have to be sourced from the inter-bank foreign exchange market, a market segment in which the rate had been ranging between 197 and 198 naira (the Nigerian currency) to the dollar. That day the CBN also announced that it would intervene in the IFEM to continue to provide foreign exchange liquidity support for the naira. The Bank has kept its promise, imposing a de facto peg of 196 to 199 naira to the dollar. It has also continued to make a window available for BDC operators to purchase dollars twice a week, as part of efforts to support the naira and narrow the gap between the official and parallel markets. However, the gap between the open and controlled foreign exchange market has since only widened.

payment of the current account transactions involving the items contained in the circular), to import those items "using their own funds, without any recourse to the Nigerian foreign exchange markets."[103]

4.4.2 *Analysis of the Measure*

4.4.2.1 The Measure May Be Outside the Scope of GATT Art. XI

GATT Art. XI, which sets out a general prohibition of quantitative restrictions, is not limited to border measures that set a specific numerical ceiling and is applicable to prohibitions or restrictions made effective through quotas, import or export licenses or "other measures." GATT Art. XI:1 states:

> No prohibitions or restrictions other than duties, taxes or other charges, whether made effective through quotas, import or export licences or other measures, shall be instituted or maintained by any contracting party on the importation of any product of the territory of any other contracting party or on the exportation or sale for export of any product destined for the territory of any other contracting party.

To determine whether a breach of GATT Article XI:1 has occurred, it is necessary to establish that (i) the measure at issue falls within the purview of measures covered by the Article and (ii) the measure constitutes a "prohibition" or a "restriction" on the importation or exportation of any product of the territory of any other contracting party.

The first question to be answered for the purposes of finding a violation under GATT Art. XI is whether the Forex Measure can be considered an "other measure." WTO panels[104] have given GATT Article XI:1 a broad scope. For example, several panels found that the prohibition applied to a wide spectrum of measures including, a system of minimum import licenses,[105] import restrictions made effective through an import monopoly and through State trading operations,[106] and restrictions on

[103] CNB Circular, *supra* note 102.

[104] And to a certain extent the Appellate Body.

[105] Panel Report, *EEC—Minimum Import Prices*, ¶3.1, L/4687 - 25S/68 (Oct. 18, 1978).

[106] Panel Report, *Korea—Various Measures on Beef*, ¶751, WT/DS161/R, WT/DS169/R (July 31, 2000).

ports of entry.[107] Given the broadness of scope, and taking into account that the Forex Measure is not "duties, taxes or other charges" (i.e. of the type of measures explicitly excluded from the scope of GATT Art. XI:1), it is possible that it be considered to be within the meaning of GATT Art.XI. However, Nigeria could argue that the Forex Measure does not fall within the scope of the GATT Art. XI as it is a measure that is monetary in nature. Though the term "other measures" has been broadly construed, the most recent Panel Report has established that GATT Art. XI:1 *does not* cover measures that are fiscal in nature.[108] The Forex Measure is an exchange-related measure and it may be contended that such exchange-related measures are not covered by GATT Art. XI:1, which was designed for trade-related measures.

This argument is also supported by the fact that GATT has a separate provision for dealing with exchange matters, GATT Art. XV, which is entitled "Exchange Arrangements." In particular, GATT Article XV:4 contains the following obligation which may be used to suggest that GATT Art. XI and XV are mutually exclusive: "Contracting parties shall not, by exchange action, frustrate the intent of the provisions of this Agreement, nor, by trade action, the intent of the provisions of the Articles of Agreement of the International Monetary Fund."[109] Therefore, it could be maintained that GATT Article XV:4 contains an all-encompassing rule for the treatment of measures related to exchange that would rule out the application of GATT Art. XI in the context of exchange-related measures. In this way, Nigeria may find it possible to contend that the Forex Measure is outside the scope of GATT Art. XI.

The second question to be answered in order to asses a violation of GATT Art. XI:1 is the extent to which the Forex Measure is a restriction on the importation of products. In this regard, it is important to take into account that the panel in *Colombia—Ports of Entry* gave the term "restriction" a broad meaning and established that a measure's impact on the competitive opportunities available to imported products is the

[107] Panel Report, *Colombia—Ports of Entry*, ¶7.274–7.275, WT/DS366/R (Apr. 27, 2009).

[108] Panel Report, *Argentina—Measures Relating to Trade in Goods and Services*, ¶7.1069, WT/DS453/R (Sept. 30, 2015).

[109] GATT Art. XV:4.

decisive criterion.[110] The Appellate Body in its Report in *Argentina – Import Measures* indicated that not every condition or burden placed on importation will be inconsistent with Article XI and only those conditions that limit the importation of products are WTO inconsistent.[111]

It may be contended that the Forex Measure has a "limiting effect" on the imports listed in the CBN's Circular insofar as it cuts off importers from access to the foreign exchange need to import the goods. However, Nigeria may argue that the Forex Measure does not cut importers off from all foreign exchange markets, as they can still procure foreign exchange from the parallel market. Although foreign exchange in the parallel market is priced around 80–90% above currency in the official foreign exchange market,[112] the Forex Measure is neither a "prohibition," as it does not totally ban access to foreign exchange markets, nor does it have a "limiting effect" on the imports of the listed products, as importers continue to have access to foreign exchange needed to pay for the importation of the listed goods. However, to the extent that it may be claimed that the Forex Measure may impact competitive opportunities of the imports of the goods listed in the CBN's Circular, owing to the differential between the parallel and official markets, Nigeria would have a significant burden to establish that the imported products are not placed at a competitive disadvantage and hence consistent with GATT Art. XI:1.

Arguendo, even if the Forex Measure infringes the letter of GATT Art. XI, it may be argued that the Forex Measure is not in violation thereof. A defense against a violation of GATT Art. XI may be made by compelling a reading of GATT Art. XI:1 in conjunction with GATT Art. XV:4.[113] GATT Art. XV:4 provides that a WTO Member cannot, by exchange

[110] Panel Report, *Colombia—Ports of Entry*, ¶7.274–7.275, WT/DS366/R (Apr. 27, 2009).

[111] Appellate Body Report, *Argentina—Measures Affecting the Importation of Goods*, WT/DS438/AB/R, WT/DS444/AB/R, WT/DS445/AB/R (Jan. 15, 2015).

[112] Price of the Dollar in the Official Market is 197 Naira. The price of the U.S. Dollar is currently ranging between 360 and 370 Naira. *See* Central Bank of Nigeria, https://www.cbn.gov.ng/rates/ExchRateByCurrency.asp (last visited May 16, 2016); Lagos Parellel Market Rates, ABOKFX, http://abokifx.com/ (last visited May 16, 2016).

[113] It must be kept in mind that as GATT Art. XV:4 has never been invoked in WTO dispute settlement practice and hence there is no authoritative guidance available as of yet on the precise meaning of its terms. An assessment of the legality of a measure with GATT Art. XV:4 is, therefore, particularly complex as most terms used therein, specially "exchange action," remain unclear and uncertain as to their precise meaning. For

action, "frustrate the intent of the provisions of the GATT." Regarding the aspect that requires the measure to "frustrate the intent of the provisions of the GATT," such determination is likely to be made in light of the relevant Ad Note. The Ad Note provides that "[t]he word 'frustrate' is intended to indicate, for example, that infringements of the letter of any Article of this Agreement by exchange action shall not be regarded as a violation of that Article if, in practice, there is no appreciable departure from the intent of the Article."[114]

Thus, Nigeria could claim that a violation of GATT Art. XI:1 is not itself a violation of Nigeria's obligations under the WTO, provided that the Forex Measure be considered an exchange action and that the concept of "frustration" as used in GATT Art. XV:4 be read to require not only a breach but also and an appreciable departure from the intent. A harmonious interpretation of GATT Arts. XI:1 and XV:4 could compel a panel to find that a breach of WTO obligations concerning and exchange action occurs only when the requirements of GATT Art. XV.4 is satisfied.

It is pertinent to note that the argument of harmonious interpretation would have the effect of subsuming the obligations of GATT Art. XI:1 by the provisions of GATT Art. XV:4, a matter that could be controversial. However, such interpretation would also be in line with the principle of effectiveness and would take into account, for instance, that GATT Art. XV:4 is more special and is placed in the text of the Agreement following Art. XI:1. Despite the fact that the panel in *Dominican Republic—Cigarettes* did not consider the method of harmonious interpretation in determining that there was a standalone violation of GATT Art. II:I(b) involving an exchange-related measure, this argument is likely to serve as a possible and valid defense in support of the Forex Measure.[115]

instance, a Special Sub-Group established in 1954 during the Review Session, in examining the GATT provisions on balance-of-payment restrictions and GATT-IMF relations concluded that "in many instances it was difficult or impossible to define clearly whether a government measure is financial or trade in character and frequently it is both." *See* L/332/Rev.1 & Addenda, adopted on Mar. 2, 4 and 5, 1955, 3S/170, 196, ¶ 2.

[114] GATT Art. XV:4.

[115] *See generally* Panel Report, *Dominican Republic—Measures Affecting the Importation and Internal Sale of* Cigarettes, WT/DS302/R (Nov. 26, 2004).

4.4.2.2 *The Measure May Be a WTO-Consistent Exchange Action*

As stated above, GATT Art. XV:4 provides that a WTO Member cannot, by exchange action, frustrate the intent of the provisions of the GATT nor, by trade action, frustrate the intent of the provisions of the Articles of Agreement of the IMF. A claim brought under GATT Art. XV:4, requires two aspects: (a) whether the measure is an "exchange action" and (b) whether it "frustrates the intent of the provisions of the GATT."[116]

As regards the first aspect, two arguments may be advanced. First, the interpretation of the term "exchange action" is broad as it is likely to cover an extensive catalogue of measures relating to exchange. References in the Agreement to exchange related terms include "exchange matters," "exchange controls," "exchange restrictions," "multiple exchange rates," "foreign exchange arrangements," and "special exchange agreement," among others. Thus, it may be argued that had the drafters of the GATT intended to give GATT Art. XV:4 a narrow meaning, they would not have chosen a term as potentially far-reaching as "exchange action." Hence, considering that the Forex Measure is an exchange related measure it is likely to be an "exchange action."

Second, it could be argued that the CBN's measure is an "exchange restriction," and that such measures are within the scope of GATT Art. XV:4. GATT Art. XV:9 provides an exception to "exchange restrictions." An "exchange restriction" is also likely an "exchange action" as there would otherwise have been no need to expressly refer to them within the purview of GATT Art. XV:9(a). Pursuant to Decision No. 1034-(60/27) of 1 June 1960 the Executive Directors of the IMF, the guiding principle for ascertaining whether a measure is a "restriction" (on payments and transfers for current transactions), "is whether it involved a direct governmental limitation on the availability or use of exchange as such."[117] To the extent that the Forex Measure directly limits all foreign exchange

[116] Although from the wording of GATT Art. XV:4, the prohibition of "frustration" applies to "this Agreement" (meaning the GATT), there might be an avenue for contending that its extends beyond the GATT to other WTO agreements, such as the SCM and GATS, as the GATT 1994 is an integral part of the WTO legal framework.

[117] IMF, Articles VIII and XIV, *Decision No. 1034-(60/27)* (June 1, 1962), https://www.imf.org/external/pubs/ft/sd/index.asp?decision=1034-(60/27).

that may be obtained through the official Nigerian foreign exchange market and that is used for the importation of 40 categories of listed goods, it would seem to be an exchange restriction.[118]

As regards the second aspect requiring the measure "frustrate the intent of the provisions of the GATT," such determination is likely to be made in light of the relevant Ad Note. As stated above, Ad Article XV provides that an Article's intent is frustrated, for example, when there is not only a violation of its letter but also an appreciable departure from the intent of that Article.[119] Nigeria may contend that the Forex Measure does not amount to an "appreciable departure" from the intent of GATT Art. XI as it is not an absolute ban on imports. Hence, though the measure may violate the letter of GATT Art. XI, it does not tantamount to an "appreciable departure from the intent" of that Article and is likely not in violation of GATT Art. XV:4.

4.4.3 Possible Justifications

4.4.3.1 The Measure May Be Justified as Permissible Exchange Restriction

Nigeria should undertake efforts to create the conditions necessary for a justification of its Forex Measure under GATT Art. XV:9(a). If a successful case is made, such a provision would preclude Nigeria from wrongfulness as regards to the prohibition set on foreign exchange payments for transactions involving the 40 categories of imported goods. GATT Art. XV:9(a) provides:

> Nothing in this Agreement shall preclude: (a) the use by a contracting party of exchange controls or exchange restrictions in accordance with the Articles of Agreement of the International Monetary Fund or with that contracting party's special exchange agreement with the CONTRACTING PARTIES.[120]

[118] It is to be noted that exchange arrangements in Nigeria have undergone significant changes over the past fifty years. Nigeria moved from a fixed exchange regime in the 1960s, to a (de facto) pegged arrangement between the 1970s and the mid-1980s, to a predominantly (managed) floating exchange regime from 1986 to 2015, with a formal peg having been provisionally instituted in 1994. At the end of February of last year, Nigeria shifted back to a de facto currency peg.

[119] GATT Ad Article XV.

[120] GATT Art. XV:9(a).

As recognized by the panel in *Dominican Republic—Cigarettes*, Nigeria would bear the burden of proving that the conditions of this exception or affirmative defense are met. These conditions are that (i) the measure be an "exchange control or exchange restriction," and that (ii) it be taken "in accordance with the Articles of Agreement of the IMF."[121]

As regards to the first element, the panel in *Dominican Republic—Cigarettes* reasoned that a measure is an exchange restriction only when it limits the availability or use of exchange as such for "all purposes," meaning that the measure most impose a restriction not only on the importation of goods, but also services, remittances, and dividend payments, among others.[122] Hence, in order to invoke this exception, Nigeria would have to claim that the Forex Measure limits the availability of foreign exchange for all purposes. However, the Forex Measure may not necessarily satisfy the standard established by the panel decision in *Dominican Republic—Cigarettes.*

Nigeria could claim that, notwithstanding the panel decision, the Forex Measure by its very nature is an exchange restriction based on the 1960 IMF Decision mentioned above.[123] To the extent that the Forex Measure is a "direct governmental limitation on the availability or use of exchange as such"[124] and it directly limits all foreign exchange that may be obtained through the official Nigerian foreign exchange market that is used for the importation of 40 categories of listed goods. Thus, Nigeria may attempt to distinguish the panel decision in *Dominican Republic—Cigarettes* based on the interpretation of the 1960 IMF Decision and claim that the Forex Measure is an "exchange restriction."

Finally, in order to invoke the exception of GATT Art. XV:9(a) Nigeria would have to claim that the Forex Measure is in accordance with the Articles of Agreement of the IMF. For the Forex Measure to be in such compliance, it must formally be approved by the IMF. Section 2(a) of Article VIII of the Articles of Agreement of the IMF provides that "no member shall, without the approval of the Fund, impose restrictions on

[121] GATT Art. XV:9(a); *Dominican Republic, supra* note 115, ¶7.150–7.154.

[122] *Id.* ¶7.137.

[123] *Decision No. 1034-(60/27), supra note 119.*

[124] *Id.*

the making of payments and transfers for current international transactions."[125] As of today, Nigeria has not requested any such approval from the IMF. It is therefore recommended that Nigeria begin, as soon as possible, consultations with the IMF with a view to obtaining an approval concurrent with its obligations under the Articles of Agreement of the IMF. Without such approval, it will not be feasible to invoke GATT Art. XV:9(a) as a defense for the Forex Measure.

4.4.3.2 The Measures May Be Justified Under the Balance-of-Payments Exception

In addition to finding a justification under GATT Art. XV:9(a), Nigeria should endeavor to find a workable defense for its Forex Measure under the GATT balance-of-payments exceptions.[126] As noted above in relation to the Fisheries Measures, GATT Art. XVIII:B may serve as a justification for measures taken for balance-of-payments reasons. Three considerations must be satisfied in order for GATT Art. XVIII:B to apply: (i) the scope of the exception (members and measures covered) must be satisfied, (ii) its requirements fulfilled, and (iii) all the procedures applicable for the review of a Member's balance-of-payments restrictions must be complied with.[127]

Regarding Members covered, it is likely that Nigeria be considered falling within the purview of GATT Art. XVIII:B as discussed in the Section above.[128] Regarding the measures covered, balance-of-payments measures can only be applied after several requirements are met. As mentioned above, those requirements relate to proportionality, severity, temporality, necessity, and transparency of the measure and of the balance-of-payments situation.[129]

The nature of Nigeria's current balance-of-payments situation is likely to be of the type for which GATT Art. XVIII:B was specifically designed. Even though the determination of certain requirements of GATT Art.

[125] Articles of Agreement of the International Monetary Fund, §2(a), *concluded* Dec. 27, 1945, 2 U.N.T.S. 39.

[126] Nigeria should also take note of GATT Art. XX(d) which provides and exception for measures which are necessary to secure compliance with domestic laws or regulations, which themselves are not GATT inconsistent.

[127] GATT Art. XVIII:B.

[128] *See supra* Part II.D.3.

[129] *Id.*

XVIII:B are entrusted to the IMF, as mentioned above, the fall of foreign exchange reserves in Nigeria may be claimed to be a "serious decline," it may be possible that the measures taken by Nigeria are considered as not exceeding what is necessary to address the balance-of-payments situation, and it may be contended that they are of a temporary nature. In this regard, similar to the Fisheries Measure, Nigeria may proceed to claim that the Forex Measure will not exceed what is necessary to forestall the threat of, or to stop' the decline in monetary reserves based on the participation of the imports of the 40 category of goods listed in the CBN's Circular in the current account of Nigeria. Moreover, Nigeria can begin to prepare and design a time-limit for the application of its Forex Measure, and proceed to announce a schedule for fading it out. This will allow the Forex Measure to be in conformity with GATT Art. XVIII:B.

Finally, in order to invoke GATT Art. XVIII:B as a justification for its Forex Measure, Nigeria must also comply with the procedure set out in GATT Art. XVIII:12. In this regard, as mentioned above, it should be noted that Nigeria proceed with notifying the General Council of the adoption of the Forex Measure and initiating consultations within the Committee on Balance-of-Payments Restrictions. In determining how to proceed in relation to the balance-of-payments exception, Nigeria should consider all the strict requirements that it imposes. Moreover, regardless of whether it determines that a defense under GATT Art. XV:9(a) is a more expedited and/or practicable alternative, Nigeria should bear in mind that GATT Art. XVIII:B imposes consultation obligations which it is expected to observe, as it has done so in the past when taking other balance-of-payments measures before the turn of the century.

4.4.4 Action Plan

Based on the above analysis of the Forex Measure, their compliance with GATT Art. XI:1 and GATT Art. XV:4 and possible justifications that Nigeria may pursue in its support under GATT XV and XVIII:B the following action plan is suggested for the path ahead in continuing to achieve the broader policy objectives of the Forex Measure in a WTO-consistent manner.

- Nigeria must seek to cooperate and fully consult with the IMF in order to avail itself of GATT Art. XV:9(a). Since the IMF is the organization entrusted with exchange questions, and is the organization that makes the factual and statistical findings that are required to defend the Forex Measures in the WTO, this cooperation will also be key for the purposes of invoking the exception of GATT Art. XVIII:B. Nigeria must also begin the consultation process with the Committee on Balance-of-Payments Restrictions and make any necessary amendments to the Forex Measure, in order to avail itself of the defense enshrined in GATT Art. XVIII:B and ease the concerns raised by other WTO Members.

- Nigeria may also consider amending the list on CBN's Circular such that it only covers services in which Nigeria has made no specific commitments under its GATS Schedule of Specific Commitments. Nigeria's biggest current account imports are "commercial services." Other services such as "other business services" and "government goods and services" are also a major source of imports.[130] These services are likely outside the purview of its Schedule. By eliminating goods from the list and imposing limitations on foreign exchange in respect of such non-committed services, Nigeria may be able to bring the Forex Measure out of likely WTO violation concerns.
- Nigeria may consider raising its MFN tariff on imports of the goods listed in the CBN's Circular up to the bound levels and eliminate the goods from Forex Measure. Nigeria has binding tariff commitments on agricultural products up to 150% and on non-agricultural goods up to 80%. To that end, an increase in Nigeria's MFN tariff for the imports of the listed goods up to the bound rate[131] may cause a significant reduction in the demand for such goods, thereby impacting the demand of foreign currency and offsetting the decline in foreign exchange reserves.
- Finally, Nigeria should take note that of the wording of the CBN's Circular, including references which indicate that the purpose of the Forex Measure is "encouraging local production" and "helping resuscitate domestic industries."[132] The Appellate Body in *Argentina – Import Measures* stated that the limitation on imports

[130] Nigeria 2015 Data, *supra* note 98.

[131] As regards the ECOWAS Countries, Nigeria may raise the tariff upto the highest rate permitted under the ECOWAS Treaty.

[132] CNB Circular.

for purposes of a GATT Art. XI violation need not be demonstrated by quantifying the effects of a measure. Instead, its limiting effects can be established through the "design, architecture, and revealing structure of the measure at issue." Hence, Nigeria should consider avoiding such reference in the Forex Measure.

4.5 Conclusion

4.5.1 Certain Measures Regarding the Oil and Gas Industry

In 2010, Nigeria introduced the Nigerian Oil and Gas Industry Content Development Act ("Act"). Among other things, the Act aims to stimulate the Nigeria economy by increasing the percentage of local employment and growing the value-added in the economy through the efficient utilization of local services.

An analysis of the Act reveals four measures that, at first sight, may raise potential concerns with respect to Nigeria's national treatment obligations under the WTO. *Measure 1* mandates that operators and contractors comply with minimum content requirements and give first consideration to goods and services listed in the Schedule to the Act. *Measure 2* mandates that the government give first consideration to "Nigerian independent operators" with respect to certain activities. *Measure 3* mandates that the government, operators, and contractors give exclusive consideration to "Indigenous Nigerian service companies" in respect of certain activities. *Measure 4* mandates that operators and contractors give first consideration to Nigerians for employment and training.

Based on the text of the relevant sections of the Act, Nigeria may claim that Measures 2, 3, and 4 are likely outside the scope of the GATT and TRIMs because they relate to trade in services and not goods. Nigeria has not undertaken any specific commitments in its Schedule of Specific Commitments under the GATS in oil and gas services and therefore these measures may likely not violate Nigeria's WTO obligations.

Measure 1 is more complex and may have effects extending to trade in goods. However, Nigeria may contend that the definition of "Nigerian

Content" in the Act is broad, focuses on "creating value in the economy," and does not mandate preferential treatment to goods manufactured in Nigeria. Moreover, the language of the relevant sections provides the Board charged with implementing the provisions with wide discretion. Nigeria may claim that this discretion is likely to be exercised in a manner consistent with Nigeria's WTO obligations. For these reasons Nigeria may argue that the Act is consistent with the national treatment obligations codified in GATT Art. III:4 and TRIMs Art. 2.1.

Furthermore, Nigeria may rely on GATT Arts. XXI, XX, and XVIII:C to justify these measures. First, Nigeria may invoke GATT Art. XXI and claim that it considers its measures to be necessary for the protection of its essential security interests. These measures are aimed at promoting local community participation in the Niger Delta region, and thereby curb terrorist activity therein, and violence affecting international peace and security. Second, Nigeria may rely on GATT Art. XX(b) and claim that the measures are necessary for the protection of human and plant life. Nigeria may be able to establish that its measures are designed to halt the violence and prevent consequent environmental damage in the Niger Delta region by promoting participation of local communities. Lastly, Nigeria may rely on GATT Art. XVIII:C which allows developing country Members to promote the establishment and development of an industry with a view to raising their general standard of living. Nigeria, being a developing country may claim that the measures are intended to promote the substantial transformation of the Nigerian oil and gas industry to raise the standard of living of Nigerians. However, since GATT Art. XVIII:C is not a self-executing exception, Nigeria is required to satisfy the notification and procedural requirements set out in Section C.

Possible strategies that Nigeria could pursue in relation to the Act include, amending relevant sections of the Act to eliminate reference to goods, communicating and leveraging on its intent to invoke GATT Art. XXI in relevant fora, and complying with the notification and procedural requirements of GATT Art. XVIII:C.

4.5.2 Certain Measures Regarding the Importation of Fish

Nigeria has introduced measures to regulate imports of fish into Nigeria through a document titled "Proposed Guidelines." There are two measures at issue, collectively referred to as the "Fisheries Measures": Measure 1 prohibits the importation of fish other than certain permitted pelagic fish. The prohibition covers farmed fish, either frozen or smoked, and products of farmed fish into Nigeria. Measure 2 limits the importation of certain pelagic fish per importer up to the "allocated quantity" decided by the FDF in the Letter of Clearance issued to that importer.

The Fisheries Measures limit the quantities and the types of fish and fish products that can be imported into Nigeria and raise concerns regarding the obligation on quantitative restrictions contained in GATT Art. XI:1. However, GATT Art. XI:2(b) exempts measures necessary for the marketing, classification or grading of fish. Nigeria may argue that the over-importation of fish, when combined with the inadequate cold storage facilities in Nigeria, leads to the marketing of unwholesome and unhealthy fish. It may be claimed that, given the inadequacy of the cold storage capacity in Nigeria, the Fisheries Measures prevent the over-importation of fish and are necessary to ensure the safe and wholesome marketing of imported fish. Additionally, Nigeria may rely on GATT Art. XI:2(c)(i) which allows WTO Members to impose import restrictions on fisheries, so long as they are necessary for the enforcement of governmental measures which restrict the quantities of the like domestic product permitted to be marketed or produced. Nigeria's domestic fisheries laws claimed to restrict the total quantity of domestic fish permitted to be marketed in order to increase reliance on farmed fish. In the absence of the Fisheries Measures, the quantities of domestic fish marketed in Nigeria would be replaced with imported sea fish and defeat the objective of stimulating farmed fish. Hence, the Fisheries Measures are necessary for the enforcement of domestic fisheries laws.

Further, Nigeria may rely on GATT Art. XX(b), (d), and (g) to justify the Fisheries Measures. GATT Art. XX can be invoked as a justification for measures that are necessary to protect human health, or necessary to secure compliance with WTO-consistent laws, or that relate to the conservation of exhaustible natural resources. The Fisheries Measures may be contended to be necessary for the protection of human health as it contributes to limit the over-importation of fish, thereby preventing the distribution of decaying and unfit fish stored in insufficient cold storage facilities. It may also be contended that the Fisheries Measures are justified as necessary to secure compliance with WTO-consistent domestic fisheries laws that prevent the marketing of decaying and unfit fish stored in insufficient cold storage facilities. The Fisheries Measures contribute to ensuring that imported fish is also prevented from being marketed in a manner contrary to domestic fisheries laws. Nigeria could further argue that the

Fisheries Measures contribute to preserving sea fish which are exhaustible natural resources. By promoting reliance on farmed fish in lieu of sea fish, the Fisheries Measures, in conjunction with domestic fisheries laws, limit the quantity of sea fish marketed in Nigeria, thereby stimulating reliance on farmed fish in lieu of sea fish and leading to the conservation of sea fish.

Finally, the justifications of GATT Art. XX must fulfill the requirements of the chapeau which establish that the application of the measures must not constitute an arbitrary or unjustifiable discrimination between countries where the same conditions prevail, and must not tantamount to a disguised restriction on trade. Nigeria may argue that distinguishing between restricted fish and prohibited fish under the Fisheries Measures balances and preserves the consumer preferences in Nigeria while maintaining a rational relationship with the recognized objectives of the measures. Furthermore, Nigeria may also argue that as domestic fisheries laws operate to have a limiting effect on domestic fish, similar to the effect on imported fish, and that any differences are in response to the imported fish's greater reliance on cold storage facilities. Hence, it may be argued that the distinction drawn by the Fisheries Measures satisfies the chapeau of GATT Art. XX.

Lastly, Nigeria may justify the measure under the balance-of-payment exception of GATT Art. XVIII:B in view of the serious decline in its monetary reserves since 2013. By limiting the imports of fish, the Fisheries Measures may be claimed to satisfy the substantive requirements relating to severity, proportionality, and necessity of GATT Art. XVIII:B to forestall the threat of, or to stop' the decline in monetary reserves. However, Nigeria would need to incorporate a time-limit for the Fisheries Measures, in order to satisfy the temporality requirement of GATT Art. XVIII:B. Nigeria would also need to notify the General Council of the adoption of the Fisheries Measures and initiate consultations within the Committee on Balance-of-Payments Restrictions.

Possible strategies that Nigeria could pursue in relation to the Fisheries Measures include, raising MFN tariffs on imports of fish, introducing SPS or TBT measures such as inspection or certification requirements, applying trade remedies such as anti-dumping or countervailing duties or even safeguards, and complying with the substantive and procedural requirements of GATT Art. XVIII:B.

4.5.3 Measure Concerning Foreign Exchange

In 2015, Nigeria issued a circular excluding the importation of 40 categories of goods and 1 category of services from the official Nigerian foreign exchange markets ("Forex Measure"). This may cause concerns regarding the prohibition on quantitative restrictions contained in GATT Art. XI:1 and the obligation on exchange related measures contained in GATT Art. XV:4.

Nigeria may contend that the Forex Measure is outside the scope of GATT Art. XI:1 as the measure is a monetary measure and not an "other measure" within the meaning of that Article, and that exchange related measures are covered exhaustively under GATT Art. XV alone. Furthermore, Nigeria may also argue that since the 40 categories of goods can still be imported using foreign exchange from the parallel market, there is no "limiting effect" required for a violation of GATT Art. XI:1 to ensue.

Additionally, Nigeria may claim that an exchange related measure cannot violate GATT Art. XI:1 on a stand-alone basis because, as provided in GATT Art. XV:4 and its Ad Note, an infringement of the letter of an Article resulting from such measures is not WTO-inconsistent unless there is an "appreciable departure from the intent" of that Article. Nigeria may further argue that the Forex Measure is consistent with GATT Art. XV:4 and that there is no "appreciable departure from the intent" of GATT Art. XI:1, as the Forex Measure does not impose a total ban on the imports.

Nigeria may also invoke GATT Art. XV:9(a) and GATT Art. XVIII:B in justification of the Forex Measure. GATT Art. XV:9(a) allows Members to take measures that are exchange restrictions and are in accordance with the Articles of Agreement of the International Monetary Fund ("IMF"). The Forex Measure by its very nature is likely an exchange restriction. Nigeria should therefore proceed to seek approval from the IMF, as only exchange restrictions that are approved by the IMF are in conformity with the Articles of Agreement of the IMF.

Lastly, Nigeria may justify the measure under the balance-of-payment exception of GATT Art. XVIII:B in view of the serious decline in its monetary reserves since 2013. By limiting foreign exchange in relation to the imports on the CBN's Circular, the Forex Measure may be claimed to satisfy the substantive requirements relating to severity, proportionality, and necessity of GATT Art. XVIII:B to forestall the threat of, or to stop the decline in monetary reserves. However, Nigeria would need to incorporate a time-limit for the Forex Measure, in order to satisfy the temporality requirement of GATT Art. XVIII:B. Nigeria would also need to notify the General Council of the adoption of the Forex Measure and initiate consultations within the Committee on Balance-of-Payments Restrictions.

Possible strategies that Nigeria could pursue in relation to the Forex Measures include, cooperating and fully consulting with the IMF, complying with the substantive and procedural requirements of GATT Art. XVIII:B, modifying the Forex Measure to eliminate goods and include only non-GATS committed services, and raise applied MFN import tariffs up to the bound rates.

Appendix: List of Items Restricted from Foreign Exchange

1. Rice
2. Cement
3. Margarine
4. Palm kernel/palm oil products/vegetable oils
5. Meat and processed meat products
6. Vegetables and processed vegetable products
7. Poultry—chicken, eggs, turkey
8. Private airplanes/jets
9. Indian incense
10. Tinned fish in sauce (geisha)/sardines
11. Cold rolled steel sheets
12. Galvanized steel sheets
13. Roofing sheets
14. Wheelbarrows
15. Head pans
16. Metal boxes and containers
17. Enamelware
18. Steel drums
19. Steel pipes
20. Wire rods (deformed and not deformed)
21. Iron rods and reinforcing bars
22. Wire mesh
23. Steel nails
24. Security and razor wire

25. Wood particle boards and panels
26. Wood fiber boards and panels
27. Plywood boards and panels
28. Wooden doors
29. Furnitures
30. Toothpicks
31. Glass and glassware
32. Kitchen utensils
33. Tableware
34. Tiles—vitrified and ceramic
35. Textiles
36. Woven fabrics
37. Clothes
38. Plastic and rubber products, cellophane wrappers
39. Soap and cosmetics
40. Tomatoes/tomato pastes
41. Euro band/foreign currency band/share purchase

References

Appellate Body Report, *Argentina—Measures Affecting the Importation of Goods*, WT/DS438/AB/R, WT/DS444/AB/R, WT/DS445/AB/R (Jan. 15, 2015).

Appellate Body Report, *EC—Tariff Preference*, WT/DS246/AB/R (Dec. 1, 2003).

Appellate Body Report, *United States—Countervailing Duties on Certain Corrosion-Resistant Carbon Steel Flat Products from Germany*, WT/DS213/AB/R (Nov. 28, 2002).

Appellate Body Report, *United States—Laws, Regulations And Methodology for Calculating Dumping Margins ("Zeroing")*, WT/DS294/AB/R (Apr. 18, 2006).

Appellate Body Report, *United States—Tax Treatment for "Foreign Sales Corporations"*, WT/DS108/AB/RW2 (Feb. 13, 2006).

Articles of Agreement of the International Monetary Fund, *concluded* Dec. 27, 1945, 2 U.N.T.S. 39.

Comprehensive Economic and Trade Agreement, EU-CA, *concluded* Sept. 29, 2014, ANNEX 8-E, http://trade.ec.europa.eu/doclib/docs/2014/september/tradoc_152806.pdf.

Economic Community of West African States (ECOWAS), Revised Treaty of the Economic Community of West African States (ECOWAS), 24 Jul. 1993, http://www.refworld.org/docid/492182d92.html.

Panel Report, *Argentina—Measures Relating to Trade in Goods and Services*, WT/DS453/R (Sept. 30, 2015).

Panel Report, *Colombia—Ports of Entry*, WT/DS366/R (Apr. 27, 2009).

Panel Report, *EEC—Minimum Import Prices*, L/4687, 25S/68 (Oct. 18, 1978).

Panel Report, *India—Autos*, WT/DS146/R, WT/DS175/R (Dec. 21, 2001).

Panel Report, *India—Quantitative Restrictions*, WT/DS90/R (Apr. 6, 1999).

Panel Report, *Indonesia—Certain Measures Affecting the Automobile Industry*, WT/DS64/R (July 2, 1998).

Panel Report, *Korea—Various Measures on Beef*, WT/DS161/R, WT/DS169/R (Jul. 31, 2000).

CHAPTER 5

Innovative Strategies for Maximizing Aid-for-Trade Towards Enhanced Transport Infrastructure and Intra-regional Trade Facilitation: Policy Directions for Nigeria and West Africa

Abiola Abidemi Akinsanya

5.1 Introduction, Context and the Rationale

The focus in this paper on AfT to build economic infrastructure (road infrastructure) emerged from the fact that, among the six categories of AfT, economic infrastructure category continues to receive major attention from both donors and recipients. Globally, it receives the largest share of commitment and disbursement allocations from 2006 to 2015. For instance, out of the US$298.3 billion total AfT disbursed globally between 2006 and 2015, US$155 billion was allocated to economic infrastructure, with transport and storage infrastructure receiving

A. A. Akinsanya (✉)
Department of Trade, Federal Ministry of Trade and Investment,
Abuja, Nigeria

G. Odularu (ed.), *Strategic Policy Options for Bracing Nigeria for the Future of Trade*,
https://doi.org/10.1007/978-3-030-34552-5_5

US$85.2 billion, accounting for 55% share (OECD and WTO 2017). It is therefore not surprising that donor and recipient countries, particularly those in Africa such as the ECOWAS member-states with poor infrastructure, often attach greater importance to this category of AfT. Evidence suggests that in 2015, relative to Asia as the second largest recipient, Africa received US$14.1 billion of global AfT disbursement, representing 34% of the total amount disbursed (UNECA and WTO 2017). At the regional level, economic infrastructure has also received the highest share of allocations. For instance, in 2013, the sum of US$8.5 billion out of the total AfT disbursement to African region was allocated to economic infrastructure category, followed by productive sector at US$6.8 billion and trade policy and regulation at US$490 million (UNECA 2015).

Among the three subsets of economic infrastructure, namely, communications; energy generation and supply; and transport and storage infrastructure, the latter received the second largest amount in commitment (US$4.7 billion) and disbursement (US$3.7 billion) to Africa after energy in 2015 (OECD, n.d.-a). Data from the OECD CRS also shows that total AfT to transport infrastructure in Africa increased from US$1.5 billion in 2002 to US$4.7 billion in 2015. The increase in AfT commitment and disbursement allocation to transport infrastructure stimulates the quest to examine whether this increased funding provides opportunities for ECOWAS member-states to significantly improve their regional road infrastructure interconnectivity and strengthen the sub-region's economic integration objective.

Poor transport interconnectivity among ECOWAS member inhibits intra-regional trade in the region. Transport connectivity is hampered by factors including poor road infrastructure, non-tariff barriers such as excessive or multiple border checks and inefficient logistic procedures and regulations. Some of these excessive road checks and charges among ECOWAS. Consequently, exporting to countries within ECOWAS is often more time-consuming and costly than exporting to Europe or United States, which partly explains why many ECOWAS member-states often have the EU, United States or China as their major trading partners (Akpan 2014). This low level of trade between ECOWAS member-states stands in contrast to the levels of intra-regional trade in other regions such as South-East Asia.

Finance to develop and support economic infrastructure in ECOWAS, especially road infrastructure, is necessary. Despite Africa spending US$45 billion on the average annually on infrastructure development, which constitutes US$30 billion of government spending and US$15 billion from foreign sources (Foster and Briceño-Garmendia 2010), it is still not sufficient to meet its road infrastructure needs. A World Bank study on development finance to address infrastructure challenges in Africa states that US$93 billion investments are required annually to fully meet Africa's infrastructure needs (Foster and Briceño-Garmendia 2010). However, the poor financial and economic position of many ECOWAS countries continues to inhibit their capacity to build more transport (road) infrastructure. As stated earlier, many ECOWAS countries are least developed economies, and some of them are landlocked countries, which increases their dependence on road infrastructure linkages for regional trade. Their circumstances mean they must seek other sources of funding. These other sources of funding come in the form of private and public investment, and accounts for two-thirds of infrastructure finance, and ODA which includes AfT, has seen a significant growth over the last few years (Gutman et al. 2015; Foster and Briceño-Garmendia 2010).

Despite the increase in AfT allocation, transport costs continue to soar, long delays are still prevalent in transshipment of goods, and trade within the region still low (UNECA 2013a; Byiers and Lui 2013). These trends raise some questions about whether AfT can assist ECOWAS countries to meet their developmental goals, by using export-led economic growth and international trade as the means. Consequently, critics have advocated for an end to aid as a whole, which includes AfT, on the assumption that AfT has been ineffective at facilitating the development objective provided for by the WTO Doha mandate on trade and development (Evennett 2005).

It is as a result of the preceding factors that this study examines the opportunities that AfT provides in helping to enhance economic infrastructure and strengthen integration of the ECOWAS sub-region. It also examines some of the challenges in the implementation of AfT in ECOWAS, and how these can be overcome. Although, many studies have sought to examine the effectiveness of AfT (see for example Vigil and Wagner 2012; Hühne et al. 2014a; Cadot and de Melo 2014), and the role of AfT in enhancing regional integration in ECOWAS (see for example Udvari 2014; Oyejide and Bankole 2010) more generally, this study is more focused. It identifies and offers a comprehensive analysis of the challenges in order to capitalize on the opportunities that AfT offers in strengthening road infrastructure interconnectivity in ECOWAS. It also examines the challenges in implementing AfT and proffers ways to further improve its effectiveness in the region.

The article seeks to proffer answers to selected strategic challenges which confront Nigerian and West African regional development policy makers: How is AfT assisting ECOWAS members to improve their regional road interconnectivity? What are the challenges faced by ECOWAS in using AfT to enhance their road infrastructure? How do the challenges and opportunities faced by ECOWAS in using AfT to enhance their road infrastructure influence the integration of the West African sub-region?

By reviewing and analysing evidence in the literature on how or ways through which AfT is assisting to improve road infrastructure interconnectivity within ECOWAS and how these impacts on fostering regional integration in the region and Africa as a whole, this study adds to the growing body of knowledge in this area of research. It may also serve as a source of reference to policy makers and academics who may wish to advance future research on AfT and its effectiveness on-road infrastructure in Africa and ECOWAS. This study adopts a qualitative case study methodology to address its objectives. A qualitative case study (QCS) is defined as a:

> qualitative approach in which the investigator explores real-life, contemporary bounded system (a case) or multiple bounded system (cases) over-time through detailed, in-depth data collection involving multiple sources of information (e.g., observation, interviews, audio-visuals, materials, documents and reports), and reports a case description and case themes. (Creswell and Poth 2018, p. 96)

The rationale for a QCS approach is to provide a detailed analysis of the case being examined. It is commonly regarded as a form of qualitative technique however it can contain elements of quantitative research method (Pietsch 2016). Using QCS allows a study to examine one or more 'contemporary phenomenon in-depth' or 'event holistically' within certain context using more than one method (Yin 2009, p. 18; Thomas and Myers 2015, p. 7; Yin 2014). However QCS is not limited to only real-life or contemporary phenomenon, it allows examination of non-real life events by allowing journals or other documents from participants to be used to depict real-life experiences or changes in perspectives (Creswell 2013; Woodside 2010).

For this study, the contemporary phenomenon is AfT and it is examined in the context of the opportunities as well as the challenges that it presents to ECOWAS to improve road infrastructure. The QCS provides a useful tool when seeking answers to the research questions of 'how and why' which can either be a single or multiple cases, referred to as 'holistic or embedded' or 'intensive or extensive' case (Yin 2014, p. 50; Eriksson and Kovalainen 2016, p. 133; Thomas 2011, p. 75). This study adopts a single case design (ECOWAS members) to investigate how AfT is assisting to improve the region's road infrastructure. The choice of a single case (ECOWAS) is to give focus to the region's effort at reducing high transport cost caused by poor roads. However, two road examples from ECOWAS, namely, Tema-Ouagadougou-Bamako road and Enugu-Bamenda road are used to support the analysis. The selection of the two road projects is based on the availability of statistical data indicating the amount of AfT loans and grants that goes into the project from the key donor agencies like AfDB and World Bank. Also, availability of data from an interview conducted by an independent academic journalist that shows the effectiveness of the roads after completion provides background information about the roads and makes the case useful to examine. Hence, the two roads provide examples of how AfT is facilitating the improvement of road infrastructure in ECOWAS.

A qualitative case study also allows researchers to set boundaries for their studies to ensure that the data gathered remain within the area of focus (Gorman et al. 2014). Therefore, Yin (2014) notes that, with this method, case samples can be examined within specific boundaries, which could be a place or time boundary or both. This study is bounded by a place (West African/ECOWAS) and time (AfT allocations to road infrastructure from the year 2005 to 2015). Moreover, using QCS researcher can investigate the contexts or relationships and processes of the issue through a comprehensive examination of the information gathered over a given period or within a particular context (Gorman et al. 2014; Thomas 2011). In this study, the case investigates challenges and opportunities (relationship) of using AfT to facilitate improvement of road infrastructure in ECOWAS (a process). The QCS is suitable for examining issues, which has general relevance both in theory and practice as well as for comparing the strengths and criticisms of a phenomenon with theory and methods (Eriksson and Kovalainen 2016; Woodside 2010). This is why this study adopts a mix of explanatory analysis and exploratory approach. It uses explanatory approach to explain the concepts of aid and AfT and exploratory to examine the opportunities and challenges of AfT in enhancing road infrastructure among ECOWAS.

5.2 Background to the Study

5.2.1 Transport Infrastructure and Intra-regional Trade in Africa and ECOWAS

Prior studies identify poor transport infrastructure in ECOWAS as the biggest challenge to the growth of intra-regional trade and economic integration in Africa, and in the sub-region in particular (Oyejide and Bankole 2010; Akpan 2014; Deen-Swarray et al. 2014). Besides, intra-regional trade in the region remains one of the lowest in the world. For instance, in 2015 the percentage of exports traded within the African region stood at only 18%, which compares unfavourably with other regions; Asia recorded 52% in the same year while North America and Europe recorded 50 and 70%, respectively (WTO 2015, p. 27). Extant evidence shows that this poor regional trade is largely caused by inadequate and poor infrastructure interconnectivity within the region, which increases the time, costs and distance to transport goods and services from one country to another (African Development Bank [AfDB] 2011; Storeygard 2016; Mbekeani 2010; Jouanjean 2013).

Limao and Venable (2001) conclude that poor infrastructure in Africa causes transportation costs to rise by 12% and the volume of trade to decrease by 28%. These costs may be higher in ECOWAS because of infrastructural inadequacies. Evidence suggests that other barriers, like multiple informal border checks, prolonged bureaucratic delays in custom procedures and the various levies and taxes, add up to make the cost of transportation of goods and services extremely high in Africa, particularly ECOWAS (UNECA 2013a; Hoppe 2013). As a result, ECOWAS' exports are less competitive and intra-ECOWAS trade is unattractive to businessmen. These factors combined point to the need to examine how AfT could provide the opportunities for ECOWAS member-states to develop new networks of road interconnectivity or upgrade existing ones with a view to expanding the means of exchange of goods and services among them and foster economic integration. Against this backdrop, a 2014 study reveals that enhancing regional road infrastructure in ECOWAS would increase intra-ECOWAS trade annually by 4.97% valued at US$356.06 million (Akpan 2014). While Akpan's (2014) study investigates the impact of road infrastructure development in fostering regional integration, it does not examine the challenges and benefits of improving those roads using AfT. Therefore, this current study fills the void in the literature by examining the challenges and opportunities of using AfT to improve road infrastructure in ECOWAS.

Building physical infrastructure such as road infrastructure in developing countries is likely to increase their chances of accessing other markets, which is partly why a large share of AfT is often channelled towards building more economic infrastructure in developing countries (Francois and Manchin 2013). As stated earlier, AfT to build economic infrastructure continues to receive the largest share of AfT allocation to ECOWAS and Africa, with road infrastructure receiving the biggest share in ECOWAS (AfDB 2011). Besides, as fifteen of the world's forty-nine landlocked countries are located in Africa, including ECOWAS member-states such as Niger, Mali and Burkina Faso, which rely heavily on neighbouring countries to transship their goods, the opportunities that development of regional road networks using AfT can provide to the ECOWAS subregion are enormous.

In line with the preceding overview, ECOWAS is taking numerous steps to initiate and implement series of road infrastructure projects under its Transport Facilitation Project, including the West African Regional Transport and Transit Facilitation Project implemented in collaboration with the World Bank (ECOWAS 2016b). Some projects are also being implemented at the continental level under the Programme for Infrastructure Development in Africa (PIDA), which is jointly implemented by the African Union (AU), African Development Bank (AfDB), and New Partnership for Africa's Development (NEPAD). The AfDB's Infrastructure Development Fund is also a dedicated fund to support Africa's infrastructure development, in addition to those initiated by key donor partners like the European Union's Africa Infrastructure Trust Fund (AITF).

Although, some of these projects are financed with the support of AfT loans and grants, which depicts the growing influence of AfT in assisting Africa to enhance its transport infrastructure. However, ECOWAS member-states still collectively finance majority of these projects using their internal revenue and other development finance support from their regional development agencies like AfDB. A huge part of their fiscal or capital expenditure is channelled towards financing infrastructural projects and programmes including road, rail, and ICT projects. For instance, between 15 and 25% of Africa's Gross Domestic Product (GDP) has gone into financing transport infrastructure from 2005 to 2012 (AfDB 2013).

Yet, many African countries, especially those in ECOWAS, possess inadequate financial and technical capacities to fully develop their transport infrastructure. This is because most of the world's poorest nations are in Africa and the majority of them are ECOWAS member-countries. Thirty-four out of the world's forty-eight poorest nations (LDCs) are in Africa, eleven of which are ECOWAS member-states. Given that these countries are poor and are unable to fully finance their transport infrastructure projects, the AfT provides a supplementary fund to assist them to address such challenges. Therefore, it is based on the need to assist these poor countries that the AfT initiative was created by the WTO with the mandate 'to help developing countries, particularly LDCs, to build the supply-side capacity and trade-related infrastructure that they need to assist them to implement and benefit from WTO agreements and more broadly to expand their trade' (WTO 2005, para. 57). It is for this reason that this paper aims to analyse whether the AfT has fulfilled this mandate of providing opportunities for countries in ECOWAS to enhance their road infrastructure.

5.2.2 Background of AfT

AfT has existed for a long time as part of the aid. However, it evolved and gained prominence from a decision reached at the 6th WTO Ministerial conference held in Hong Kong, China in 2005. It was at this conference that WTO members agreed on the need to reform aid by having a dedicated and coherent initiative that supports trade and developmental needs of developing countries and LDCs. This decision was followed by the creation of AfT Taskforce in 2006 as a way of reforming aid so as to effectively monitor and evaluate AfT flows and activities. It is a collaborative effort of the WTO, together with multilateral and regional development agencies like the OECD, World Bank, United Nations Development Programme (UNDP), United Nations Conference on Trade and Development (UNCTAD), African Development Bank (AfDB), to mention but a few (WTO 2017). The aid it encompasses is disbursed bilaterally on a country to country basis, or multilaterally through these agencies, and they all collaborate to assess the effectiveness of AfT periodically every two years on how it is impacting on trade, growth and development globally.

The Taskforce on AfT helps donors and recipients to monitor and assess the effectiveness of AfT and this is then evaluated at global reviews, which is held biennially. These reviews often map out ways to better improve on AfT delivery and objectives. However, despite the various efforts targeted at enhancing AfT, the initiative is still met with some key challenges. These include systemic corruption, poor accountability, lack of effective coordination and ownership, divergence of economic interests, poor or inadequate definite statistical data including lack of clear distinction between ODA and AfT projects, bureaucratic and institutional problems and lack of mainstreaming AfT projects into development needs strategy.

5.2.3 Aid for Economic Infrastructure in ECOWAS

Infrastructure development is of great importance to developing countries, particularly ECOWAS, which is why it continues to be an important area in their development needs strategies. Countries have identified the role that good infrastructure, especially road networks play in facilitating competiveness, expanding trade and deepening economic integration. This is evident in the fact that, comparable to the other categories AfT, 30% of case story responses to WTO AfT global review questionnaires identify AfT to build trade-related infrastructure as their major priority, both by donors and recipients (OECD and WTO 2017). The significance of this is reflected in economic infrastructure, which often being allocated the largest share of AfT disbursement. It is an area where literature tends to have large convergence on the effectiveness of AfT (Lopez 2015); and it is of great importance to ECOWAS due to the prevalence of poor transport infrastructure networks in the sub-region, which limits their potential to fully maximize opportunities in regional trade and integration. Aid to build economic infrastructure and productive sector are more likely to facilitate growth in the long-term due to their potential to enhance production of goods and its distribution (Lopez 2015).

A study to investigate the effect of regional road infrastructure on intra-ECOWAS trade finds that an improvement in road infrastructure in ECOWAS will result in about 5% increase in intra-regional trade valued at US$345.06 million (Akpan 2014). More importantly, Mbekeani (2010) also argues that transport and communication infrastructure tend to facilitate regional integration faster in Africa than other forms of infrastructure. Africa identifies the opportunities that AfT provides in assisting developing countries to build capacities to strengthen their border measures and improve transport infrastructure that links their local producers to the global market (Jianmei et al. 2013).

AfT to build trade-related infrastructure assists developing countries to reduce transport costs on their exports through provision of funds to build roads or other infrastructure linkages. A study by Limao and Venables (2001) conclude that while the transport costs on exports arising from poor domestic infrastructure constitute 40% of costs for developing countries with coastlines, it constitutes as high as 60% of costs in landlocked countries. In Sub-Saharan Africa transport cost is higher in comparison to other regions due to poor road networks, remoteness and low population density of some areas (Storeygard 2016). Mbekeani (2010) provides evidence that transport costs on trade in Africa continue to increase at an average of 14% comparable to other developing countries at 8.6%. This tends to be higher in ECOWAS where we have a large number of the world's poorest nations. This is why Iwanow and Kirkpatrick (2009) in their study, using standard gravity model, also find that a 10% improvement in quality of infrastructure and trade facilitation in Africa would raise Africa's exports by approximately 17%, especially manufactured exports.

Improving infrastructure has also been argued to have a positive impact on exports of recipient countries. The findings in a study by Hühne et al. (2014b) show that AfT to develop economic infrastructure does not only reduce trade costs but also increase exports of recipient countries. Another research, based on panel data analysis, also indicates that AfT to develop trade-related infrastructure has the most significant capability to increase exports of recipient countries (Calì and te Velde 2011). Vigil and Wagner (2012), using gravity model, investigate and find that a 10% increase in AfT to build trade-related infrastructure will cause export performance to rise in recipient countries at an average of 10.7%.

5.3 Analysis of AfT—ECOWAS Regional Trade Nexus

This section contains results of examining two roads samples that have been developed with the support of AfT in ECOWAS and how these roads are helping to facilitate integration of the sub-region. The discussion takes from the challenges and opportunities towards investigating where AfT is providing opportunities for ECOWAS to improve its road infrastructure.

5.3.1 Overview of AfT for Building Road Infrastructure Among ECOWAS

Road infrastructure plays a significant role in facilitating trade, regional integration and development in Africa in general and ECOWAS in particular. Study shows that improving regional road infrastructure interconnectivity can increase Sub-Saharan Africa's trade by approximately US$250 billion for the next 15 years (Buys et al. 2010).It is for this reason that ECOWAS member-states are intensifying efforts towards increasing commitments and investments to improve their road infrastructure. Road infrastructure is generally regarded as the most important form of transporting goods within ECOWAS (Njoh 2009). This is partly because a large share of trade within the region is conducted informally through the various roads interlinks. Evidence also suggests that about 80% of total freight logistics and movement of persons in Africa are transported using road infrastructure (United States International Trade Commission [USITC] 2009). The importance of roads for the transport of goods in Africa has meant that road infrastructure consistently received the largest share of AfT commitment and disbursement between the year 2002 and 2015. AfT disbursement to support road infrastructure in Africa rose from US 917 million in 2002 to US 2990.1 in 2015 (OECD, n.d.-a). Consequently, disbursements to road infrastructure to ECOWAS member-states also increased considerably. As illustrated in Fig. 5.1, and an increasing proportion of this funds was disbursed through regional economic bodies, constituting 9% between 2006–2008 to over 12% from 2011 to 2013 (UNECA 2015). These funds helped build some major roads among ECOWAS member-states such as Tema-Ouagadougou-Bamako road and Enugu-Bamenda road which are examined as case studies in this project.

5.3.2 Road Sample One: Tema-Ouagadougou-Bamako Highway Road

This road project entails the development of a 311 kilometre portion of Tema-Ouagadougou-Bamako highway road, which connects Sakoinse road, Ouagadougou, Burkina Faso; and Heremakono road, Bamako, Mali; to Tamale road, Buipe, Ghana's Tema seaport (World Bank 2015). The project was implemented under the World Bank's West Africa Transport and Transit Facilitation (WATT) infrastructure initiative and the sum of US$197.2 million was allocated for developing and maintaining the

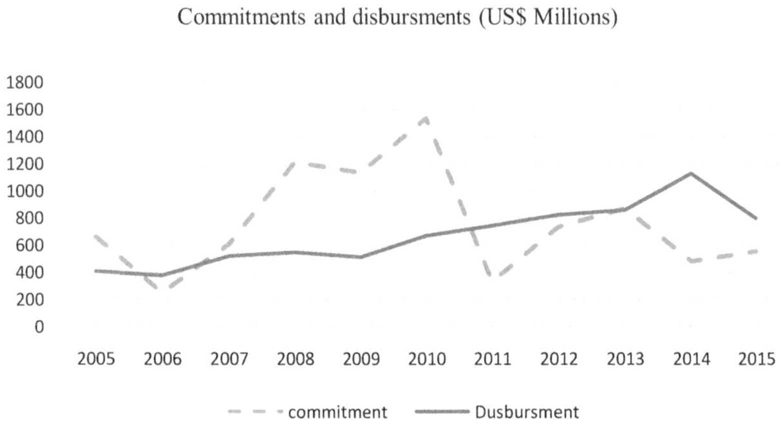

Fig. 5.1 Total AfT to road infrastructure among ECOWAS members, 2005–2015 (*Source* OECD CRS database. Retrieved from http://stats.oecd.org/qwids/; http://www.oecd.org/dac/aft/Aid-for-trade-sector-codes.pdf on 5 September 2017)

road as well as digital upgrading of Mali and Burkina Faso's cargo system (Independent Evaluation Group [IEG] 2016). The fund for the project comprises US$190 million grants from International Development Association [IDA], a subsidiary of World Bank; other financial support from AfDB, the EU, West African Development Bank, United States Agency for International Development (USAID), Japan International Cooperation Agency (JICA) and Arab Bank for Economic Development in Africa, as well as counterpart funding from Mali and Ghana at US$6.33 million and US$20 million, respectively (IEG 2016).

The road is important to the sub-region as it is one of the major roads that connect ECOWAS through Trans-Coastal West African highway corridor to Africa's comprehensive Trans-African Highway (TAH) initiative, which connects the whole of the African continent (AfDB and UNECA 2003). Moreover, it is especially important to Mali and Burkina Faso because both countries, particularly Mali, have the highest transport costs in ECOWAS (Briceno-Garmendia et al. 2011; UNECA 2013a). Burkina Faso and Mali are both landlocked countries, which depend on the seaports of neighbouring countries like Ghana, Togo, Senegal and Cote d'ivoire to transport their goods. Transport costs are 50% higher in Burkina Faso, Mali and Niger when compared to other ECOWAS member-states with coastal links (World Bank 2008). These higher costs are consistent with the overall higher transport costs in Africa, which are 36% higher than other developing countries (Barka 2012).

The particular costs and inefficiencies that the *Tema – Ouagadougou – Bamako highway road* was built to address were examined prior to the upgrade and showed that due to the unpredictability caused by the poor road, it took about a week or more for trucks to move from Tema through Ouagadougou to Bamako instead of the expected 2–4 days (USITC 2009).

A USAID study conducted to assess the impact of this road on the sub-region's trade between 2008 and 2012 shows that there is already an improvement in transport and logistics efficiency along the road (United States Agency for International Development [USAID] and West African Trade Hub [WATH] 2013). The findings also reveal that there is a 9% reduction in transport and logistics costs, and efficiency in transiting time for cargo movement also increased by 50% including reduction of corrupt practices on the road corridor by 50%. Some of these improvements may be attributable to the digitalization of the trucking system. In essence, the road has demonstrated effectiveness to reduce trade cost and integrate the economy of the ECOWAS countries.

However, the effectiveness of the road network has led to an increase in utilization of the road (USAID and WATH 2013). Nevertheless, traffic flow can indicate increased commercial activities, which, in turn, can signify economic growth. The road has also helped to reduce the transit time in moving containerized cargo from Tema to Burkina Faso from 7 to about 5 days, and from Tema to Bamako from 15 to 5 days, as well as reducing trucking time at Tema port from 48 to 24 hours (IEG 2016). Therefore, the road have helped to integrate these countries as they have become interdependent on one another for their economic activities. Road infrastructure being a major means through which AfT directly have positive impact on integration and trade through easing movement of goods and people. With the road, more than 90% of truck operators are now able to access Tema-Burkina Faso route within 2–5 days compared to period before the upgrade when only around 35% of truck operators could access the road from within 5 days (IEG 2016). On the Ouagadougou-Bamako route, the number of heavy trucks plying the road daily grew from 516 in 2011 to 685 in 2015, constituting a 25% increase.

5.3.3 *Road Sample 2: Enugu-Bamenda, Connects ECOWAS (West Africa) to Central Africa*

The Enugu-Bamenda road is a project facilitated with the support of AfT to underscore the strong commitment ECOWAS has towards strengthening regional integration among its members. The road is a 443 kilometre highway, which connects ECOWAS through Enugu, Nigeria; to Central Africa through Bamenda, Cameroon. The road, which costs over US$423 million was largely financed by the AfDB, which provided US$288 million in loans and over US$25 million in grants, with the remainder provided by the World Bank, Japan International Cooperation Agency (JICA), the EU, China, the Governments of Nigeria and Cameroon as well as ECOWAS (AfDB 2017a). Thus the AfDB loans and grants constitute 74% of the funding for this project, which demonstrates how AfT disbursed through regional institutions has increased. It is not surprising that the World Bank, the EU, AfDB and JICA are the major financiers of this road project, because these donors are the largest providers of AfT disbursements to Africa's economic infrastructure in 2015 (OECD and WTO 2017). The road is both strategic to ECOWAS in particular and Africa in general as it helps to link ECOWAS and Central Africa to the Trans-African Highway (TAH) through the Lagos (West Africa)–Mombassa (East Africa) corridor (ECOWAS 2016a; AfDB 2017a). The road integrates fifteen ECOWAS members with the ten members that make up Economic Community of Central African States (ECCAS), thereby deepening the integration of the African continent and facilitating intra-African trade.

The road has helped to reduce trade costs emanating from delays in transit time to transport goods between ECOWAS and Central Africa. For instance, prior to building the road, traders spent between 15 and 20 days on the road between Cameroon and Nigeria, especially during rainy season and could take about a month on return trip, which usually cost between US$268 and US$358. However, it now takes less than a day, approximately 5 hours to transport goods from Bamenda, Cameroon to Onitsha, Nigeria, with cost reduced to only about US$179 (Nkemngu 2017).

In all, it has helped to increase trade, household income, job opportunities and private sector development in the two countries and beyond as feeder roads from different areas within the two countries connect to this road to reach the city markets in West Africa and Central Africa (United

States Fund for Central African States Development Commission 2016). The increased trade has also provided the two countries with increased revenue from custom duties as well as improves Nigeria and Cameroon's socio-political relations in the aftermath of the Bakassi Peninsula maritime's dispute (ECOWAS 2015). In all, these roads, together with all the corridor roads identified by the African Union, would help to increase the efficiency of Africa's road infrastructure by approximately US$172 billion and facilitate the actualization of the African Common market by 2028 (AfDB, AU, and NEPAD 2010). However, despite the opportunities that AfT provides to increase road infrastructure in ECOWAS, this paper finds that, in doing so, it comes with some challenges which are discussed below.

5.4 Challenges of Building These Roads with the Support of AfT

Drawing from the challenges and the opportunities of aid and AfT identified, this section examines those challenges and opportunities as well as other ones in the context of the two road projects identified in the results of this research.

High cost of constructing the roads: Building roads, especially roads that benefits more than one country, like any other forms of infrastructure development comes at a huge cost. For instance, the preparation costs of erecting regional infrastructure is 70% higher than the cost of constructing national infrastructure projects (Moulot 2017). Improving regional roads in Africa would cost an estimated US$20 billion to initiate and an additional US$1 billion yearly for maintenance (Buys et al. 2010). This level of expenditure amounts to an annual investment of 15% of Africa's GDP in order to fully improve its infrastructure (Calderon and Serven 2010; AfDB 2013). The high cost of road infrastructure is one of the reasons loans and grants continue to constitute the largest part of infrastructure funding in Africa (Infrastructure Consortium for Africa [ICA] 2016). For instance, the Tema-Ouagadougou-Bamako road cost over US$190 million in loans and grants from the World Bank alone, in addition to loans and grants from other donors.

The high cost seems to also partly influence the delay in the planning and construction of the Enugu-Bamenda. This is because the road was first proposed over thirty years as part of the transcontinental highway link between ECOWAS through Lagos, Nigeria to East Africa through Mombassa, Kenya (AfDB 2017a). Another issue that sometimes influence the high cost in using AfT to build road emanates from the inconsistency in estimating the financial cost for roads projects in Africa. For instance, extant evidence suggests that road infrastructure in Africa costs more to complete in practice than what is actually estimated in the costing appraisals (AfDB 2014). Findings from an examination of 172 road projects in Africa shows that actual value cost of completing road projects is often greater than the value costs estimated in project appraisals report, as there are 48% chances that the costs in the project completion report would be greater than the cost in the project appraisal reports. A way out of this high-cost menace is for ECOWAS to explore alternative forms of development financing for its road projects such as investing remittances into infrastructure through selling of remittances bond to attract fund.

High indebtedness: The use of AfT to meet the financial demands of road infrastructure, means ECOWAS members end up being significantly indebted as a result of the concessional loans, which form part of AfT. Although the concessional loans are disbursed at discounted rates, many ECOWAS members still find repayment difficult, extending the life of the loan and resulting in high levels of indebtedness. For instance, loans represent 73% of total infrastructure funding in Africa in 2015, followed by grants at 12% (ICA 2016). More specifically, ECOWAS members, including Gambia, Burkina Faso and Cote D'Ivoire are some of the largest recipients of African Development Bank's infrastructure concessional, non-concessional loans and grants (AfDB 2017b). With these countries Ghana, Senegal, Nigeria, Burkina Faso and Cote D'Ivoire are also among the largest recipients of AfT disbursements to road infrastructure in 2015 (see Table 5.1 in the appendix), while Benin, Burkina Faso, Cote D'Ivoire, Gambia and Ghana are among heavily indebted poor countries (World Bank 2017). However, the level of indebtedness caused by AfT is still minimal relative to other forms of ODA because AfT contains more grants elements of over 25%. For instance, in 2013 grants accounted for nearly 55% of total AfT allocations to Africa while concessional loans were 40% (UNECA 2013a). Moreover, AfT is established on the need to provide 'predictable and non-debt creating funding' to developing countries (UNCTAD 2009, p. 18). This notwithstanding, ECOWAS members which are directly linked to the two roads will continually have to repay these loans which cost well over US$620 million in total.

In order to reduce the burden of indebtedness, developing countries proposed a new dedicated fund that provides the grants and concessional loans through a different channel away from being a subset of ODA, however, the proposal was rejected by donors. A way out of this would be for ECOWAS to intensify efforts to increase private sector investment (both local and foreign) into road infrastructure, as it has for telecommunication infrastructure. Overall, private investment in infrastructure still remains low in ECOWAS and Africa in general, constituting US$7.5 billion at 8.9% share in 2015 (ICA 2016).

Stringent conditionality and complex procedures: Another problem associated with using AfT to build road infrastructure is that the conditions or requirements to access the ODA loans and grants, which constitute AfT are often rigorous and challenging and can reflect the interests of the donor countries. Some of the requirements sometimes entail imposing policy or regulatory reforms on recipient countries. For instance, HIV/AIDS action plan was included as sub-components of criteria for the Tema-Ouagadougou-Bamako road (IEG 2016), while OECD donors also include environmental, biodiversity and gender issues as factors in their AfT sub-components as indicated in the OECD CRS micro-data (OECD, n.d.). These factors tend to influence the two road projects because these roads are largely funded with financial support from OECD countries through the World Bank and AfDB.

As a result of this conditionality, oftentimes low-income countries in Africa experience difficulty in accessing concessional loans for infrastructure development (Bertelsmann-Scott et al. 2016). The United States has adopted this method at times and allocated AfT and trade preferences as conditions or a form of reward to recipients with good governance (Gnangnong 2017). For instance, countries like Zimbabwe and Sudan are not beneficiaries of the AGOA due to their varying policy conditions and ideology. The U.S. policy here is a good example of how a donor country may allocate AFT in accordance with its own priorities and interests. Also, road infrastructure projects are implemented according to planned timelines. However, complex, technical and legal procedures in the disbursement of AfT often make it difficult for African countries to implement the projects within the estimated timelines (Moulot 2017). The rigorous requirements and procedures that can accompany AFT mean that African countries are exploring innovative financing like public–private partnership financing for its regional infrastructure projects (Akinkugbe 2013).

Financial challenges and delays in disbursing AfT fund: Poor financial capacity of ECOWAS members, especially LDCs, limits building more roads, because ECOWAS members have to prioritize between addressing other developmental needs, such as providing health and electricity infrastructure. More so, the inability of African countries to remit their own counterpart funding causes delay in the implementation of infrastructure projects (Bertelsmann-Scott et al. 2016). Ghana, for instance, contributed less than the amount (US$20 million) that was allotted to her for the development of the Tema-Ouagadougou-Bamako (IEG 2016). Donors, while trying to be prudent in their financial expenditure, also cut down on their aid budget thereby resulting in late disbursement, inconsistency or discontinuation of AfT. The budgetary cut consequently reduces donors' ability to provide adequate concessional loans and grants thus making ECOWAS members resort more to non-concessional loans, which increases their debt profiles and hampers their development objectives.

The procedures for mobilizing and disbursing funds, especially concessional loans and grants also take a longer time (Moulot 2017). The factors outlined combine to inhibit effective coordination. Hence, creating alternative sources of funding like raising internal taxes would help address these challenges (Gutman et al. 2015). Similarly, the difficulty in getting regional partners to harmonize their national interests with regional development needs and commit to building infrastructure projects often add to the delay because of their varying economic infrastructure priorities (Byiers and Lui 2013).

Multiple checkpoints, charges and corrupt practices on the regional road interlink: These factors also inhibit road infrastructure development and reaping the benefits of completed project. USAID and WATH (2013) show that there is a negative effect of excessive cross-border road checkpoints on trade in West Africa. The objective of building regional road infrastructure is to facilitate intra-regional trade and deepen integration. However, multiple cross-border checkpoints hinder the effectiveness of using AfT to build road infrastructure thereby adding to trade costs in ECOWAS. Multiple road checks and charges are highly prevalent in ECOWAS and Central Africa with some countries having checkpoints in every 30 kilometres distance or less, thereby constituting additional 10% cost to trade (Arvis et al. 2010). For instance, on the Tema-Ouagadougou-Bamako road, a truck transporting grain from Koutiala, Mali to Dakar, Senegal would pass through about 100 road checkpoints, which often require payment of charges, taxes and bribes totaling about

US$437 for the journey (Barka 2012). Similarly, on the Enugu-Bamenda road which connects ECOWAS with CEMAC, the total number of taxes and charges on these road checkpoints represents over 50% of trading costs between the two sub-regions because both are different regional blocs and adopts varying charges (Hoppe 2013). All these add up to make inland transportation of goods in Africa account for the largest share of total trade cost at over 70% (UNECA 2013b). This is why evidence suggests that one day reduction in transit time to move goods in Africa would increase Africa's exports by 7% (Freund and Rocha 2011). Therefore, supporting road infrastructure with requisite measures and policies aimed at reducing roadblocks and border checkpoints would help to enhance the effectiveness of roads infrastructure (Christ and Ferrantino 2011).

Inadequate statistical data on AfT and on-road infrastructure: The OECD-Creditor Reporting System (CRS) remains the resource point for data on AfT, which are mainly reported by donors. There is no aggregate data on AfT that donors or development partners provide to regional economic bodies like ECOWAS secretariat as a whole except to individual member-states. More so, AfT provided by non-OECD/DAC members such as China and India, which are significant providers of bilateral AfT to Africa and ECOWAS's infrastructure are not reflected in AfT data. For instance, the Enugu-Bamenda road were built by two Chinese companies, namely, China Communications Construction Company (CCCC) on the Cameroonian side and China Civil Engineering Construction Corporation (CCECC) on the Nigerian side (Nkemngu 2017). China also increased its investment and ODA commitments to Africa's infrastructure from US$3.1 billion in 2014 to US$20.9 billion in 2015, making it the largest external financier of Africa's infrastructure development (ICA 2016). However, China does not distinguish between investment fund and aid fund to infrastructure development and thus calculates both as aid because it believes both are meant for improving economic development of recipient countries (Tan-Mullins et al. 2010).

The insufficiencies of the data create various challenges for ECOWAS nations. For instance, data reported to OECD CRS is insufficient to effectively measure the broader impact of AfT, especially at the regional level because the reporting system focuses more on allocation of the AfT fund rather than on the outcome of AfT projects (Byiers and Lui 2013). In addition, the composition of AfT is too broad and poorly defined, which makes it difficult to distinguish national AfT projects from regional projects, especially as regional road projects often require its planning and legal procedures being performed at the national level (Byiers and Lui 2013). The unclear distinction between loans allocated to trade-related sector and non-trade sector (World Bank 2013) is also a major challenge when using AfT to build road infrastructure as this may distort AfT planning and allocation processes. This tends to create uncertainty on the scope and coverage of what constitutes AfT among total ODA flows. Poor transparency of infrastructure data in Africa, which are often not publicized (Gutman et al. 2015), while its vagueness and discrepancies adds to the problem of using it to plan for AfT allocation and strategies to road infrastructure (Buys et al. 2010). Similarly, the absence of a universal and broad data on economic infrastructure over a long period of time makes it challenging to conduct comprehensive analysis (Donaubauer et al. 2016). The OECD also acknowledges the disparity in its AfT calculations and data relative to calculations by other development agencies such as the World Bank. The OECD CRS often include in its AfT calculation investments to transport or other economic infrastructure funded through aid even if the impacts of the infrastructure does not directly affect trade or trade-related (OECD 2011).

5.5 Opportunities of Using AfT to Build Road Infrastructure in ECOWAS

Additional source of finance: AfT provides additional source of funding to ECOWAS, which enables building and upgrading their road infrastructure. The significance of this funding is reflected in the increase in the total AfT disbursed to support road infrastructure in ECOWAS from US$408 million in 2005 to US$794.3 million in 2015 (see Table 5.1 in the appendix). Top bilateral donors to road infrastructure in Africa are EU members (OECD, n.d.). However, for ECOWAS members, bilateral donors vary from country to country. For example, Nigeria's top donors in 2015 are Denmark, France, Japan, IDA (World Bank) and AfDB, while Ghana's top donors in the same year are Belgium, Denmark, France, Switzerland, Germany and Japan (OECD, n.d.). This shows that ECOWAS members are able to draw AfT funding from varieties of sources.

Aside non-OECD members, China is the largest bilateral contributor to Africa's infrastructure funding. Also, the EU, the World Bank and AfDB collectively are the largest providers of external sources of funding to transport infrastructure development in Africa (Gutman et al.

2015). For instance, the Enugu-Bamenda and Tema-Ouagadougou-Bamako road projects have the World Bank, AfDB, EU, JICA and USAID as the top multilateral providers of AfT funding through concessional loans and grants. The World Bank continues to be the largest multilateral AfT donor to infrastructure development with about two-thirds of its financial support being allocated to building roads and highways (World Bank 2013). These funds help to complement ECOWAS Governments' financing of road infrastructure. Similarly, the European Commission, through its Africa Infrastructure Trust Fund (AITF), has also disbursed in grants to Africa a total of €698.4 million since the inception of the fund in 2007, of which ECOWAS receives the second largest amount (i.e., €183.6 million) after East Africa (i.e., €415.1 million) (EC-AITF Report 2017). In all, the AITF grants have helped to support the construction and improvement of 1,798 km roads in Africa.

However, government funding still accounts for the largest share of infrastructure financing in ECOWAS and Africa in general, with commitment from 44 African Governments reaching US$28.4 billion in 2015 (Infrastructure Consortium in Africa [ICA] 2016). Africa spends a minimum of US$45 billion annually on infrastructure development and US$30 billion of it is sourced internally while US$15 billion is derived from external sources (Foster and Briceño-Garmendia 2010). The additional funding through AfT has helped to increase the number and efficiency of road infrastructure within ECOWAS. This is because a 10% increase in AfT to economic infrastructure leads to a 1% growth in the quantity of infrastructure (Vigil and Wagner 2012). However, since a share of this finance comes from loans, this partly contributes to the indebtedness of ECOWAS members.

Enhances economic growth and inclusive development: AfT to build road infrastructure in ECOWAS has also helped to enhance economic growth and development through improved roads which facilitates trade. ECOWAS is often faced with poor and inadequate economic infrastructure. However, with access to increased AfT, this has helped in building more road infrastructure, which eases movement of goods and services, integrates the region and improves the welfare of the countries. Improving transport infrastructure increases country's openness to trade, which consequently facilitate growth because an improvement in transport infrastructure by one standard deviation leads to a 0.27% rise in openness to trade (Donaubauer et al. 2016). If it is regional roads or rural roads in Africa, it increases the country's overall economic performance by 3–5% because it facilitates movement of agricultural produce and connects them to the market, and could be as high as 4–6% if the roads are in the central regions where economic activities are higher (Calmette and Kilkenny 2012). More so, infrastructural improvement has proved to have positive impact on the economic development of Sub-Saharan African countries in the long-term without increasing inequality level of those countries (Calderon and Serven 2010). In particular, developing road infrastructure tend to be a catalyst for enhancing inclusive growth as it helps to link the rural poor to the global market and provides them access to increased investments and technology acquisition (Kanbur and Rauniyar 2010). For instance, Enugu-Bamenda highway, which links ECOWAS to Economic Community of Central African States (ECCAS), Central African market, also connects ECOWAS to the Dakar-N'Djamena highway corridor which is one of the major corridors that connects the entire African market to the global market.

Aid to infrastructure, especially grants, provides the opportunities for countries to enhance their cross-border transport infrastructure, which aids development (Mun and Nakagawa 2008) and improves economic welfare by increasing activities that boost domestic consumption (Djajić 2009; Donaubauer et al. 2016). It is for this reason that from definition of AfT, ODA must contain element of grants for it to be classified as AfT. Grants are forms of assistance in cash, goods or services in which recipients are not obliged to pay back (OECD 2013). Figure 5.2 shows that grants account for a significant sum of the total AfT to roads infrastructure in ECOWAS, thereby helping to improve economic welfare of member-states. The detailed amounts are depicted in Table 5.3 of the appendix.

Corridor development, regional integration and logistic services improvement: Using AfT to build road infrastructure in ECOWAS provides opportunities for corridor development, strengthening regional integration and improving logistic services within the sub-region. Road corridor is a concept, which allows private sector participation and financing in the implementation process of AfT infrastructure projects through linking private investments with donors or development partners, together with trade policy and infrastructure projects (Byiers and Lui 2013). AfT enables developing countries like ECOWAS to jointly

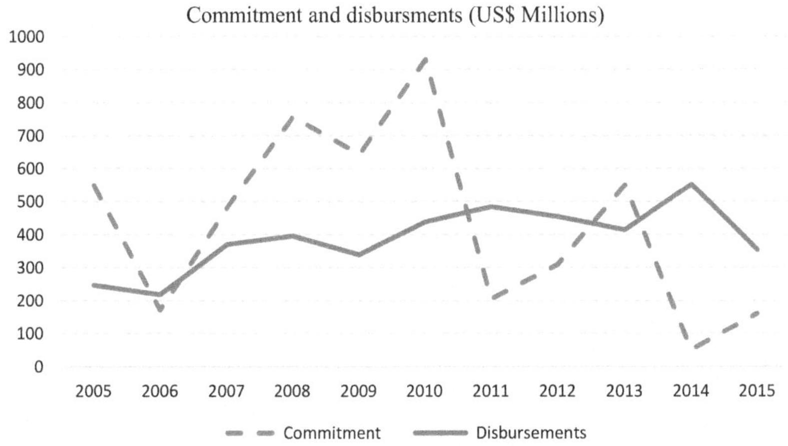

Fig. 5.2 Sum of grants in total AfT to road infrastructure to ECOWAS members, 2005–2015 (*Source* OECD CRS database. Retrieved from http://stats.oecd.org/qwids/; http://www.oecd.org/dac/aft/Aid-for-trade-sector-codes.pdf, on 16 September 2017)

make effort and commitments by putting resources together for implementation of infrastructure projects with the support of other stakeholders. It helps countries to harmonize their interests to collectively support and build regional transport infrastructure (Mun and Nakagawa 2008). For instance, AfT from development partners contributed to facilitate the construction of Tema-Ouagadougou-Bamako corridor road by assisting regional members to prioritize their infrastructure needs in line with the broader regional goal.

AfT and the corridors approach both help to enhance integration of the West African sub-region by linking ECOWAS members transport infrastructure together to facilitate movement of goods and people. The two roads examined in this research together with Dakar-N'Djamena are good examples of regional road corridors. The EU often supports ECOWAS greatly in this regard by providing AfT to support regional integration through its European Development Fund (EDF). This is because the EU itself used infrastructure development to facilitate its regional integration (Crescenzi and Rodríguez-Pose 2012) which is why it is one of the largest providers of AfT to ECOWAS' integration and infrastructure development. For instance, it provided the sum of €65.8 million in concessional loans and grants to support the West African Transport and Transit Facilitation project under which the Tema-Ouagadougou-Bamako corridor was completed (AfDB 2011).

Improving logistic infrastructure and services: AfT to road infrastructure allows ECOWAS to improve the efficiency of its logistics infrastructure and services. The road does not only facilitate trade within ECOWAS member-states, it also helps to increase the efficiency of logistic and land freights services. For instance, part of the World Bank support on Tema-Ouagadougou-Bamako corridor development includes upgrading of trucking system and facilities in the three countries (IEG 2016). Improvement of logistic is important to ECOWAS because some of its members have some of the world's poorest logistic infrastructure and services as indicated in the Logistic Performance Index (LPI) (see Table 5.2). The LPI evaluates and ranks the logistic infrastructure of countries which includes trucking system for efficiently moving goods from one country to another, with 5 being the highest ranked and 1 as the lowest.

5.6 Conclusion and Recommendations

5.6.1 Introduction

This section summarizes the findings of this research and proffers recommendations on how ECOWAS members can better address the challenges in using AfT to meet infrastructural needs in order to increase their benefits from the initiative. Based on the findings, this paper has provided innovative options on how AfT could improve their regional road infrastructure and strengthen integration in West Africa. Further, it has proffered recommendations on how to better improve the effectiveness of AfT in ECOWAS. This study uses multiple sources to collect and analyse data derived from reports like those prepared by the WTO and OECD that review global AfT. Additionally, documents like journal articles, newspaper articles and books provide existing information. The existing literature was sourced from online databases like EBSCOhost, ScienceDirect and Wiley Online library using Boolean search engine. The review helps to bring out divergent perspectives on AfT, by identifying areas where it is providing opportunities and areas where it is challenging to implement. Statistical data on AfT and road infrastructure were extracted from archival or past factual records of OECD CRS database, including World Bank, AfDB, UNECA and ECOWAS. The statistical data from these organizations analyses the trends in AfT flows to road infrastructure to ECOWAS members from 2005 to 2015.

5.6.2 Conclusion

Findings from this research reveal the opportunities that AfT provides to ECOWAS by granting them additional sources of finance to support the development of their road infrastructure. These opportunities vary from ability to access other markets through improving road linkages, logistics improvement and transport corridor development, with the aim of deepening integration, assisting them to benefit from the global value chain and facilitating growth and development. However, the research finds that using AfT to enhance infrastructure in ECOWAS, also comes with challenges like having to deal with donor interests over theirs, ineffective coordination of AfT projects by both donor and recipients, poor and incoherent data on road infrastructure. The problem of multiple checkpoints and taxes also add to transport cost and delays in movement of goods thereby undermining the efficiency of the road infrastructure. It is for this reason that supporting AfT with the requisite domestic policies and regulations would help address this inefficiency and enable ECOWAS to fully utilize the opportunities in AfT to enhance its road infrastructure. Increasing private sector investment in road infrastructure would complement Government effort and reduce dependence on AfT and indebtedness of ECOWAS member-states.

5.6.3 Recommendations

This study helps to show areas where AfT is playing significant role in assisting ECOWAS to improve its road infrastructure in order to further strengthen integration of West African sub-region and Africa in general. It is for this reason that this study proposed the need for ECOWAS to support its AfT needs with requisite effective economic policies, reforms and regulations in order for it to benefit more from the opportunities that AfT provides. These includes policy and reforms like effective border regulations that reduces the number of road checkpoints among ECOWAS members in order to reduce transport cost and facilitate movement of goods and people; tax holidays or lower interests rates to investors in road infrastructure; or tariff waivers for the importation of road infrastructure equipment and machinery.

Improving investment climate would encourage the private sector to play complementary role is collaborating with the government through public–private partnership (PPP) or fully invest in road infrastructure development like it does in the telecommunication sector. Adopting road toll fee collection on major roads and investing in digital system of toll collection would provide an alternative source of getting finance to maintain the roads and reduce indebtedness of ECOWAS members arising from using external sources of finance or foreign aid to develop their infrastructure. It will reduce the dependence on ECOWAS members, especially members which have foreign aid constituting about half of their GDP. Remittances can also serve as another alternative source of funding for ECOWAS.

To further benefit more from AfT, ECOWAS member-states would need to mainstream and prioritize trade into their national development strategies. This is because AfT is targeted at assisting countries to achieve growth and development through increased export performance. Prioritizing trade-related infrastructure in their development plan would enable them to benefit more as this is a requirement for benefiting from AfT.

Data disparity between two key development agencies, the OECD and World Bank on what constitute AfT and AfT projects should be harmonized to eliminate distorted data. The OECD database, which is the resource centre for data on ODA and AfT should be enhanced to give clear distinction on the definition of AfT and what constitute AfT projects and programmes.

5.6.4 *Limitations and Areas of Further Research*

There is no aggregate data on AfT flows to each sub-regions only for SSA as a whole which is why the data is recorded on a country basis. Also, this research focuses mainly on OECD members due to availability of data, hence non-OECD members like China, India which are large Aft donors to ECOWAS and Africa's infrastructure development in general are not examined in this paper.

Appendix

See Tables 5.1, 5.2, and 5.3.

Table 5.1 Total AfT to road infrastructure to ECOWAS members, 2005–2015

Road	*2005*	*2006*	*2007*	*2008*	*2009*	*2010*	*2011*	*2012*	*2013*	*2014*	*2015*
	***Commitments**, US$ millions (current price)*										
Benin	99.7	68.3	16.4	105.8	56.1	145.8	–	33.3	2.6	2.2	1.0
Burkina Faso	–	5.7	0.0	33.9	288.0	96.0	17.4	78.2	124.8	85.3	25.2
Cape Verde	94.7	9.1	58.0	16.1	83.6	0.2	7.4	–	12.4	–	–
Cote D'Ivoire	–	0.0	–	35.7	0.0	30.4	97.3	79.2	38.1	0.0	174.2
Gambia	51.0	–	6.2	–	–	37.1	12.0	100.0	45.0	26.4	2.0
Ghana	106.8	35.5	272.2	175.1	344.8	465.0	27.7	20.1	14.7	26.8	1.8
Guinea	12.2	24.3	93.10	0.6	13.0	0.5	–	0.0	131.0	1.0	32.7
Guinea Bissau	0.0	3.1	13.3	–	4.2	0.0	–	–	–	–	3.1
Liberia	–	4.7	–	12.2	165.0	19.1	94.2	51.0	119.2	22.2	125.7
Mali	40.1	0.3	35.6	242.8	34.3	30.0	–	0.0	48.4	–	–
Niger	110.0	32.4	7.5	144.6	6	11.0	30.9	37.9	101.2	89.4	35.0
Nigeria	–	–	39.5	345.9	34.5	157.8	–	198.0	0.0	0.0	0.0
Senegal	113.1	63.0	35.6	80.8	104.4	391.7	31.3	38.2	51.8	207.0	66.3
Sierra Leone	35.1	3.0	27.4	17.4	0.0	55.0	–	73.4	150.8	–	51.1
Togo	–	0.3	2.7	–	1.8	97.0	14.1	27.3	30.6	22.3	36.7
Total	662.7	249.5	607.0	1210.9	1140.0	1535.3	331.8	736.5	870.0	482.4	554.7
	***Disbursements**, US$ millions (current price)*										
Benin	26.7	15.1	50.6	88.2	67.8	61.4	59.4	65.0	66.9	73.0	52.7
Burkina Fso	29.1	47.7	103.0	25.4	30.6	20.7	22.9	53.1	96.0	166.3	75.9
Cape Verde	28.8	28.4	25.7	50.3	35.3	42.3	35.6	36.6	17.0	9.3	5.2
Cote D'Ivoire	0.1	1.0	–	6.1	17.0	24.7	16.3	39.1	16.5	43.0	57.0
Gambia	0.7	0.4	6.4	6.4	9.7	19.4	37.4	19.2	18.5	28.6	2.0

(continued)

Table 5.1 (continued)

Road	*2005*	*2006*	*2007*	*2008*	*2009*	*2010*	*2011*	*2012*	*2013*	*2014*	*2015*
Ghana	160.5	133.6	103.2	98.5	99.0	110.0	203.3	217.7	161.2	200.2	166.4
Guinea	5.4	8.9	12.3	33.1	24.2	48.4	28.4	23.1	31.0	28.7	17.6
Guinea Bissau	0.8	6.7	15.8	16.1	14.3	1.4	1.0	0.2	0.6	0.5	–
Liberia	–	0.1	1.8	8.3	18.3	61.0	38.1	50.5	33.8	43.1	26.3
Mali	53.1	34.2	62.6	38.8	3.5	45.2	70.8	45.0	21.5	21.6	13.4
Niger	3.5	4.6	44.0	59.3	37.2	51.7	19.1	30.4	46.3	48.2	36.0
Nigeria	24.8	29.8	32.4	22.7	34.1	34.0	41.1	111.7	175.1	184.7	125.4
Senegal	50.7	44.4	49.5	74.8	89.0	106.6	103.4	65.6	93.5	223.6	140.5
Sierra Leone	18.3	15.5	9.7	18.0	30.2	38.7	44.4	41.6	53.8	30.8	30.2
Togo	5.5	5.8	–	0.0	0.2	1.5	20.7	22.0	23.5	24.0	46.6
Total	408.0	376.0	516.9	546.0	510.0	666.3	741.3	820.6	854.6	1124.6	794.1

Source OECD CRS database, n.d., viewed from http://stats.oecd.org/qwids/; http://www.oecd.org/dac/aft/Aid-for-trade-sector-codes.pdf, accessed on 5 September 2017

Table 5.2 Sum of grants in total AfT to road infrastructure to ECOWAS members, 2005–2015

	2005	*2006*	*2007*	*2008*	*2009*	*2010*	*2011*	*2012*	*2013*	*2014*	*2015*
	***Commitments**, US$ millions (current price)*										
Benin	89.2	69.3	16.4	93.8	35.1	47.1	–	24.2	2.6	2.2	1.0
BurkinaFaso	–	5.7	0.0	5.4	240.1	96.0	17.4	45.3	44.0	28.0	0.2
Cape Verde	28.2	9.1	2.7	12.4	0.0	0.2	0.0	–	0.1	–	–
Cote D'Ivoire	–	0.0	–	35.7	0.0	19.0	97.3	79.2	0.0	0.0	42.1
Gambia	51.0	–	6.2	–	–	37.1	–	100.0	14.0	1.4	1.0
Ghana	78.2	35.5	240.2	118.7	136.6	234.4	27.7	20.1	14.7	1.8	1.8
Guinea	12.2	24.3	93.1	0.6	8.0	0.5	–	0.0	123.5	0.9	0.0
Guinea Bissau	0.0	3.1	13.3	–	4.2	0.0	–	–	–	–	1.6
Liberia	–	4.7	–	12.2	164.5	19.1	16.4	1.0	75.6	12.2	32.2
Mali	31.2	0.3	35.6	238.1	23.6	10.7	–	0.0	44.0	–	–
Niger	110.0	0.0	7.5	144.6	6	1.0	20.9	–	85.0	–	–
Nigeria	–	–	–	–	–	1.7	–	0.0	0.3	0.0	0.0
Senegal	113.1	15.2	35.6	80.8	23.8	326.0	21.2	3.5	4.6	3.2	2.7
Sierra Leone	35.1	3.0	27.4	14.2	0.0	55.0	–	35.3	136.7	–	51.1
Togo	–	0.3	2.7	–	1.8	83.0	4.1	0.0	5.6	0.3	26.7
Total	548.1	170.4	480.8	756.6	643.5	930.0	205.0	308.6	550.4	50.0	160.5
	***Disbursements**, US$ millions (current price)*										
Benin	26.0	12.2	38.0	75.2	57.5	50.4	55.0	48.8	34.0	26.0	24.2
Burkina Faso	20.5	39.4	90.7	14.6	12.6	2.2	2.0	37.7	84.7	138.1	36.1
Cape Verde	12.0	8.1	9.4	28.6	13.0	7.1	0.5	–	0.0	–	–
Cote D'Ivoire	0.3	0.5	–	3.0	11.1	17.1	12.3	27.8	10.0	37.5	32.0
Gambia	0.1	–	6.2	6.2	8.3	15.7	34.8	17.0	8.6	23.7	1.4

(continued)

Table 5.2 (continued)

	2005	*2006*	*2007*	*2008*	*2009*	*2010*	*2011*	*2012*	*2013*	*2014*	*2015*
Ghana	99.1	77.6	55.3	62.8	65.1	73.4	147.2	130.4	71.5	85.0	52.8
Guinea	3.1	6.6	8.8	27.7	24.2	46.2	23.3	14.3	19.6	27.5	12.3
Guinea Bissau	0.2	6.7	15.8	16.1	14.3	1.4	0.6	0.2	0.6	0.5	–
Liberia	–	0.1	1.8	8.3	18.3	60.9	38.1	44.8	28.5	31.0	10.4
Mali	37.8	20.2	61.4	33.2	2.2	38.7	63.3	3.0	3.2	18.9	12.7
Niger	3.5	4.6	43.9	59.3	22.6	38.6	9.2	21.7	40.0	42.5	20.1
Nigeria	–	–	–	0.0	–	0.0	–	0.0	0.0	0.1	0.2
Senegal	21.6	22.3	29.7	42.4	59.2	49.3	43.3	31.3	58.6	86.5	105.4
Sierra Leone	17.0	14.1	8.3	17.5	30.2	34.7	33.9	30.1	35.7	19.5	17.7
Togo	5.5	5.8	–	0.3	0.2	1.5	20.7	19.7	19.0	14.4	27.6
Total	246.6	218.1	369.2	395.0	338.5	437.3	483.5	453.7	413.7	551.2	352.8

Source OECD CRS database, n.d., viewed from http://stats.oecd.org/qwids/; http://www.oecd.org/dac/aft/Aid-for-trade-sector-codes.pdf, accessed on 16 September 2017

Table 5.3 Logistic Performance Index (LPI), and doing business ranking of ECOWAS members

Country	*Logistic Performance Index (2016)*				*World Bank doing business ranking (2017)*	
	LPI ranking 2016	LPI score	Quality of trade-related infrastructure	Logistic competence (of trucking and logistic services)	Doing business ranking 2017	Trading across border
Burkina-Faso	81	2.75	2.67	2.78	146	104
Ghana	88	2.66	2.48	2.54	108	154
Nigeria	90	2.63	2.40	2.74	169	181
Togo	92	2.62	2.24	2.46	154	117
Cote D'Ivoire	95	2.60	2.46	2.62	142	150
Niger	100	2.56	2.22	2.50	150	132
Mali	109	2.50	2.30	2.46	141	89
Benin	115	2.43	2.39	2.47	155	133
Guinea Bissau	128	2.37	1.91	2.07	172	153
Guinea	129	2.36	2.01	2.54	163	162
Senegal	132	2.33	2.23	2.39	147	130
Liberia	142	2.20	2.01	2.07	174	185
Sierra Leone	155	2.03	2.07	1.85	148	169
Gambia	Data not available (NA)				145	112
Cape Verde					129	113

Source https://lpi.worldbank.org/international/global; http://www.doingbusiness.org/rankings

References

African Development Bank. (2011). *Regional integration strategy paper for West Africa 2011–2015.* Retrieved from https://www.afdb.org/fileadmin/uploads/afdb/Documents/Policy-Documents/RISP%20for%20West%20Africa%20-%20REV%202.pdf.

African Development Bank. (2013). *Improved infrastructure to support Africa's competitiveness.* Retrieved from https://www.afdb.org/en/blogs/afdb-championing-inclusive-growth-across-africa/post/improved-infrastructure-to-support-africas-competitiveness-11755/.

African Development Bank. (2014). *Study on road infrastructure costs: Analysis of unit costs and cost overrun of road infrastructure projects in Africa.* Retrieved from https://www.afdb.org/fileadmin/uploads/afdb/Documents/Publications/Study_on_Road_Infrastructure_Costs_Analysis_of_Unit_Costs_and_Cost_Overruns_of_Road_Infrastructure_Projects_in_Africa.pdf.

African Development Bank. (2017a). *Enugu-Bamenda road, tool of regional integration and African Development Bank success story.* Retrieved from https://www.afdb.org/en/projects-and-operations/selected-projects/enugu-bamenda-road-tool-of-regional-integration-and-afdb-successstory-119/.

African Development Bank Group. (2017b). *Africa development fund recipient countries: Eligibility criteria.* Retrieved from https://www.afdb.org/en/about-us/corporate-information/african-development-fund-adf/adf-recipient-countries.

African Development Bank & United Nations Economic Commission for Africa. (2003). *Review of the implementation status of the trans-African highways and the missing links.* Retrieved from https://www.afdb.org/fileadmin/uploads/afdb/Documents/Project-and-Operations/00473235-EN-TAH-FINAL-VOL1.PDF.

African Union, African Development Bank & New Partnership for Africa's Development. (2010). *Programme for Infrastructure Development in Africa (PIDA): Interconnecting, integrating and transforming a continent.* Retrieved from https://www.afdb.org/fileadmin/uploads/afdb/Documents/Project-and-Operations/PIDA%20note%20English%20for%20web%200208.pdf.

Akinkugbe, O. D. (2013). The dilemma of public-private partnerships as a vehicle for the provision of regional transport infrastructure development in Africa. *Law and Development Review, 6*(2), 3–27. https://doi.org/10.1515/ldr-2013-0018.

Akpan, U. (2014). Impact of regional road infrastructure improvement on intra-regional trade in ECOWAS. *African Development Review, 26*(2), 64–76. https://doi.org/10.1111/1467-8268.12093.

Arvis, J., Raballand, G., & Marteau, J. (2010). *The cost of being landlocked: Logistics costs and supply chain reliability.* https://doi.org/10.1596/978-0-8213-8408-4.

Barka, H. B. (2012). *Border posts, checkpoints and intra-African trade: Challenges and solutions.* Retrieved from https://www.afdb.org/fileadmin/uploads/afdb/Documents/Publications/INTRA%20AFRICAN%20TRADE_INTRA%20AFRICAN%20TRADE.pdf.

Bertelsmann-Scott, T., Markowitz, C., & Parshotam, A. (2016). Mapping current trends in infrastructure financing in low-income countries in Africa within the context of the African development fund. *Global Economic Governance Africa Discussion Paper.* Retrieved from http://www.gegafrica.org/publications/mapping-current-trends-in-infrastructure-financing-in-low-income-countries-in-africa-within-the-context-of-the-african-development-fund.

Briceno-Garmendia, C., Dominguez, C., & Pushak, N. (2011). *Mali infrastructure: A continental perspective—Africa infrastructure country diagnostic (AICD) country report.* Retrieved from http://hdl.handle.net/10986/27311.

Buys, P., Deichmann, U., & Wheeler, D. (2010). Road network upgrading and overland trade expansion in Sub-Saharan Africa. *Journal of African Economies, 19*(3), 399–432. https://doi.org/10.1093/jae/ejq006.

Byiers, B., & Lui, D. (2013). Selected current issues in aid for trade: Regional aid for trade effectiveness and corridors. In M. Rassaque & D. W. te Velde (Eds.), *Assessing aid for trade: Effectiveness, current issues and future directions* (pp. 183–207). https://dx.doi.org/10.14217/9781848591646-en.

Cadot, O., & de Melo, J. (2014). Evaluation in aid for trade: Introduction to the symposium. *World Economy, 37*(4), 511–515. https://doi.org/10.1111/twec.12137.

Calderon, C., & Serven, L. (2010). Infrastructure and economic development. *Journal of African Economics, 19*(1), i13–i87. Retrieved from https://doi-org.ezproxy.lib.monash.edu.au/10.1093/jae/ejp022.

Calì, M., & te Velde, D. W. (2011). Does aid for trade really improve trade performance? *World Development, 39*(5), 725–740. https://doi.org/10.1016/j.worlddev.2010.09.018.

Calmette, M., & Kilkenny, M. (2012). Rural roads versus African famines. *The Annals of Regional Science, 49*(2), 373–396. https://doi.org/10.1007/s00168-011-0455-3.

Christ, N., & Ferrantino, M. (2011). Land transport for export: The effects of cost, time, and uncertainty in Sub-Saharan Africa. *World Development, 39*(10), 1749–1759. https://doi.org/10.1016/j.worlddev.2011.04.028.

Crescenzi, R., & Rodríguez-Pose, A. (2012). Infrastructure and regional growth in the European Union. *Papers in Regional Science, 91*(3), 487–513. https://doi.org/10.1111/j.1435-5957.2012.00439.x.

Creswell, J. W. (2013). *Qualitative inquiry and research design: Choosing among five approaches.* Riverside, CA: Sage.

Creswell, J. W., & Poth, C. N. (2018). *Quantitative inquiry and research design: Choosing among five approaches*. Thousand Oaks, CA: Sage.
Deen-Swarray, M., Adekunle, B., & Odularu, G. (2014). Policy recipe for fostering regional integration through infrastructure development and coordination in West Africa. In D. Seck (Ed.), *Regional economic integration in West Africa* (pp. 29–56). https://doi.org/10.1007/978-3-319-01282-7.
Djajić, S. (2009). Foreign aid, infrastructure development and welfare: An intertemporal analysis. *Review of Development Economics, 13*(3), 393–402. https://doi.org/10.1111/j.1467-9361.2009.00497.x.
Donaubauer, J., Meyer, B., & Nunnenkamp, P. (2016). A new global index of infrastructure: Construction, rankings and applications. *World Economy, 39*(2), 236–259. https://doi.org/10.1111/twec.12290.
Economic Community of West African States. (2015). *High-level experts field supervision mission to Nigeria–Cameroun transport facilitation programme*. Retrieved from http://www.ecowas.int/high-level-experts-field-supervision-mission-to-nigeria-cameroun-transport-facilitation-programme/.
Economic Community of West African States. (2016a). *Transport*. Retrieved from http://www.ecowas.int/transport/.
Economic Community of West African States. (2016b). *Infrastructure*. Retrieved from http://www.ecowas.int/ecowas-sectors/infrastructure/.
Eriksson, P., & Kovalainen, A. (2016). *Qualitative methods in business research* (2nd ed.). London, UK: Sage.
European Commission & Africa Infrastructure Trust Fund. (2017). *EU-Africa infrastructure trust fund 2016, annual report*. Retrieved from http://www.eib.org/attachments/country/eu_africa_infrastructure_trust_fund_annual_report_2016_en.pdf.
Evenett, S. J. (2005). Some tough love on 'aid for trade'. *Intereconomics, 40*(6), 326–329. http://dx.doi.org/10.1007/s10272-005-0163-2.
Foster, V., & Briceño-Garmendia, C. (2010). *Africa's infrastructure: A time for transformation*. Retrieved from http://documents.worldbank.org/curated/en/246961468003355256/Africas-infrastructure-a-time-for-transformation.
Francois, J., & Manchin, M. (2013). Institutions, infrastructure, and trade. *World Development, 46*, 165–175. http://dx.doi.org/10.1016/j.worlddev.2013.02.009.
Freund, C., & Rocha, N. (2011). What constrains Africa's exports? *World Bank Economic Review, 25*(3), 361–386. https://doi.org/10.1093/wber/1hr016.
Gnangnong, S. (2017). Relative trade preferential margin and aid for trade allocation. *The International Trade Journal*, 1–28. https://doi.org/10.1080/08853908.2017.1353455.
Gorman, K. O., Lochrie, S., & Watson, A. (2014). Research philosophy and case study. In K. O. Gorman & R. Macintosh (Eds.), *Research methods for*

business and management: A guide to writing your dissertation. Oxford, UK: Goodfellow Publishers Limited.

Gutman, J., Sy, A., & Chattopadhyay, S. (2015). *Financing African infrastructure: Can the world deliver?* Retrieved from https://www.brookings.edu/wp-content/uploads/2016/07/AGIFinancingAfricanInfrastructure_FinalWebv2.pdf.

Hoppe, M. (2013). Unblocking border gridlock. *International Trade Forum* (3), 28–29. Retrieved from http://web.b.ebscohost.com.ezproxy.lib.monash.edu.au/ehost/detail/detail?vid=0&sid=dca8b50f-3629-4752-ab5975dd894814af%40sessionmgr120&bdata=JnNpdGU9ZWhvc3QtbGl2ZSZzY29wZT1zaXRl#AN=96548586&db=bth.

Hühne, P., Meyer, B., & Nunnenkamp, P. (2014a). Does aid for trade from the north promote south–south trade? *Applied Economics Letters, 21*(17), 1230–1233. https://doi.org/10.1080/13504851.2014.922665.

Hühne, P., Meyer, B., & Nunnenkamp, P. (2014b). Who benefits from aid for trade? Comparing the effects on recipient versus donor exports. *Journal of Development Studies, 50*(9), 1275–1288. https://doi.org/10.1080/00220388.2014.903246.

Independent Evaluation Group. (2016). *Africa: West Africa regional transport and transit facilitation project*. Retrieved from http://documents.worldbank.org/curated/en/501471468204256879/Africa-West-Africa-Regional-Transport-And-Transit-Facilitation-Project.

Infrastructure Consortium for Africa. (2016). *Infrastructure financing trends in Africa—2015*. Retrieved from https://www.icafrica.org/fileadmin/documents/Annual_Reports/ICA_2015_annual_report.pdf.

Iwanow, T., & Kirkpatrick, C. (2009). Trade facilitation and manufactured exports: Is Africa different? *World Development, 37*(6), 1039–1050. https://doi.org/10.1016/j.worlddev.2008.09.014.

Jianmei, H., Li, F., & Jiming, G. (2013, November). *The research on aid for trade in Africa*. Paper presented at the 2013 International Conference on Information Technology and Applications (ITA), Chengdu, China. https://doi.org/10.1109/ita.2013.100.

Jouanjean, M.-A. (2013). Aid for trade and development. In M. Rassaque & D. te Velde (Eds.), *Assessing aid for trade: Effectiveness, current issues and future directions* (pp. 275–290). http://dx.doi.org/10.14217/9781848591646-en.

Kanbur, R., & Rauniyar, G. (2010). Conceptualizing inclusive development: With applications to rural infrastructure and development assistance. *Journal of the Asia Pacific Economy, 15*(4), 437–454. https://doi.org/10.1080/13547860.2010.516163.

Limao, N., & Venables, A. J. (2001). Infrastructure, geographical disadvantage, transport costs, and trade. *The World Bank Economic Review, 15*(3), 451–479. https://doi.org/10.1093/wber/15.3.451.

Lopez, L. (2015). Corruption and international aid allocation: A complex dance. *Journal of Economic Development, 40*(1), 35–61.

Luke, D., Monge-Roffarello, L., & Varma, S. (2009). Perspectives on aid for trade. In P. Lombaerder & P. Lakshmi (Eds.), *Aid for trade: Global and regional perspective, 2nd world report on regional integration* (pp. 29–38). https://doi.org/10.1007/978-1-4020-9455-2_3.

Mbekeani, K. (2010). Infrastructure, trade expansion and regional integration: Global experience and lessons for Africa. *Journal of African economies, 19*, 88–113. https://doi.org/10.1093/jae/ejp021.

Moulot, J. (2017). *Financing of major continental, regional and national infrastructure: Opportunities and challenges.* Paper presented at the First Ordinary Session of the African Union Specialized Technical Committee on Transport, Intercontinental and interregional infrastructures, Energy and Tourism, Lome Togo. Retrieved from https://au.int/sites/default/files/documents/32249-doc-financing_major_infrastructure-stc_lome_-moulot.pdf.

Mun, S., & Nakagawa, S. (2008). Cross-border transport infrastructure and aid policies. *The Annals of Regional Science, 42*(2), 465–486. https://doi.org/10.1007/s00168-007-0169-8.

Njoh, A. J. (2009). The development theory of transportation infrastructure examined in the context of Central and West Africa. *Review of Black Political Economy, 36*(3), 227–243. https://doi.org/10.1007/s12114-009-9044-4.

Nkemngu, A. (2017). *Cameroon–Nigeria trade: The transformative power of Chinese built Bamenda–Enugu, Kumba–Mamfe road corridor.* Retrieved from http://cameroonjournal.com/2017/08/17/cameroon-nigeria-trade-the-transformative-power-of-chinese-built-bamenda-enugu-kumba-mamfe-road-corridor/.

Organization for Economic Cooperation and Development. (2011). *Strengthening accountability in aid for trade: The development dimension.* http://dx.doi.org/10.1787/9789264123212-en.

Organization for Economic Cooperation and Development. (2013). *Glossary of statistical terms: grants.* Retrieved from https://stats.oecd.org/glossary/detail.asp?ID=1143.

Organization for Economic Cooperation and Development. (n.d.). *Credit reporting system (CRS) micro-data.* Retrieved from http://stats.oecd.org/qwids/microdata.html?q=1:1+2:240+3:79+4:1+5:3+6:2015+7:1+8:85+9:85&ds=CRS1&f=json.

Organization for Economic Cooperation and Development. (n.d.-a). *Credit reporting system (CRS).* Retrieved from http://stats.oecd.org/qwids/; http://www.oecd.org/dac/aft/Aid-for-trade-sector-codes.pdf. Accessed on 19 August 2017.

Organization for Economic Cooperation and Development & World Trade Organization. (2017). *Aid for trade at a glance 2017: Promoting trade, inclusiveness and connectivity for sustainable development.* https://doi.org/10.1787/aid_glance-2017-en.

Oyejide, T. A., & Bankole, A. S. (2010). *Aids for trade and regional integration in West Africa.* Paper presented at the United Nations Economic Commission for Africa Expert Forum, Addis Ababa, Ethiopia. Retrieved from https://www.researchgate.net/publication/266454585_Aid_for_Trade_and_Regional_Integration_in_West_Africa.

Pietsch, W. (2016). Two modes of reasoning with case studies. In T. Sauer & R. Scholl (Eds.), *The philosophy of historical case studies* (pp. 49–67). https://doi.org/10.1007/978-3-319-30229-4.

Storeygard, A. (2016). Farther on down the road: Transport costs, trade and urban growth in Sub-Saharan Africa. *The Review of Economic Studies, 83*(3), 1263–1295. https://doi.org/10.1093/restud/rdw020.

Tan-Mullins, M., Mohan, G., & Power, M. (2010). Redefining 'aid' in the China–Africa context. *Development and Change, 41*(5), 857–881. https://doi.org/10.1111/j.1467-7660.2010.01662.x.

Thomas, G. (2011). *How to do your case study: A guide for students and researchers.* London, UK: Sage.

Thomas, G., & Myers, K. (2015). *The anatomy of case study.* London, UK: Sage.

Udvari, B. (2014, September). *Aid for trade: Does it enhance the intra-trade of Sub-Saharan African integrations?* Paper presented at the 16th Annual Conference of ETSG, Munich. Retrieved from http://publicatio.bibl.u-szeged.hu/7088/1/etsg_2014.pdf.

United Nations Conference on Trade and Development. (2009). Aid for trade and development. In P. Lombaerder & P. Lakshmi (Eds.), *Aid for trade: Global and regional perspective, 2nd world report on regional integration* (pp. 5–27). https://doi.org/10.1007/978-1-4020-9455-2_2.

United Nations Economic Commission for Africa. (2013a). *Building trade capacities for Africa's transformation: A critical review of aid for trade.* Retrieved from http://hdl.handle.net/10855/22153.

United Nations Economic Commission for Africa. (2013b). *Trade facilitation from an African perspective.* Retrieved fromhttps://www.uneca.org/sites/default/files/PublicationFiles/trade_facilitation_eng.pdf.

United Nations Economic Commission for Africa. (2015). *Reducing trade costs to support Africa's transformation: The role of aid for trade.* Retrieved from https://www.wto.org/english/tratop_e/devel_e/a4t_e/global_review15prog_e/uneca_final.pdf.

United Nations Economic Commission for Africa & World Trade Organization. (2017). *Promoting connectivity in Africa: The role of aid for trade in boosting intra-African trade executive summary.* Retrieved from https://www.wto.org/english/tratope/devel_e/a4t_e/gr17_e/aft_2017_africa_report_exec_summary_eng_fn_rev.pdf.

United States Agency for International Development & West African Trade Hub. (2013). *Trends in transport and logistics on the Tema-Ouagadougou-Bamako corridor, West Africa trade hub technical report no. 51*. Retrieved from http://www.Borderlesswa.com/sites/default/files/resources/nov14/1305%20Tema-Ouaga-Bamako%20Trends%20in%20Transport.

United States Fund for Central African States Development Commission. (2016). *Project—Regional integration road project*. Retrieved from http://usf-casdc.org/projects/.

United States International Trade Commission. (2009). *Sub-Saharan Africa: Effects of infrastructure conditions on exports competitiveness, third annual report* (No. 332–477). Retrieved from https://www.usitc.gov/publications/332/pub4071.pdf.

Vijil, M., & Wagner, L. (2012). Does aid for trade enhance export performance? Investigating the infrastructure hannel. *World Economy, 35*(7), 838–868. https://doi.org/10.1111/j.1467-9701.2012.01437.x.

Woodside, A. G. (2010). *Case study research: Theory, methods and practice*. Bingley, UK: Emerald Group Publishing Ltd.

World Bank. (2008). *World Bank supports transport improvements in West African States*. Retrieved from http://web.worldbank.org/external/default/main?pagePK=34370&piPK=&theSitePK=4607&menuPK=34463&contentMDK=21815573.

World Bank. (2013). *What is the World Bank doing on aid for trade?* (No. 83234). Retrieved from http://documents.worldbank.org/curated/en/966251468326183873/What-is-the-World-Bank–doing-on-aid-for-trade.

World Bank. (2015). *Implementation status and results: West Africa regional transport and transit facilitation project (P079749)*. Retrieved from http://documents.worldbank.org/curated/en/662911468004848946/pdf/ISR-Disclosable-P079749-04-08-2015-1428518903338.pdf.

World Bank. (2017). *Heavily indebted poor countries (HIPC)*. Retrieved from https://data.worldbank.org/region/heavily-indebted-poor-countries-hipc?view=chart.

World Trade Organization. (2005). *Ministerial declaration*. Retrieved from https://www.wto.org/english/thewto_e/minist_e/min05_e/final_text_e.htm#aid_for_trade.

World Trade Organization. (2015). *International trade statistics 2015*. Retrieved from https://www.wto.org/english/res_e/statis_e/its2015_e/its2015_e.pdf.

World Trade Organization. (2017). *Aid for trade*. Retrieved from https://www.wto.org/english/tratop_e/devel_e/a4t_e/aid4trade_e.htm.

Yin, R. (2009). *Case study research: Design and methods* (4th ed.). Thousand Oaks, CA: Sage.

Yin, R. (2014). *Case study research: Design and methods* (5th ed.). Thousand Oaks, CA: Sage.

CHAPTER 6

Harnessing the AfCFTA for Economic Diversification in Nigeria: The Role of Trade Logistics and Infrastructure

Oluwasola E. Omoju and Emily E. Ikhide

6.1 Background

Economists have long regarded the role of trade liberalisation in economic diversification and regional development (Robinson and Thierfelder 1999; Shafaeddin 2005). Hence, the launch of the African Continental Free Trade Agreement (AfCFTA) is expected to boost intra-African trade and promote regional development. A major thrust of the agreement is the removal of tariffs from about 90% of goods, enhancing free flow of goods and services across the continent. According to the United Nations Economic Commission for Africa (UNECA), the agreement has the potential to boost intra-African trade by 52% by 2022, compared with the trade levels in 2010 (UNECA 2018). As of July 2019, 54 countries have signed the agreement and the agreement is currently in force.

O. E. Omoju (✉) · E. E. Ikhide
National Institute for Legislative and Democratic Studies,
Abuja, Nigeria
e-mail: shollcy@yahoo.co.uk

G. Odularu (ed.), *Strategic Policy Options for Bracing Nigeria for the Future of Trade*,
https://doi.org/10.1007/978-3-030-34552-5_6

Before the Nigerian government signed the agreement on 7 July 2019, there were concerns about the distribution of the costs and benefits of the agreement among the participating countries. According to the Nigerian government and other major stakeholders (the Manufacturers Association of Nigeria, Chambers of Commerce and the Nigeria Labour Congress), the AfCFTA would stifle local manufacturing and encourage anti-competitive practices such as dumping. There are also concerns about its effects on government revenue from import taxes. A study by the United Nations Conference on Trade and Development (UNCTAD) found that the elimination of all tariff among African countries would reduce government revenue across the continent by $4.1 billion annually, but would create an annual welfare gain of $16.1 billion in the long term (Saygili et al. 2018).

The argument that the agreement would stifle local manufacturing capacity in Nigeria is partly premised on a number of factors including but not limited to rules of origin, dumping, vulnerability of local industries and competitiveness of Nigeria's products in the international market. This note argues that the agreement has the potential to enhance Nigeria's economic diversification efforts, but the country needs major domestic adjustments, especially with respect to trade logistics and infrastructure, that reduce (increase) the costs (ease) of doing business and exporting for it to benefit from the export expansion that will be engendered by the agreement. It highlights the current state of trade logistics and infrastructure using available secondary data.

6.2 Stylized Facts on the Nigerian Economy and Export Dynamics

The Nigerian economy is the largest in Africa, surpassing the South African economy after the rebasing of the GDP in 2014. According to the World Bank's World Development Indicators, Nigeria's GDP stands at $375 billion in 2017. The economy experienced significant expansion in the years leading to 2013 due to high oil prices and supportive macroeconomic environment. In line with the expansion of the economy, the structural composition of the economy has also changed significantly over the years as shown in Fig. 6.1. According to the available data, the contribution of the petroleum, manufacturing and agriculture sectors to the economy has fallen over the years, while those of the service and trade

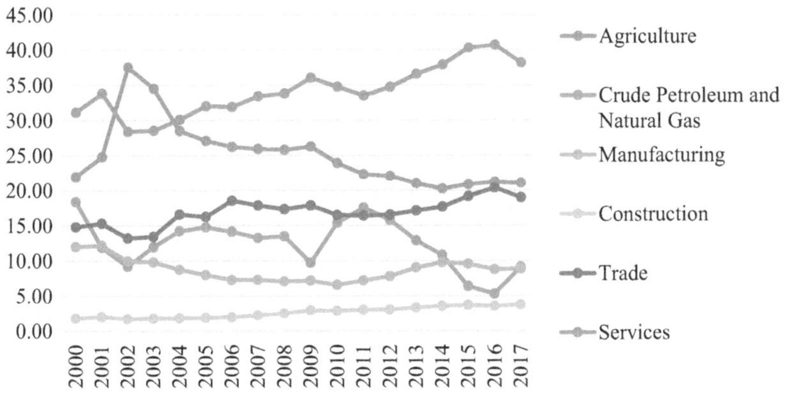

Fig. 6.1 Sectoral contribution to Nigeria's GDP, 2000–2017 (*Source* Data from the Central Bank of Nigeria's Statistical Bulletin)

sectors have experienced an upward trend. The diversification of the economy from over-reliance on oil and primary commodities is a stated goal of the government, as it seeks to reverse the resource curse and "Dutch disease" syndromes and develop other critical sectors of the economy in order to promote balanced and sustainable development.

The export structure of the Nigerian economy is dominated by crude oil and gas exports. According to data from the Central Bank of Nigeria's Statistical Bulletin, oil-related exports account for 92% of total exports in 2017, subjecting the economy to macroeconomic shocks during periods of volatility in international oil prices. Additional data from the World Bank's World Integrated Trade Solution (WITS) database classifies Nigeria's exports into raw materials (82.3%), intermediate goods (2.3%), consumer goods (14.8%) and capital goods (0.35%). Efforts to diversify the export base of the economy from primary commodities are gathering steam, and the contributions of the non-oil sector to exports are expected to increase with the AfCFTA.

The number of Nigeria's export partners and products, which is a measure of export diversification, has declined significantly in recent years. In 2013, Nigeria has 148 trading partners but this has reduced to 116 partners by 2017 (Fig. 6.2). Similarly, Nigeria exports varieties of 1228 products in 2013 but has reduced to only 328 products by 2017. The declining trend of export products and partners signals concentration of

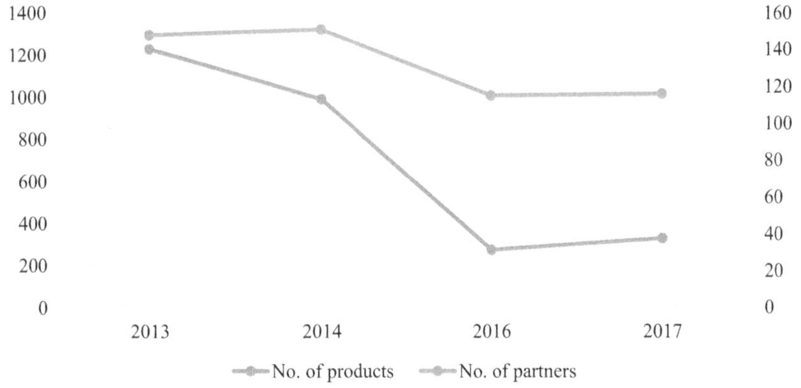

Fig. 6.2 Number of Nigerian export products and partners, 2013–2017 (*Source* World Bank's WITS Database [World Bank 2019])

Nigeria's exports products and trading partners, which could undermine economic development in the long term.

Currently, the top destinations of Nigerian exports are outside the continent (Fig. 6.3). India accounts for the largest proportion of Nigeria's exports at 17.9%, followed by the United States at 12.8%, Spain (9.9%), Netherlands (8.5%) and France (7.7%). The AfCFTA is poised to boost

Fig. 6.3 Nigeria: Top five export destinations (*Source* World Bank [2019])

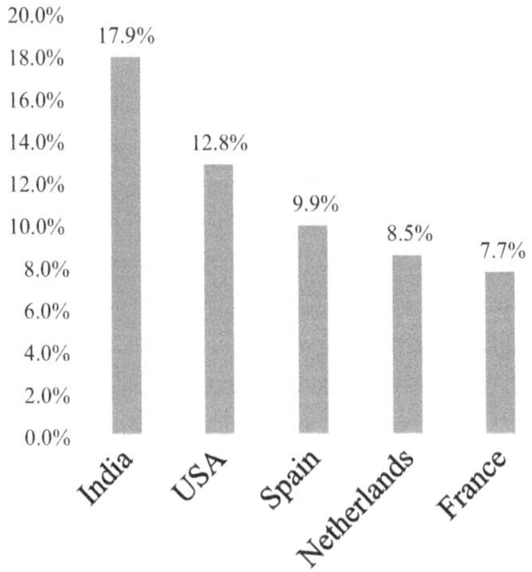

intra-African trade and regional integration. Nigeria exports to African destinations have also witnessed some modest increases in recent years. Data from the UN International Trade Centre cited by the Trade Law Centre shows that Nigeria exported goods worth about $4.9 billion to other African countries in 2017, accounting for 12% of the country's total exports. The major African destinations of Nigeria's exports are shown in Fig. 6.4. The commodities exported composed of crude oil which accounts for 83%, petroleum gas (4.7%), electrical energy (2.1%), tobaccos and cigarettes (2.05), vessels and other floating structure (1.82%) and cement (1.07%). Other notable intra-Africa Nigerian exports include petroleum oil (excluding crude), pasta, mineral or chemical fertilisers and insecticides and herbicides.

The AfCFTA is expected to increase the number of exported commodities due to the opening of new markets. However, the state of trade logistics and infrastructure in Nigeria vis-à-vis other African countries need to be revisited to ascertain the competitiveness of Nigeria's export within the framework of the agreement. The next section examines some of the core trade logistics and infrastructure indicators that could enhance or undermine Nigeria's export potentials.

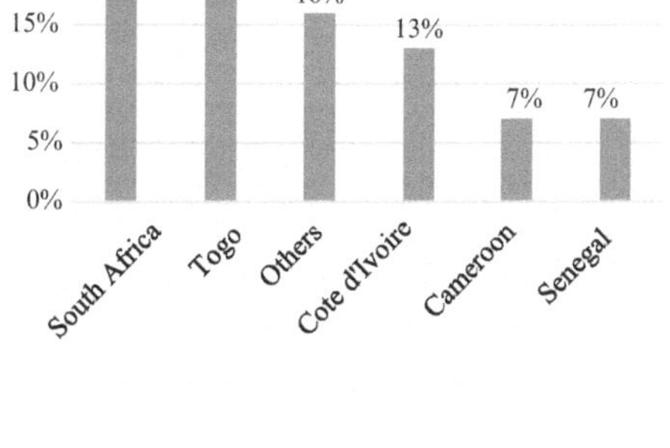

Fig. 6.4 African destination of Nigeria's exports (*Source* Trade Law Centre [2018])

6.3 Trade Infrastructure and Competitiveness of Nigeria's Export

The Nigerian economy is less competitive than a number of other economies in the continent as shown in Fig. 6.5. This to some extent suggests that goods produced in these countries may be cheaper in the international market relative to those produced in Nigeria. In addition, the competitiveness of the economy has significantly declined in the past few years, with the score declining from 3.70 in 2012/2013 to 3.30 in 2017/2018 (Fig. 6.6). The low competitiveness of the economy is due to several factors including unconducive macroeconomic environment, poor infrastructure, weak institutions and other governance issues (Schwab 2017). The components of the global competitiveness index, except market size, good market and labour market efficiency, are poor and declining. These include infrastructure (2.0/7.0), institutions (3.2/7.0), macroeconomic environment (3.5/7.0), technological readiness (3.0/7.0) and innovation (2.8/7.0).

Infrastructure plays a prominent role in enhancing the competitiveness of the economy. All things being equal, the cost of doing business

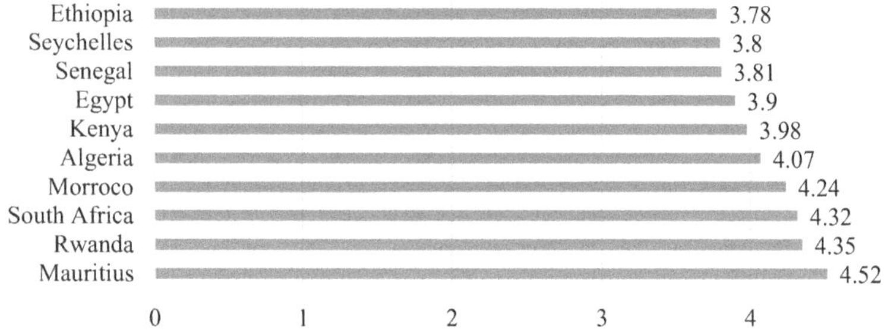

Fig. 6.5 Global Competitive Index score for selected African countries (*Source* Schwab [2017]; Scores ranges from 1 to 7)

Fig. 6.6 Trend of Global Competitiveness Index for Nigeria (*Source* Schwab [2017]; Scores range from 1 to 7)

would be lower with better infrastructure, and hence would enhance the competitiveness of locally made goods in the international and regional markets.

Effective modes of transport enable entrepreneurs to get their goods and services to market in a secure and timely manner, facilitate the movement of labour and encourage foreign direct investment. Economies also depend on electricity supplies that are free from interruptions and shortages so businesses and factories can work unimpeded (AfDB 2013). In addition, a solid and extensive telecommunication network allows for a rapid and free flow of information, which increases overall economic efficiency by ensuring that businesses can communicate and make timely decisions, taking into account all available relevant information.

Productivity growth and competitiveness are higher in countries with an adequate supply of infrastructure. Analysis by the AfDB (2013) shows that there is a positive relationship between infrastructure investment and economic growth—solid infrastructure accelerates annual growth convergence rates by as much as 13% and also increases per capita annual growth by almost 1%. But the quality of Nigeria's infrastructure is poor (Fig. 6.7) and insufficient to induce significant cost reduction required to promote competitiveness.

Thus, the low quality of infrastructure in Nigeria vis-à-vis other countries in the region (as shown in Fig. 6.8) places Nigerian exports at a

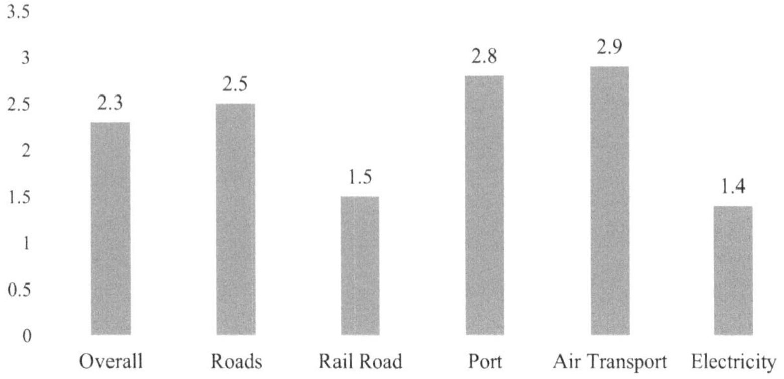

Fig. 6.7 Quality of different infrastructure types in Nigeria (*Source* Schwab [2017]; Scores range from 1 to 7)

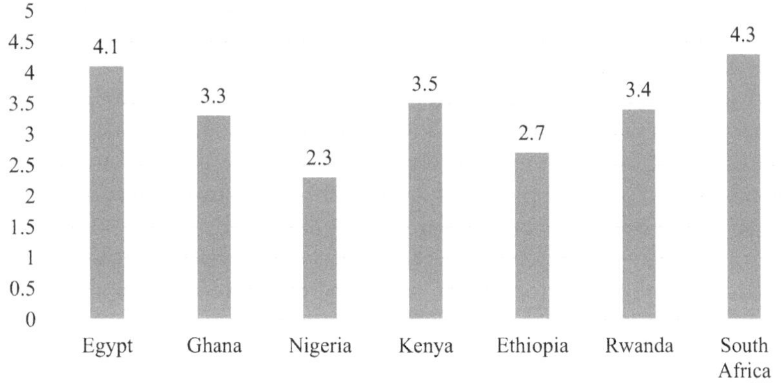

Fig. 6.8 Comparison of Infrastructure Quality in selected African countries (*Source* Schwab [2017]; Scores range from 1 to 7)

competitive disadvantage. Moreover, the time delay and cost of transporting goods from other parts of Nigeria to the Apapa Ports Complex is enormous partly due to poor road infrastructure and traffic gridlock in the Apapa Port area (LCCI 2019; Okon 2019).

In addition to infrastructure challenges, trade logistics, which encompasses logistics quality and competence, tracking and tracing and timeliness, also poses threats to the competitiveness of Nigerian exports in the proposed free trade area. According to Anabel Gonzalez, Senior Director for the World Bank Group's Trade and Competitiveness Global Practice (World Bank 2016), "logistics performance both in international trade and domestically is central to countries' economic growth and competitiveness. Efficient logistics connects people and firms to markets and opportunities, and helps achieve higher levels of productivity and welfare".

Nigeria performed poorly in every area of trade logistics. A recent data from the World Bank's Logistics Performance Index (LPI) (World Bank 2018) shows that Nigeria ranks 103 among 167 countries, with an average logistics performance index score of 2.59 out of 5.0. The score for logistics quality and competence (2.54), tracking and tracing (2.73) and timeliness (3.10) are low. Nigeria's low logistics performance vis-à-vis other African countries would undermine export competitiveness and ultimately the capability of Nigerian exports to easily penetrate other markets. The logistics performance index of Nigeria (2.59) is lower compared to Ghana (2.60), Benin (2.65), Rwanda (2.90) and Kenya (2.93). In terms of timeliness for example, importing and exporting in Nigeria requires at least consultation with six different agencies compared to Benin and other African countries which require an average of three agencies.

In terms of customs and border efficiency and administration, Nigeria's performance is also low, implying inefficiency at borders and increased difficulties in importing and exporting goods. According to the LPI, the performance of Nigerian customs services and procedures is rated at 2.15 out of 5.0. The poor performance of the custom services and procedures is also confirmed by the Global Enabling Trade Index (WEF 2016). According to the index, Nigeria scored 3.32 (out of 7.00) in 2016 in efficiency and transparency of border administration compared to 3.35 in 2014. This shows a worrisome decline in the efficiency of the border system. The performance of the border system is poor if compared with other African countries such as Kenya (4.44), Ghana (4.18), The Gambia (4.11), Ethiopia (4.00) and Senegal (3.89).

The performances of Nigeria in the subcomponents of the border administration are shown in Table 6.1, and poor relative to some other African countries. For example, the total time to comply with export documentation and border procedures totalled 266 hours and cost US$1036

Table 6.1 Efficiency and transparency of border administration

Indicators	*Score*	*Rank*
Customs services index 0–1 (best)	0.49	85
Efficiency of the clearance process 1–5 (best)	2.5	88
Time to import: Documentary compliance hours	172.7	124
Time to import: Border compliance hours	283.7	132
Cost to import: Documentary compliance US$	564.3	128
Cost to import: Border compliance US$	1076.8	127
Time to export: Documentary compliance hours	131.4	123
Time to export: Border compliance hours	135.4	130
Cost to export: Documentary compliance US$	250.0	120
Cost to export: Border compliance US$	785.7	125

Source WEF Enabling Trade Index (WEF 2016)

compared to 139 hours and US$293 for Rwanda and 168 hours and US$598 for South Africa. This places additional time and financial costs on Nigerian exporters, especially exporters of time-sensitive or perishable items.

A recent report by MoverDB (2019) notes that it costs more to ship goods to Nigeria from New York (USA) than any other destinations globally, regardless of the distance. The report finds that shipping a 20-foot container from New York (USA) to Apapa Port (Lagos) costs US$4982 compared to US$2542 for Cape Town (South Africa), US$2797 for Sydney (Australia) and US$3086 for Jeddah (Saudi Arabia). The report attributes the gap in costs to entrenched inefficiency—slow pace of inspection and offloading of ships, congestions and bottleneck—at the local destination ports.

The Global Enabling Trade Index, relying on a survey conducted for businesses and exporters in Nigeria, summarises the problematic factors for exporting in Nigeria in the order of importance as follows: Access to trade finance, inappropriate production technology and skills, difficulties in meeting quality/quantity requirements of buyers, access to imported inputs at competitive prices, high costs or delays caused by domestic transportation, identifying potential markets and buyers, technical requirements and standards abroad, burdensome procedures at foreign borders and corruptions at foreign borders. Others include high costs or delays caused by international transportation, tariff barriers abroad and rules of origin requirements abroad. This should serve as a basis for policy makers to design measures to enhance the competitiveness of Nigerian exports.

6.4 Conclusion and Recommendations

Following the signing of the AfCFTA, there is a need for the Nigerian government to improve on the various factors that would enhance the competitiveness of Nigerian exports in the African market. Issues such as infrastructure, trade logistics and custom administration need to be looked into in order to reduce the time and cost of producing and exporting Nigerian-made goods. There is need to boost financial investment in critical transport, electricity and port infrastructure through public-private partnerships.

As it is, the Lagos port complex has reached its economically viable carrying capacity in terms of facilities and transportation linkages. Any further investment to shore up the Lagos Port complex would amount to sunk cost as it is most unlikely to be cost-effective because of the spatial binding constraint and deeply entrenched inefficiencies which have a significant add-on impact on the non-competitiveness of Nigerian exports. Thus, measures to boost the competitiveness of Nigerian exports in the medium-long term must include leveraging private domestic and foreign investment to rapidly develop other coastal and inland ports to decongest the Lagos Port complex.

A major weakness in Nigeria's trade policy management arsenal is the absence of a trade remedy infrastructure. This has hampered the country's ability to manage and adjust its trade policy to emerging dynamics in the light of its experience in implementing bilateral and multilateral trade agreements. Happily, work is being done to strengthen capacity in this area with the establishment of the Nigerian Office for Trade Negotiations (NOTN).

Nigeria needs to mainstream trade facilitation into its overall trade agenda. The country should prioritise the implementation of the World Trade Organization (WTO) Trade Facilitation Agreement (TFA) to identify areas in which it could apply for technical and financial supports from WTO and UNCTAD to build capacity to relax constraints militating against its export competitiveness. The government should also improve on port reforms to enhance efficiency in port operations and custom administration. In this respect, emphasis should be placed on streamlining the exporting processes and procedures and eliminating the activities of middlemen and irrelevant government agencies. Other factors such as availability of trade financing, skills development and better production technologies and compliance with quality and quantity requirements should also be at the forefront of considerations. Overall, the government should aim at creating stable macroeconomic environment. These will benefit Nigeria's external trade performance and competitiveness within and outside the AfCFTA.

Economies that are open to trade and investment and provide appropriate, pro-development safeguards will prosper, flourish and develop. Nigeria cannot be an exception and is poised to benefit from the AfCFTA if appropriate measures are taken to improve trade infrastructure and logistics that reduce the costs of doing business and exporting.

References

African Development Bank (2013). Improved infrastructure to support Africa. https://www.afdb.org/en/blogs/afdb-championing-inclusive-growth-across-africa/post/improved-infrastructure-to-support-africas-competitiveness-11755/.

LCCI (2019). Maritime ports: Reform in Nigeria—Feedback from the OPS. Lagos Chamber of Commerce and Industry, Lagos, Nigeria.

MoverDB (2019). 2019 Overseas cargo & freight costs from the United States. https://moverdb.com/freight-costs-usa/.

Okon, A. (2019, July 1). NPA sets up committee on Apapa gridlock. *The Punch Newspaper*. https://punchng.com/npa-sets-up-committee-on-apapa-gridlock/.

Robinson, S., and Thierfelder, K. (1999). Trade liberalisation and regional integration: The search for large numbers. TMD Discussion Paper No. 34, Trade and Macroeconomics Division, International Food Policy Research Institute, Washington, DC.

Saygili, M., Peters, R., and Knebel, C. (2018). African Continental Free Trade Area: Challenges and opportunities of tariff reductions. UNCTAD Research Paper No. 15, United Nations Conference on Trade and Development, Geneva, Switzerland.

Schwab, K. (2017). The Global Competitiveness Report, 2017–2018. Insight Report, World Economic Forum, Cologny, Switzerland.

Shafaeddin, S. M. (2005). Trade liberalisation and economic reform in developing countries or de-industrialisation? UNCTAD Discussion Papers No. 179, United Nations Conference on Trade and Development, Geneva, Switzerland.
Trade Law Center (2018, September). Nigeria: Intra-Africa trade and tariff profile. Trade Data Update, Issue No. 20, Trade Law Center, Western Cape, South Africa.
UNECA (2018, May 18). Continental Free Trade Area deal set to boost intra-African trade, says Ambassador Quartey. Communication Section, United Nations Economic Commission for Africa, Addis Ababa, Ethiopia.
WEF (2016). The Global Enabling Trade Report 2016. World Economic Forum, Cologny, Switzerland.
World Bank (2016). Germany tops 2016 logistics performance index. The World Bank Group. http://www.worldbank.org/en/news/press-release/2016/06/28/germany-tops-2016-logistics-performance-index.
World Bank (2018). Connecting to compete 2018: Trade logistics in the global economy—The Logistics Performance Index and its Indicators, The World Bank, Washington, DC.
World Bank (2019). World Integrated Trade Solution. https://wits.worldbank.org/CountryProfile/en/Country/NGA/Year/LTST/Summary.

CHAPTER 7

Sequencing and Negotiating Nigeria's Regional and International Trade Agreements in the Digital Age: Issues and Policy Prescriptions

Jonathan Adeyemi Aremu

7.1 Introduction

Since Adam Smith (1776) published ***The Wealth of Nations***, the vast majority of economists have accepted the proposition that free trade among nations improves overall economic welfare. Free trade, defined as the absence of tariffs, quotas or other governmental impediments, encourages each country to specialize in the production of goods it has a comparative advantage (i.e. where it can produce cheaply and efficiently relative to other countries). Such specialization enables all countries to achieve higher real incomes. There are ample evidences to justify that no country has achieved economic success in terms of substantial increases

J. A. Aremu (✉)
Professor of International Economic Relations, Covenant University (CU), Ota, Nigeria
e-mail: jonathan.aremu@covenantuniversity.edu.ng

G. Odularu (ed.), *Strategic Policy Options for Bracing Nigeria for the Future of Trade*,
https://doi.org/10.1007/978-3-030-34552-5_7

in living standards for its people, without being open to the rest of the world via trade (Vijayasri, 2013).

The possible interrelationship of trade and development policy sets a challenge for the task of policymaking and negotiating prioritization for countries like Nigeria. This is because, trade can lead to growth which can in turn lead to development and poverty reduction in the economy. However, the relationship from trade to structural change and increased income, and thus to growth and then from growth to poverty reduction does not occur automatically. The main intervening variable controlling the relationships between increased income or structural change and growth and between growth and poverty is effective and appropriate government policy (including, but not limited to, policy on trade).

In spite of the current globalization (which is the opening of people and nation states to a more interconnected and interdependent world with relatively free movement of capital, goods and services across the globe), there are still a proliferation of bilateral and regional trading arrangements simultaneously accompanying the multilateral trading system under the World Trade Organization (WTO). The multiplicity of such trade and investment agreements have resulted in (a) continuous reduction of tariff and non-tariff barriers, (b)fewer restrictions on inward foreign direct investments (FDI) and (c) the narrowing of regulatory differences on trade and investments across Member States engaged in the various pacts beyond the WTO provisions.

While most economists support free trade, they differ on how best to make an economy transit from tariff and quota regimes to free trade regime (Coughlin, 2002). Under these circumstances, they have recognized three basic approaches to trade reform as: unilateral, multilateral and bilateral or regional.

a. **Unilateral tariff reductions** are made independently and without reciprocal action by other countries. The advantage of unilateral free trade is that a country can reap the benefits of free trade immediately. Countries that lower trade barriers by themselves do not have to postpone reform nor do they try to persuade other nations to follow suit.
b. **Multilateral, regional or bilateral** approaches—dismantling trade barriers in concert with other countries—have two advantages over unilateral approaches. **Firstly**, the economic gains from international trade are reinforced and enhanced when many countries or

> regions agree to a mutual reduction in trade barriers. **Secondly**, regional or multilateral reductions in trade barriers may reduce political opposition to free trade in each of the countries involved (that is because groups that otherwise would oppose or be indifferent to trade reform might join the campaign for free trade if they see opportunities for exporting to the other countries in the trade agreement). Free trade agreements between countries or regions are a useful "***steppingstone***" for liberalizing multilateral trading systems.

Perhaps, the best possible outcome of trade negotiations is a multilateral agreement that includes all major trading countries. Such approach would widen the coverage of participants so as to achieve the greatest possible gains from international trade. That was why immediately after World War II, the General Agreement on Tariffs and Trade (GATT), became the world's most important multilateral trade negotiation arrangement. GATT was set up in reaction to the waves of protectionism that crippled world trade during—and helped extend—the Great Depression of the 1930s. However, in 1995, the GATT became part of the WTO, charged with overseeing four international trade agreements: (a) the GATT, (b) the General Agreement on Trade in Services (GATS), (c) agreements on Trade-Related Intellectual Property Rights (TRIPS) and (d) Trade-Related Investment Measures (TRIMS).

Although the WTO embodies the principle of non-discrimination in international trade, Article XXIV of the GATT permits the formation of free-trade areas (FTAs) and customs unions (CU) among WTO members (Kanal Saggi, 2005). An FTA occurs when a group of countries eliminate all tariffs on trade with one another but retain autonomy in determining their tariffs with non-members; while a customs union is formed when a group of countries not only eliminate all tariffs on trade among themselves but also go further to maintain a common external tariff (CET) on trade with countries outside the union. While it is true that such regional arrangements promote greater trade among the contracting parties, critics quickly point out that regional approaches to trade liberalization may undermine the efficiency of multilateral approach under the WTO. Nigeria's economic development depends among others, on how the country can make use of opportunities presented by trade liberalization at national, regional and multilateral levels. Such opportunities include: enhanced domestic productivity, efficiency, improved quality and low prices of goods and services that will ultimately lead to improved consumer welfare and higher export revenue.

With the globalization of the world economy and the multiplication of international agreements that are ever-expanding in scope and depth, the question of appropriate sequencing Nigeria into the various trade negotiations is becoming a serious challenge. The effective participation of the country in these trade negotiations and agreements would not only depend on: (a) the long-term development of the domestic capacity to identify trade and development objectives, (b) formulate policy positions, (c) establish appropriate negotiation strategies; as well as (d) appropriately sequencing the order of negotiating these increasing number of agreements in line with the objectives of the **National Trade Policy and the National Economic Recovery Growth Plan** (NERGP) of Nigeria.

This lecture is examining how Nigeria can sequence her trade negotiation towards the growth of the economy. This lecture is divided into six parts. Part I briefly examines the historical antecedences leading to the current global trading arrangements. Part II looks into the various issues faced by developing countries (DCs) and least developing countries (LDCs), particularly Nigeria, while Part III examines the various global architecture to address these issues. With an aid of practical approach, Part IV attempts to look into how Nigeria can formulate national trade policy to answer to the demands of the current multiplicity of trade negotiations at regional, continental and multilateral levels. With a national trade policy, the lecture looks into how an appropriate sequencing of Nigeria's trade negotiation should be pursued to make the country ready to be integrated into the globalized trading environment in Part V. Part VI concludes the lecture with recommendations.

7.2 Historical Antecedences Leading to the Current Global Trading Arrangements

Since Adam Smith emerged with the benefits of the division of labour and David Ricardo built on it through the theory of comparative advantage of international trade among nations, the modern world has become increasingly more economically integrated. Consequently, the volume and value of international trade have expanded, and trade agreements have equally increased in complexity across the globe. Initially, the doctrine of **mercantilism** dominated the trade policies of the major European powers for most of the sixteenth century through to the end of the eighteenth century. Under mercantilist doctrine, the main objective of engaging in international trade was to obtain a **"favourable" balance of trade**, by which the value of a country's exports should exceed the value of her imports vis a vis others. The mercantilist approach to international trade discouraged trade agreements between nations as each government assisted its own domestic industry through the use of tariffs and quotas on imports, as well as the prohibition of exporting tools, capital equipment, skilled labour or anything that might help foreign nations compete with such domestic production of manufactured goods.

7.2.1 Development of Multilateral Trading System

According to Morrison (2017) **mercantilist trade policy** occurred with the establishment of the British Navigation Act of 1651. Under the Act, foreign ships were not allowed to take part in coastal trade in England, and all imports from continental Europe were required to be carried by either British ships or ships that were registered in the country where the goods were produced. However, with the writings of both Adam Smith and David Ricardo, in which both argued for the desirability of imports that can only be acquired through exports, a re-thinking emerged towards a freer trade. The foundational theories of international trade of both economists gained increasing momentum and helped to spread a trend towards more liberalized trade. Unfortunately, the trend towards a more liberalized multilateral trading system slowed down by the late nineteenth century when the world economy fell into a severe depression in 1873. The depression which lasted until 1877, served to increase pressure for greater domestic protection. One good thing was that most of the protectionist measures were mild compared to the earlier mercantilist period thus international trade flows continued to grow.

Unfortunately again, the rise of nationalist ideologies and dismal economic conditions following the World War I served to disrupt world trade and thus dismantled the trading networks that had characterized the previous century. The new wave of protectionist trade barriers moved the newly formed League of Nations to organize the First World Economic Conference in 1927 that targeted how to have a better multilateral trade agreement. Despite this, the economic insecurity and persistence of nationalism of the period created the conditions for the outbreak of World War II. Immediately, the United States (US) and Britain emerged from

World War II as the two great economic superpowers, both of them felt the need for a more cooperative and open international trading system. They initiated the establishment of International Monetary Fund (IMF), World Bank and International Trade Organization (ITO) as an outcome of the 1944 Bretton Woods Agreement. While the IMF and World Bank were established and they played the pivotal roles assigned to them under the new international framework, the ITO failed to materialize (it was blocked by USA), and its plan to oversee the development of a non-preferential multilateral trading order was later taken up by the GATT Article in the ITO in 1947.

Since the foundation of GATT in 1947, negotiations have become an important part of the international trading system, though the interest of developing countries were not factored in from the beginning. These negotiations have become more complex, and expanded to encompass previously excluded areas like agriculture, **investment**, services, intellectual property issues and regulatory standards (see Table 7.1). GATT remained in effect until the signature by 123 nations in Marrakesh, Morocco was achieved on 14 April 1994; thus, concluding the Uruguay Round Agreements that established the WTO on 1 January 1995. The WTO therefore not only became the successor of GATT but also the original GATT text (GATT 1947) still remained under the WTO framework.

With the ushering in of a new era of multilateral trade negotiations, many developing countries, including Nigeria, enlisted not only in the WTO but have also been participating in the various Ministerial Conferences (Table 7.2) of the organization for the following reasons:

i. **Beggar-thy-neighbour reasons**—this occurs when a country knows that its domestic policies can be nullified if they do not belong;
ii. Nigeria believes that a good government should implement economic policy that is time consistent to be relevant to emerging world affairs, and being a member of WTO satisfy this desire;
iii. Membership of WTO provides a way of mitigating the undesirable trade and investment actions coming from other countries;
iv. To allow Nigerian products to have secured and improved international market access in spite of her limited power within the global space;

Table 7.1 GATT trade rounds 1947–1994

Name	*Start*	*Duration*	*Countries*	*Subjects covered*	*Achievements*
Geneva	April 1947	7 months	23	Tariffs	Signing of GATT, 45,000 tariffs concessions
Annecy	April 1949	5 months	34	Tariffs	Countries exchanged some 5000 tariffs concessions
Torquay	September 1950	8 months	34	Tariffs	Countries exchanged some 8700 tariffs concessions,
Geneva	January 1956	5 months	22	Tariffs, admission of Japan	$2.5 billion in tariff reductions
Dillon	September 1960	11 months	45	Tariffs	Tariff concessions worth $4.9 billion of world trade
Kennedy	May 1964	37 months	48	Tariffs, anti-dumping	Tariff concessions worth $40 billion of world trade
Tokyo	September 1973	74 months	102	Tariffs, non-tariff measures, "framework" agreements	Tariff reductions worth more than $300 billion achieved
Uruguay	September 1986	87 months	123	Tariffs, non-tariff measures, rules, services, intellectual property, dispute settlement, textiles, agriculture, creation of WTO, etc.	The round led to the creation of WTO, and extended the range of trade negotiations, leading to major reductions in tariffs (about 40%) and agricultural subsidies, an agreement to allow full access for **textiles** and clothing from developing countries, and an extension of intellectual property rights

Source World Trade Organization

Table 7.2 World Trade Organization ministerial conferences since inception

S/No of M/C	*Date*	*Host city*
1	9–13 December 1996	Singapore
2	18–20 May 1998	Geneva, Switzerland
3	30 November–3 December 1999	Seattle, United States
4	9–14 November 2001	Doha, Qatar
5	10–14 September 2003	Cancun, Mexico
6	13–18 December 2005	Hong Kong
7	30 November–2 December 2009	Geneva, Switzerland
8	15–17 December 2011	Geneva, Switzerland
9	3–6 December 2013	Bali, Indonesia
10	15–18 December 2015	Nairobi, Kenya
11	11–14 December 2017	Buenos Aires, Argentina

Source World Trade Organization

v. WTO permits a nation to operate predictable, secure and transparent trade and commercial policy;

vi. Membership of WTO signals to the world that a nation operates **best practices** in trade policy;

vii. It allows weaker countries, like Nigeria, to be shielded from unfair treatment under most favoured nation (MFN) and national treatment (NT) principles of WTO;

viii. Membership of WTO allows a nation to participate in the shaping global trade rules;

ix. The Dispute Settlement Body (DSB) of the WTO provides an acceptable way of resolving trade disputes which has always littered human history;

x. The fact of a single set of rules within the WTO apply to all countries simplifies the entire global trading system;

xi. By lowering tariff and non-tariff barriers, WTO allows the cost of production across the world to be reduced and therefore beneficial to Nigerian economy as well;
xii. The basic principles of WTO make the system economically efficient to operate than individual national trading principles and
xiii. Membership of WTO provides a good basis for government to defend its trade policy domestically.

7.3 Emergence of Multilateral Regionalism

Though the GATT was established to lower tariffs among Member States, thereby providing a foundation for the expansion of multilateral trade, the period that followed it saw the prediction of Bhagwati (1993), just before the WTO, becoming self-fulfilled as there were increasing waves of more regional trade agreements (RTAs). In less than five years after the GATT was established, Europe began a programme of regional economic integration through the creation of the European Coal and Steel Community in 1951, which eventually evolved into what we know today as the European Union (EU). Europe's regionalism not only helped to push the GATT agenda forward but other countries were also encouraged to put in place similar economic integration arrangements for further tariff reductions among their own groupings as well so as to compete with the preferential trade that European partnership engendered (Bergsten, 2002).

Arashiro, Marin and Chacoff (2005) questioned the rationale for the current rush towards RTAs under multilateral environment, in which some pair or group of countries announce their intention to enter into one form of regional arrangement or another all the time. In spite of the presence of WTO, virtually all countries of the world are members of one form of economic integration or another; and many belong to more than one. Current world trade situation is to a large degree characterized by trade policy initiatives that are simultaneously being pursued at the global, regional and bilateral levels with a number of governments adopting a trade policy that moves on multiple fronts of negotiations. This is best known as **competitive liberalization**, in which global, regional and bilateral trade negotiations are seen as complementing one another towards multilateralism. Over a third of the world trade takes place within

RTAs varying widely in their depth of phases and principles, but all having the objective of reducing barriers to trade between member countries but discrimination against non-member countries.

Initially, most of these agreements were targeted merely at removing tariffs on intra-bloc trade in goods in line with Jacob Viner (1950) basis for economic integration, but as time goes on many of them go beyond that Viner's model to cover non-tariff barriers (NTBs) and in fact to extend liberalization to investment and to other sociopolitical and economic policies (Krishna, 1998). At their deepest phase many of the economic integrations have the goal of an **economic union** involving the construction of shared executive, judicial and legislative institutions.

Consequently, regionalism did not necessarily grow at the expense of multilateralism, but in conjunction with it. In addition, the push for regionalism was equally due to a growing need for countries to go beyond the GATT of WTO's provisions, and at a much quicker pace. After the breakup of the Soviet Union, the EU extended its economic integration to include Central and Eastern European nations; and in the mid-1990s, it established some bilateral trade agreements with Middle Eastern countries. The United States also pursued its own trade negotiations, forming an agreement with Israel in 1985, as well as the trilateral North American Free Trade Agreement (NAFTA) with Mexico and Canada in the early 1990s. Many other significant regional agreements also took off in South America, Africa and Asia. While the WTO seeks to extend the multilateral trade initiatives of the GATT, recent numerous economic integrations are ushering in a stage of what Ethier (1998) called "**multilateralizing regionalism**". This has made the history of international trade and integration to look like a struggle between protectionism and free trade, in which both them are growing side by side (Table 7.3).

While regional agreement between countries of homogeneous economic development level is understandable, those among North–South appear confusing. As a second-best option, RTAs provide an alternative route to ensuring greater market access in key economies of the world. In addition, RTAs are also attractive since they offer a possibility of incorporating commitments on participating members that are far in excess of those found or being negotiated under the WTO Agreements. Despite their global popularity, the following emerging questions, among numerous others, confront increasing expansion of RTAs:

Table 7.3 The phases of economic integration

	Free trade between member state	*Common external tariff*	*Free movement of factors of production*	*Harmonization of economic policy*	*Centralization of economic & monetary policy*
Free-trade area	Yes	No	No	No	No
Customs union	Yes	Yes	No	No	No
Common market	Yes	Yes	Yes	Yes	No
Economic union	Yes	Yes	Yes	Yes	Yes

Source Author's analysis

i. Are there distinct characteristics to (a) North-North, (b) North–South and (c) South-South RTA?
ii. What does the trend to regionalism mean for the multilateral trading system of the WTO?
iii. If increasing emergence of RTAs implies a weakening of the WTO, what are the developmental implications for the various economic integrations among developing countries including Nigeria and between developed and developing countries?
iv. Beyond issues of trade creation and trade diversion as outcomes for such increasing number of economic integrations, what are the implications of the rules-based elements of the current RTAs particularly with respect to: investment, intellectual property rights, competition policy, trade facilitation, etc., in their protocols, particularly on developing countries such as we have under the African Continental Free Trade Area-AfCFTA?
v. Are countries using RTAs as they were used in the past, to strategically negotiate their positions better at the multilateral level; if so, can Nigeria engage RTAs for the same purpose?
vi. Since provisions in an RTA clause are stricter than the WTO rules, especially in North–South RTAs, to what extent are the North–South RTAs developmentally oriented, particularly when one considers the economic negotiations between the European Union

(EU) and the African, Caribbean Pacific (ACP) under the economic partnership agreement (EPA)?

In spite of these unresolved issues confronting the continuous emergence of RTAs, (a) many countries are increasingly making RTAs a central objective of their trade policy which may take priority over multilateral trade objectives; (b) RTAs are becoming more complex, in many cases establishing regulatory regimes that go beyond multilaterally agreed trade regulations; (c) the emergence of trade agreements among developing and least developed countries, like the Economic Community of West African States (ECOWAS) may be evidence of strengthened "South-South" cooperation; (d) RTAs are generally expanding and consolidating, on one hand, there are a growing number of cross-regional RTAs which account for a large proportion of the total increase in RTAs, while on the other hand, regional trading blocks that span continents are becoming common phenomenon; and (e) lastly, there are regional blocks with overlapping jurisdictions.

7.4 Regionalism in World Trade Organization Agreement

Perhaps, the WTO already envisaged regionalizing of multilateralism as Article XXIV of the GATT plus the Understanding on Interpretation of the Article (Understanding RTAs) of WTO sets forth the basic principles for RTAs. The provisions of the GATT in the WTO apply to **customs** territories, which are any territory with respect to which separate tariffs or **other regulations of commerce** are maintained for a substantial part of the trade of such territory with other territories. Thus, for the purpose of the WTO, customs territories could be sovereign states or non-sovereign entities such as the European Union (EU), ECOWAS with the implementation of common external tariff (CET). As can be understood from the language of Article XXIV (5) and (8), GATT deals with RTAs as exceptions but only with FTAs and Customs union and not with common market (a higher level of economic integration). Let us examine FTAs and Customs Union of WTO further.

7.4.1 Free-Trade Areas

Article XXIV (8) (b) defines FTAs to mean:

> a group of two or more customs territories in which the duties and other restrictive regulations of commerce (except, where necessary, those permitted under Article XI, Xii, XIII, XIV, XV and XX) are eliminated on substantially all the trade between the constituent territories in products originating in such territories.

Hence, an FTA brings together two or more customs territories to form a group that eliminates duties and ORRCs on SAT among the constituent territories. To this extent, FTAs are similar to customs unions; but they do not require liberalization for products that do not originate from the constituent territories like customs union. In addition, FTAs do not require a CET as in customs union. Furthermore, and legally, FTA does not entail the substitution of a single customs territory for two or more customs territories in the sense of customs union.

7.4.2 Customs Union

Article XXIV (8) (a), in the same fashion, defines customs union to mean:

> the substitution of a single customs territory for two or more customs territories, so that duties and other restrictive regulations of commerce (except, where necessary, those permitted under Articles XI, XII, XIII, XIV, XV and XX) are eliminated with respect to substantially all the trade between the constituent territories of the union or at least with respect to substantially all the trade with respect to substantially all the trade in products originating in such territories.

Accordingly, a customs union substitutes two or more customs territories with one customs territory and eliminates duties and other restrictive regulations of commerce (ORRCs) on substantially all the trade (SAT) between the constituent territories either: Irrespective of origin of products, i.e. whether products originate from the member territories or not, or Only for products originating from such territories. In addition to paragraph 8 (a) (ii) requires each member of a customs union to apply substantially the same duties and other regulations of commerce (CET) to the trade of third parties to the customs union.

7.4.3 Interim Agreement in an FTA

Article XXIV of the GATT does not expressly define an interim agreement for the formation of an FTA and customs union. However, subparagraphs 5 (a) and (b) put it as a transitional agreement leading to the formation of an FTA or a customs union. Paragraph (c) requires interim agreements to include a plan and schedule for the formation of a customs union on free-trade areas within a reasonable length of time. Evidently, the formation of such RTAs on interim entails significant trade policy coordination among the parties as well as extensive changes to domestic regulations affecting trade. In addition, such interim agreements provide members of an RTA with a breathing space to prepare properly because of the understanding that it is impossible to form an RTA overnight.

7.4.4 Internal and External Requirements of an RTA

The definitional provisions of an RTA (whether FTA or customs union) presented above are based on some internal and external requirements. **Internal requirements** in the case of customs union are provided in Article XXIV: 8 (a) (i). while for an FTA, the internal requirements are conditioned on Article XXIV: 8 (b). **External requirements**, however, refer to the obligation of an RTA not to raise barriers to the trade of other WTO members which are not members of the RTA (Article XXIV: 4–5). For customs union, the requirements of "substantially the same duties and other regulations of commerce" in respect of third parties as well is regarded as an external trade requirement.

7.4.5 Role of Transnational Corporations in the Multilateral and Regionalism of Trade

From the traditional economic theory, international trade was conducted through arm's-length trade by trading firms located in different countries, which did not involve foreign direct investment (FDI). In reality, trade has been increasingly conducted by transnational corporations (TNCs) in the form of intra-firm trade at the global level. The WTO (1996) estimates that intra-firm trade conducted by TNCs at the global level accounts for about one-third of annual world trade, and exports by TNCs to non-affiliates account for another third of world trade. Intra-firm trade has become an important international business mode for TNCs to distribute or allocate intermediate goods, materials and/or final goods around the world for production and/or distribution purposes.

As global production and corporate structures of TNCs have evolved over the years, their investments have become a sophisticated set of financial transactions that are hard to monitor both by the home and host countries. The increasing fragmentation of production and the creation of global value chains (GVCs) result in TNCs governing such chains to break up their businesses in smaller parts. In so doing, they take advantage of the most favourable production locations for each production part of their final product as well as disposing of certain parts deemed non-core and focus on others. As a result, TNCs and their affiliates (that is: their branches, subsidiaries and associates) often have multiple passports across multiple jurisdictions.

According to Aremu (2005), the legal structures surrounding the intra-firm relationships, including trade within the various affiliates of TNCs could be very tedious. For instance, it is often doubtful that if enterprise **A** has a partial ownership of subsidiary **B**, which itself has a subsidiary **C** whose existence depends on **B**, not **A**, that **C** should not be included as part of **A**'s FDI. While company **A** could be said to have complete control over its subsidiaries, it may be for this reason that it decided to invest in **C** through **B**. It is common to see a TNC build some intra-enterprise transactions in the area of transferring of products, capital resources, personnel and in fact technology among its affiliates via an established sophisticated numerous links and trade.

In a typical TNC—system where the economic ambition is merely upstream integration (i.e. vertical backward integration), the parent firm is likely to constitute an important market for the products from its affiliates while in the case of a TNC—system that is pursuing a complex integration, the flow of goods and services can be seen to be multidirectional (i.e. from the parent firm to affiliates and from affiliates to the parent company or among the affiliates).

The integrated production network systems of the TNCs have been facilitated by the current wave of trade liberalization with a consequent reduction in trade barriers between countries that are members of WTO, leading to specialization by different parts of a TNC production system. This development is practically more noticeable among European Union countries where components, sub-assemblies and semi-finished products particularly in the automobile industry have built closely knit supply chains across several countries. No doubt, the growing role of international production in the world economy is enlarging the geographical spread of TNCs. Apart from **trade mis-pricing** between their affiliates to strip off the capital of an affiliate located in a high tax jurisdiction to a low tax jurisdiction, TNCs move capital abroad and conceal it through the seemingly **process of international trade**, with the help of secrecy jurisdictions, and accountants and lawyers. Trade mis-pricing is most effectively exploited by the TNCs because: (a) a TNCs operate through affiliates scattered across the globe, which enable them to exploit **transfer pricing** and (b) having multiple affiliates that can front for the TNCs provide opportunity for their unlimited number of registration in multiple tax havens and secrecy jurisdictions in order to conceal their operations in trading activities. The activities of TNCs within the global setting have made trade negotiation extremely complex, particularly for DCs and the LDCs.

For Nigeria, effectively managing the interface between both regional and multilateral trade initiatives requires greater synergy between national development objectives and external commitments. Central to this challenge facing the country is how to design and implement an appropriate and **strategic pacing and sequencing** of national, regional and multilateral trade liberalization, so as to maximize development gains from all of them. It should be noted that simultaneous participation in a web of RTAs while at the same time engaging in the evolving multilateral trading system (MTS) of the WTO could lead to overlapping agendas that could affect sensitive development policies of the country as well as overload the limited negotiating capacity of the national economy.

7.5 Various Trade Negotiations Facing Nigeria

Today, Nigeria is faced with many trade cooperation arrangements that have assumed increasing importance as the building block for the creation of larger markets and increasing trade flows, (inflow and outflows) into and from the country. The essence of these trading arrangements includes: (a) providing the required solidarity in forging bargaining power under the current globalization of economic activities; (b) creation of larger more viable markets through merging of relatively weak and fragmented markets of DCs and LDCs; (c) preservation of regional markets from unnecessary incursions from the global market place and (d) locking-in of national trade liberalization of the country into international best practices at regional and multilateral levels. Such regional and international agreements are expected to stimulate productivity and competitiveness of Nigerian economy through economies of scale and lower transaction costs. Most important among the trade agreements Nigeria is currently faced with are: ECOWAS-Common Trade Policy; EPA with EU; AEC with AU Members—AfCFTA; and Multilateral Negotiations at WTO. While the goal of Nigeria's participation in these arrangements is for the maximization of advantages of inherent opportunities in them, the sequence of engaging in them is yet to be agreed upon, neither does the country have a current trade policy that could address the sequence of negotiating them.

7.5.1 ECOWAS Economic Integration Agreement

ECOWAS was established in Lagos, on 28 May 1975 to integrate economic activities of Member States as a borderless region where the entire population has access to its abundant resources and is able to exploit same through the creation of opportunities under a sustainable environment. A revised version of the Treaty was agreed to on 24 July 1993 in Cotonou. Considered as one of the pillar regional blocs of the continent-wide African Economic Community (AEC), the goal of ECOWAS is to achieve "collective self-sufficiency" for its Member States by creating a single large trading bloc through the building of a full economic union.

The community has achieved some level of success with respect to ECOWAS Trade liberalization Scheme (ETLS) i.e. the regional FTA; The customs union phase was established with common external tariff (CET) with 5-bands since 2015, and it is on its way to becoming a Common Market by allowing the Interregional flow of factors of production in the emerging ECOWAS Single Market Economy. Currently, substantial harmonization of policies on trade, investment, finance and agriculture, is ongoing in preparation for the emerging common market by 2020. There is no Common Trade Policy (CTP) yet, as Nigerian Government declined from its take-off a year ago (2018) due to inadequate consultation in the country. Nigeria is a party to so many regional agreements, As the largest economy and market in the African sub-region, it is important for the country to position itself for mutually beneficial trade within and beyond the ECOWAS community.

7.5.2 EU/ECOWAS Economic Partnership Agreement

ECOWAS has been negotiating an EPA with the European Union (EU) since 2004. As presented by the EU, the EPA intends to foster the gradual integration of the ACP countries into the global economy on the basis of an open, transparent and predictable framework for trade and investment. Towards the end December 2007 (deadline for conclusion of EPA) when it appeared that the negotiations cannot be concluded as scheduled, EU sent individual national draft to Ghana and Côte d'Ivoire (the 2 non-LDCs) to initiate an interim EPA each; a decision against the objectives of CPA. Côte d'Ivoire and Ghana signed an interim agreement each with EU on the 7 and 13 December respectively.

The objective of the regional EPA negotiators was to conclude negotiations before October 2014, to ensure the continuity of the trade preferences to Côte d'Ivoire and Ghana, to guarantee a single trade regime for the region with the EU and thus safeguard regional integration achievements. At the conclusion of the negotiation of the EPA agreement in 2014, Nigeria declined signing the EPA with the EU, though it is an intra-regional process, establishing a CET in West Africa as a prerequisite to the signature of the EPA between the EU and ECOWAS. The Nigerian position has had a strong impact on the implementation of the EPA in the region. In fact, the EPA talks have led to the application of several different tariff regimes in the region that are much less advantageous for Nigeria. For instance, non-reciprocal market access applied to "everything but arms" (EBA) for the thirteen LDCs in the West. For not signing EPA, Nigerian government is concerned about the following questions:

i. How to manage the expected loses of fiscal revenue when Nigeria finally ratify the EPAs the way it is now;
ii. Will Nigeria's trade liberalization with a more economically powerful and homogeneous EU not be in the larger interest of the EU alone;
iii. How to curb deflection of EU products from entering Nigerian market through the LDCs and the non-LDCs that acceded to either EBA or interim EPA respectively even if Nigeria does not accede to EPA;
iv. How to cope with more competition against Nigerian products in ECOWAS intra-Community trade (ETLS), particularly as Morocco comes;

v. How to deal with limited negotiation capability of Nigeria to negotiate on the matter, since ECOWAS negotiation appears not acceptable to Nigeria and
vi. Can Nigeria not look for separate EPA with EU?

7.5.3 *African Economic Community Treaty*

Among the objectives of Organization of African Union (OAU) Charter was to address Africa's peculiar situation of underdevelopment. In 1980 the OAU Extraordinary Summit adopted the **Lagos Plan of Action**, as a major step towards that goal. The commitments in the Lagos Plan of Action translated into Abuja Treaty, in June 1991 when the OAU Heads of State and Government established the **African Economic Community** (AEC). The AEC Treaty has been in operation since May 1994 when the required number of instruments of ratification for its coming into force were deposited with the Secretary General of the OAU/AEC. According to UNECA (2017), when AEC entered in force in 1994, a roadmap of six phases economic integration was agreed upon as follows: Stage I Creation of regional blocs (that is, the Regional Economic Communities or RECs); Stage II Strengthening of intra-regional integration and the harmonization between the blocs; Stage III Establishment of free-trade areas and customs unions in each the RECs; Stage IV Creation of a continental free-trade area and customs union; Stage V Creation of an African common market; Stage VI Establishment of an African economic monetary union and a parliament. Among the objectives of AfCFTA are to:

a. create a single continental market for goods and services, with free movement of business persons and investments, and thus pave the way for accelerating the establishment of the Customs Union;
b. expand intra-African trade through better harmonization and coordination of trade liberalization and facilitation and instruments across the RECs and across Africa in general and
c. enhance competitiveness at the industry and enterprise level through exploitation of opportunities for scale production, continental market access and better reallocation of resources.

Nigeria is a signatory to the Treaty establishing the AEC, during the 18th Ordinary Session of Assembly of the African Union (Addis Ababa,

Ethiopia, 23–30 January 2012), the summit adopted a "Decision on boosting intra-African trade and fast tracking the Continental Free Trade Area". Negotiations were subsequently launched by the Assembly in June 2015 and effective negotiations started in July 2016 after a preparatory phase. The AfCFTA Agreement and its Protocols were negotiated by all the membership of the African Union. The signing of **Stage 1** comprising the following protocols of the AfCFTA took place during the 10th Extraordinary Summit of the Assembly of the AU on 21 March 2018 in Kigali

- the Agreement Establishing the AfCFTA,
- the Protocol on Trade in Goods,
- the Protocol on Trade in Services and
- the Protocol on Rules and Procedures for the Settlement of Disputes

Paradoxically, Nigeria, which was instrumental in garnering support to finalize the AfCFTA in the build-up to March 2018, did not sign until 7 July 2019; after the commencement of the implementation of the continental initiative on the 30 May 2019, when the minimum ratification threshold had been reached. As at middle of September, the country is yet to submit her accession ratification.

7.5.4 World Trade Organization Agreement

Nigeria has been participating well in all the Ministerial Conferences of WTO, since it was created in 1995. However, the country has never had a decisive role in the WTO system and this may be much more damaging now than ever before, because of these reasons: (a) the WTO is increasingly spreading its coverage to new areas and thus reducing national sovereignty of Member States; (b) the impact of the WTO agreements (as compared to the GATT) and their operation is much wider and deeper for Nigeria's economy to fully comprehend; (c) thirdly and perhaps the most important, Nigeria's economy is much more vulnerable to external shocks due to her weakness. Consequently, Nigeria as well as the other DCs and LDCs have raised issues of inadequacies and inequities in the WTO agreements, including the timeframes in which they have to implement the agreements into national laws.

Along with other developing countries, Nigeria, has questioned certain aspects relating to the implementation of agreements in the WTO Agreement. The challenges confronting Nigeria in its bid to comply with the WTO agreements are multi-dimensional and cover policy, legal and economic terrains. In the area of policymaking, for example, the challenges range from bad government policies to lack of political will. In addition, it is becoming difficult for the DCs and LDCs to negotiate effectively with the mechanisms of "***green room meetings***", which are being used to reduce the number of countries actively participating in many important deliberations of the WTO. "***The WTO is an organization in which all decisions are taken by consensus; where every member government, holds the equivalent of a UN Security Council veto. But there is also no denying that some members are more equal than others when it comes to influence***" (WTO/ D.G, 2016).

From this statement, discussions and negotiations at the WTO do not take place on a level playing field in terms of both power and negotiating capacity among WTO Members. The decision-making is theoretically on the basis of equality, with each Member being entitled to one vote (in the event of decision-making by voting) or with the effective right to veto (in the case of consensus decision-making), However, both power and capacity imbalances may essentially negate this fundamental legal equality to participate in decision-making provided for in WTO law. From the outcome of the 11th World Trade Organization (WTO) Ministerial Conference (MC 11), it is clear that the credibility of various International Trade Theories about the benefits of free trade is put in doubt, while the negotiating function of the WTO to guarantee efficient and effective trading among its Member States is gradually being questioned. We are now facing the inability of both the Trade Theories and the multilateral trade arrangements, under the WTO, to adapt and adjust to emerging global trade priorities as expected.

According to Grassley and Wyden (2019), the negotiating process at the WTO has largely broken down. Under the old GATT system, from 1947 to 1994, there were eight negotiating rounds—each of which led to lower tariffs and fewer trade barriers among all GATT members. To this day, the basic rules that govern global trade were negotiated under the GATT. But in the 24 years since the WTO began operation, there has been no new significant multilateral market access agreement. Much work of WTO remains to be done in terms of lowering tariffs—primarily in countries that consider themselves developing. Numerous WTO members continue to have very high "bound" tariff rates that allow them to maintain tariffs significantly above the bound rates that apply to the United States. For example, the average bound tariff rate for all goods in the United States is 3.4%. In Brazil, it is 31.4%. In India, it is 48.5%. In Indonesia, it is 37.1%. Too many WTO members are not living up to current obligations.

The ultimate questions facing Nigeria as well as other LDCs and DCs under these webs of negotiations coming at the same time are numerous (Odell, 2003); among them are: **firstly**, what determines the outcome of a trade negotiation involving these group of nations? **Secondly**, how can they gain more or lose less in future from these negotiations? **Thirdly**, what should shape the negotiation process to make them beneficial to these groups of nations? **Fourthly**, how can we use international rules (designed by developed countries) of WTO to shape better strategies or responses to these nations plight? **Fifthly**, could change in the domestic institutions of Nigeria as well as in these groups of countries permit them to use a wider range of external strategies to achieve better deals in both regional and multilateral trade negotiations?

7.6 Resolving Issues Confronting LDCs and DCs in Global Trade

As expected, the position of Nigeria, as well as other DCs and LDCs under the existing global trade arrangements can be summed up as less favourable than those of their developed economies (DEs) counterparts. The competitiveness of the Nigerian economy and that of the other DCs and LDCs in the global markets is very low compared to that of the DEs since DCs and LDCs tend to export products with less value added, less technologically advanced, lower quality and definitely lower price. During the second half of twentieth century, when GATT was established, only a few DCs participated in the trade rounds while majority of them are unable to use the significant liberalization in global trade regime to their own advantage.

When Nigeria, along with other DCs and LDCs engaged in trade cooperation with other countries, through trade agreements, they always believed that the trade concessions they granted should be reciprocated with trade concessions that they will receive. Despite their expectations, in the last century, it became apparent that they have not been able to compete with DEs with equal level of exchange of trade concessions. For this reason, there emerged many unilateral and international initiatives to grant asymmetrical trade concessions to these DCs and LDCs with most of these favourable concessions designated for LDCs.

7.6.1 General System of Preferences

The first of such programmes was developed by United Nations Conference on Trade and Development (UNCTAD), known as ***Generalised System of Preferences*** (GSP). The GSP is a generalized, non-reciprocal and nondiscriminatory preference scheme beneficial to developing countries (also known as preference receiving countries or beneficiary countries) extended by developed countries (also known as preference giving countries or donor countries). It involves reduced MFN Tariffs or duty-free entry of eligible products exported by beneficiary countries to the markets of donor countries. The main objectives of granting trade preferences to developing countries are to: (a) enhance their export earnings; (b) promote industrialization ;and (c) encourage the diversification of their economies. The idea of GSP was proposed at the first meeting of the UNCTAD with a view to assisting the developing countries in their exports and development efforts. In 1971, the GATT enacted two waivers to the MFN that permitted tariff preferences to be granted to developing country goods.

Most of the GSP product coverage include agricultural and industrial exports with a few but often notable exceptions. The exceptions established by the US GSP include textiles and apparel, certain footwear, certain leather products (handbags, luggage), certain watches and watch parts, canned tuna, petroleum and petroleum products. From the perspective of developing countries as a group, GSP programmes have been a mixed success. On one hand, most rich countries have complied with the obligation to generalize their programmes by offering benefits to a large swath of beneficiaries, generally including nearly every non-OECD member state. Criticism has been raised noting that most GSP programmes are not completely generalized with respect to products, and this is by design. That is, they do not cover products of greatest export interest to low-income developing countries lacking natural resources.

While this appeared to be a welcome idea as it was adopted by multilateral initiative, however, its application is a unilateral option by each DE. That is, each DE decides on its own whether it is willing to extend

GSP trade concessions to the DCs and LDCs and in what extent the trade concession will be given. Also, each DE has the prerogative of making its own list of countries to benefit from such GSP initiative; that is, it is an exception in the Most Favoured Nation (MFN) principle in international trade. According to Pomfret (1986) sometimes DEs have used the GSP preferences as a tool of political pressure on LDCs and DCs beneficiaries. Under Lome Conventions (I–IV), the European Union (EU) have a non-reciprocal specific trade regime for African, Caribbean and Pacific (ACP) countries that were once colonies of European metropolis, granting them significant trade benefits in the framework of the four Conventions and later Cotonou Partnership Agreement (CPA). For a specific group of LDCs the EU put in place a programme of trade concessions known as "Everything but Arms" (EBA) meaning that these LDCs can export their products tariff and quota free to EU market, except arms. Also, United States also put in place Africa Growth Opportunity Act (AGOA) giving the countries from Africa special and preferential access to US market.

But the problem of Nigeria as well as other DCs and LDCs is that they cannot fully use the granted trade concessions of the GSP since they do not have what to export to DEs markets. In addition, trade liberalization under international bilateral and multilateral trade agreements refers only to domestic products (i.e. products that have been mostly produced by domestic inputs of a country). In order to benefit from such trade concessions, the exporters from beneficiary countries that have been granted these concessions have to prove domestic origin of products with Certificates of Rules of origin (ROO). Usually domestic content of product inputs required for a product to be recognized domestic origin is 50%. Such condition has been very hard for many LDCs and DCs with limited natural resources to produce. In fact, in many situations, the level of technological development is also a limiting factor to produce products that can be sold on DEs markets. This is why International Trade Centre (ITC), the joint organ of WTO and UNCTAD, is a focal organ established to assists DCs and LDCs to build better export products so that these countries can fully benefit from the various regional and global trade liberalization.

7.6.2 *Doha Development Agenda*

The Doha Development Agenda (DDA) which was adopted during the IV WTO Ministerial Conference, held in Doha in 2001, was among the initiatives to solving some problems facing LDCs and DCs in multilateral trading environment. After the establishment of the WTO, LDCs and DCs discovered that to be integrated appropriately in the multilateral liberalization process, there must be further adjustment to the global trading system. These countries see DDA as the main way for them to find their place in modern international trade and to increase their part in the volume and value of the international trade, working that way for its overall development. While DDA negotiations were very optimistic and dynamic in all areas, however, 2005 and 2006 were years of crisis in the negotiating process and by 2008 the Great Global economic crisis came, which negatively affected negotiating process. And all these had negative implications on the expected outcome from Doha negotiations. Accordingly, both Bjornskov and Kim (2002) raised an alarm of where the developing countries could go, should DDA failed. As it appears, DDA has not totally died but under **intensive care**.

7.6.3 South-South and North–South Economic Integrations

Das (2002) suggested that one of the ways to strengthen developing countries position is through South-South economic integration or cooperation. The importance of this idea was further stressed with the Accra Accord (UNCTAD, 2008) which was adopted during the XII UNCTAD‘s Conference. To this end, the ***Economic Cooperation and Integration among Developing Countries (ECIDC)***, a specialized unit, for coordinating activities oriented towards developing relations between LDCs and DCs, was established by UNCTAD's Secretary General in July 2009. The inability to answer to the demands of the DDA equally provoked the loss of confidence in the multilateral trading system of the WTO, thus leading to increase in the number of RTAs mostly in the form of the FTA. Today, RTAs are no longer along geographical contiguity of contracting parties nor among countries of homogeneous economic development levels. Today, RTAs are wider and deeper integration in contents beyond the multilateral trading system of the WTO; and they consist of trade liberalization for the goods and services; investment, competition and intellectual properties protocols in addition to regulatory harmonization as a part of the broader scope of behind the border measures.

Two different directions of such RTAs are recognized, namely: (a) the **North–South RTAs** and (b) the **South-South RTAs**. The major differences in these two directions are in the reasons for engagement in such agreements. With the transformation of ECOWAS Secretariat to a Commission in 2007, Nigeria and Member countries are becoming oriented towards increasing among themselves under an **intra-regional trade** through many protocols. However, the share of such intra-trade is still not as high as it could be. With the recent desire under the African Continental Free Trade Area (AfCFTA) initiative, another similar term became important in international trade, known as **inter-trade**, or inter-regional trade, meaning the existence and the increasing role of trade between regional economic communities (RECs) within Africa in line with the African Economic Community (AEC) Treaty of 1991. In addition to this is the development of trading initiatives between the RECs of Africa and different RTAs (e.g. EU) under the economic partnership agreement (EPA). Under such North–South economic integration (that is EPA), however, Zartman and Zartman (1987) maintained that such arrangement might be likened to "David ***and Goliath***" relationship if the capacity of negotiation of DCs are not improved.

Along the intra-regional and interregional economic integration is also the rising role of transnational corporations (TNCs) from DCs, or South countries investing their capital in other South countries (for instance, South African companies investing in Nigeria like Shoprite and DSTV). The South countries are not waiting only for TNCs investments from DEs, thus the need for common investment protocols within a REC (e.g. ECOWAS Common Investment Code and Policy) and among the RECs (e.g. Pan African Investment Code of AU).

7.6.4 World Trade Organization's Trade Facilitation Agreement

Recall that during the XII Session of UNCTAD which was held in Accra, Ghana in April 2008, among those issues that were deliberated upon as constraints to sustainable expansion of South-South economic integration were (a) inadequate transport infrastructure and (b) lack of trade facilitation measures. (UNCTAD, 2008). The Session would be remembered as a UNCTAD's that pointed out the complex field of **Trade Facilitation** as a new battle-field for DCs conquering the competitiveness and a better position in the international trade engagement. It is discovered that only some of DCs from South-East Asian economies and China had good opportunities to attract FDI and to produce and export manufactured goods to DEs.

The main reason why the other DCs, including Nigeria are not able to take the leading role is due to lack of effective trade and transport facilitation structure; that is, ***hard and soft infrastructure***, which mainly consists of developed transport infrastructure and logistics services. Hitherto, about thirty years ago, most DCs and LDCs exported mostly raw materials and semi-finished goods, but at the beginning of the new century, this structure has been changed as there is a greater demand for just-in-time deliveries of these products which has provoked the increase of the share of air transportation together with the increase of transportation costs demanding that the DCs and LDCs need more effective and efficient transport and trade capacity as well to be integrated into the modern trading system.

While the increasing South-South economic integration is important in economic sense, also of importance is the improvement of these countries political position for strengthening their trade negotiating position, especially with DEs and in the multilateral trading system of the WTO. To this end, WTO has joined its efforts to facilitate trade for its members by, providing a multilateral platform for negotiations and launching a multilateral initiative for building trade capacity in these countries. After nearly two decades, the Agreement on Trade Facilitation was adopted at the WTO's 9th Ministerial Conference in Bali, Indonesia, in December 2013. However, the Trade Facilitation Committee was created on 22 February 2017, the ratification of 2/3 of WTO Members ratified the TFA. Given the current integrated and global nature of the supply chain, the WTO' Trade Facilitation has some characteristics and benefits in addition to the following:

i. provide a framework for addressing crosscutting trade issues;
ii. garner support and cooperation of the international trading community and border agencies (in terms of resources and expertise);
iii. provide an impetus for capacity building;
iv. increase predictability for business and governments and
v. help locks in domestic reforms.

Both LDCs and DCs are included in the process of the Trade Facilitation negotiations involving "***a group of different policies with the main aim to reduce trade transaction costs***" via two main groupings: (a) *Hard infrastructure*— related to Physical infrastructure and Information and

Communication Technologies (ICT) and (b) *Soft infrastructure*—related to soft infrastructure consists of Border and transport efficiency and the Business and regulatory environment (Wilson and Portugal-Perez, 2010).

The development of quality maritime ports, airports, roads and rail infrastructure, increased use of *Information and Communication Technologies* (ICT), as a part of hard infrastructure would enable the improvement of efficiency and reduction of transaction costs. *Border and transport efficiency, as soft infrastructure* consists of efficiency of customs and other border agencies, single window port operation system as well as the transport quality, not quantified with the quality of roads and ports, but with time, costs and number of documents which are necessary for export and import procedures. One important contribution to increase the level of Border and transport efficiency is **multimodal transport**, which will enhance the realization of *just-in-time* deliveries and *door-to-door* concept of trade. Yet another component of soft infrastructure is *Business and regulatory environment*, which is very important to show the presence of irregular payments, corruption or favouritism. All these elements of the hard and soft infrastructure have an important impact on freight costs as a percentage of import values in many countries.

Nigeria's instrument of acceptance of WTO/TFA was submitted to the Director-General, WTO, Roberto Azevêdo in Davos on 16 January 2017. The Trade Facilitation Agreement entered into force on 22 February 2017 when the WTO obtained acceptance of the Agreement from two-thirds of its 164 Members. Nigeria was 107th Member to ratify. Since 10 of November 2014, Nigeria submitted its Category A notification to the WTO outlining the substantive provisions of the TFA it intends to implement upon entry into force of the Agreement. Nigeria's ratification of the Trade Facilitation Agreement is a reflection of the economy's commitment to the WTO and a rules-based economy as well as evidence of the country's commitment to rapidly implement the creation of an enabling environment for business.

7.6.5 *Aid for Trade Initiative*

Trade liberalization is a key ingredient for economic success and for improved living standards. For developing countries, the reductions of trade barriers have enabled them to integrate into global markets and to share in the prosperity generated by the multilateral trading system. However, simply opening an economy to international trade is not enough, these nations require additional assistance to help them build trade-related capacity in information, policies, procedures, institutions and infrastructure. That is why at the beginning of twenty-first century, particularly since the Doha Negotiation and the 3rd Ministerial Conference at Cancun, WTO realized the need to assist LDCs and the DCs on trade capacity issues.

At the WTO's (2005) Hong Kong Ministerial Conference, Member countries agreed to increase aid to support developing countries in expanding their trade and benefit from improved market access, the Aid for Trade Initiative was launched as an integral part of regular official development assistance to help developing countries overcome the supply-side and trade-related infrastructure constraints that inhibit their ability to benefit from market access opportunities. When trade liberalization is accompanied by regulatory reform and supported by aid for trade, it will help attract domestic and foreign investment, thereby stimulating economic growth and poverty alleviation. Though it is not a development agency, like the World Bank Group, it was stress at the launching:

> Aid for Trade should aim to help DCs and particularly LDCs, to build the supply-side capacity and trade-related infrastructure that they need to assist them to implement and benefit from WTO Agreements and more broadly to expand their trade. (WTO, 2005)

It is important to note that Aid for Trade cannot be a substitute for the development benefits that will result from a successful conclusion to the DDA, but it can be a valuable complement to it (WTO, 2006). EU (EC, 2009) defines it as the "development assistance provided in support of partner countries' efforts to develop the basic economic infrastructure and tools they need to expand their trade". It is an initiative to assist DCs and LDCs to increase export of goods and services, to integrate into the multilateral trading system and to benefit from liberalized trade and increased market access. The funds are not completely new, rather they are a part of Official Development Assistance (ODA), which are now channelled for trade needs of LDCs and DCs under the following components:

i. **Technical trade-related assistance**—assistance to develop trade strategies, negotiation trade agreements, etc.;
ii. **Trade-related infrastructure**—assistance in building infrastructure to connect to global economy;

iii. **Productive capacity building**—trade development assistance to industries to build on their competitive advantages;
iv. **Trade-related adjustment assistance**—assistance to DCs and LDCs with costs of tariff reductions, etc.; and
v. **Other trade-related needs**—assistance with areas defined in development strategies of DCs.

7.7 Formulating Nigeria's Trade Policy

When appropriately harnessed, developments in the international environment provide, to a large extent a unique opportunity for the achievement of national macroeconomic policy objectives. Such opportunities, among others, include: (a) benefits arising from globalization and liberalization; (b) trade expansion and rapid economic growth and (c) technological innovation summed up in the digital revolution that is transforming the means and reducing the costs of human interaction as well as declines in the cost of production. In spite of these, if internal weaknesses in a domestic economy are not well addressed so that such opportunities can make positive contributions, the benefits from openness to international environment would become a ***dreamlike contemplation***. Therefore, the process of national economic transformation via an open market system poses new challenges on the need to have national domestic policy that will be sensitive to the demands of emerging international settings. Economists believe that countries that are open to international trade tend to grow faster, innovate, improve productivity and provide higher income and more opportunities for their people.

Trade is not an end in itself but a means for achieving higher welfare to society, than would be possible without trade. The function of the trade sector, therefore, is to integrate a country into the global economy through trade, through structural transformation of the national economy and product/market diversification. This is why trade theory recognizes that effective integration of any country into the global economy through trade and global value chains would involve an appropriate **Trade Policy** that defines standards, goals, rules and regulations that pertain to trade relations of a country with the rest of the world. Nigeria's trade policy has evolved and been shaped by changes in its socio-economic regime and political philosophy since independence to transform the economy from a supply constrained one into a competitive export-led economy that is responsive to integrating the productive sector into the global economy through appropriate trade liberalization sequence.

With globalization, international business environment has been subjected to radical shifts in relationships resulting from technological changes and emphasis on good political and corporate governance; with consequent effects on global economic interactions, particularly trade and investment. Today, economies are opening up to trade and previous small national markets are merging into larger entities through various shapes of economic integration schemes. Competition is intensifying as transnational corporations (TNCs) as well as even smaller firms are becoming more innovative. In addition, rapid developments in Information and Communication Technology (ICT) have led multiplicity of communication media with wide and instantaneous outreaches at relatively low cost. The ultimate result of these developments is the increasing awareness of customer expectations, at the touch of a button, that are forcing the business world to strive for higher quality, lower prices, quick and better services.

7.7.1 Importance of a Trade Policy for Nigeria

The last trade policy for Nigeria was that of 2001/2002. An attempt was made to develop one in 2001 but could not be concluded. Nigeria urgently requires a good trade policy that will go beyond the traditional focus on tariffs and quantitative restrictions and changes in relative prices but (a) captures the deeper transformational and production issues in the economy, (b) emphasizes the role of the government as implementer of trade policy and that of the private sector as the engine of growth as well as partners in the formulation and implementation process, (c) sets new and modern rules on how to increase competitiveness of the economy at national, regional and multilateral levels, (d) establishes how these trade rules are developed, coordinated and implemented, (e) elevates the role of the private sector from its dormant level to that of a partner in the formulation and implementation processes, (f) creates opportunities for the development of the private sector to perform its assigned role, and (g) promotes a new philosophy of economic management based on serious commitment to openness as dictated by the emerging realities at regional, continental and multilateral trading environment.

Nigeria's trade policy is expected to address the critical issues facing the country as highlighted in the National Economic Recovery Growth Plan (NERGP) particularly at:

i. highlighting the central role and contribution of Nigeria's trade policy towards the attainment of the objectives of the NERGP Vision;
ii. harmonizing and consolidating consensus of opinions from relevant stakeholders on trade development issues that will entrench sustainable policy shift from the current protected and controlled market economy towards a competitive market economy at regional, continental and multilateral levels;
iii. identifying appropriate measures for the development of the domestic production at the various sectors as well as marketing strategies as a tool of inclusion and broad-based participation in economic activity based on improved market-infrastructure, technology diffusion and access to market information;
iv. aligning national trade policy development agenda with those of regional, continental and international trade obligations of the Nigerian economy, in addition to maximizing the benefits of participation in such regional and international trade arrangements;
v. adopting an appropriate framework of measures for the interim safeguarding of domestic industry and economic activity threatened by liberalization including identification of sectors to be protected, the rationale and costs of protection and the maximum duration for protection;
vi. developing the strategy of how best to address the national supply-side constraints that inhibit expansion of trade within the domestic and global market as the route towards rapid economic development;
vii. stimulating and encouraging value-adding activities on primary exports as a means of increasing national earnings and income flows even on the basis of existing output levels. Stimulating of investment flows into export-oriented areas in which Nigeria has comparative advantages as a strategy for inducing the introduction of technology and innovation into production systems as the basis for economic competitiveness and

viii. attaining and sustaining long-term current account balance and balance of payments through effective utilization of complementarities in regional and international trading arrangements as a means of increasing exports combined with initiatives for higher efficiency in the utilization of imports.

7.7.2 *Strategies in Nigeria's Trade Policy Formulation*

Given the importance of trade to Nigeria's economic well-being, the emerging questions are: How should Nigerian government get itself organized? What objectives need to be set, what institutional arrangements are desirable, what are the relevant timeframes for different negotiations and how often should reviews be built in to ensure continuing coherence in the light of evolving events in each of the fora? What is the regional dimension to Nigeria's trade strategy? Are current regional arrangements at ECOWAS level supportive of our national strategy? How might the regional trade arrangements be realigned or changed to suit Nigeria's need? What are the domestic and external obstacles that need to be overcome—and what is a realistic approach and timetable for achieving this? Having outlined the above prerequisites to guide the Nigeria's Trade Policy formulation, the next agenda is to appropriately synchronize them within the NERGP. At both the national and international levels, the mechanics of trade policymaking are fairly straightforward. What is less clear is how national and international policies should be designed in a mutually supportive way that does not overly restrict national policy space yet respect regional and international trade obligations. This is usually through **negotiation** of trade agreements at regional and multilateral levels. In economic negotiations, like trade, countries tend to take **mercantilist approach** (*seeking "gains" for their exporters and minimizing "losses" for their domestic suppliers*). However, before developing national negotiation objectives, there is need to understand the areas and limit to negotiate, and these areas can be grouped into four (two of them primarily domestic and two primarily international).

i. **Wholly domestic**: Some policies fall wholly within a government's competence, such as those on domestic markets that determine how far any change in import or export prices are passed on to consumers and producers

ii. **Largely domestic**: Other policies are largely a domestic preserve but **within parameters set externally**; this would be the case, for example, with domestic arrangements that are influenced by WTO rules such as on allowable domestic subsidies, or changes to tariff rates agreed with aid donors as part of policy-based lending.
iii. **Externally negotiated**: These are policies that are negotiated externally between the developing country governments and other countries or actors—with the European Union (EU), for example on EPAs, or with other countries as part of the WTO negotiations.
iv. **Externally non-negotiated**: These are policy changes in which a developing country government, like Nigeria's, is not a negotiating party and hence, has no direct control such as preferences. For instance, the EU's changes to its agricultural policy and autonomous changes to private sector practice; (if Nigeria is able to influence them at all, it would only be through persuasion).

Clearly, of high priority must be to ensure that the policies set domestically are the right ones as Nigeria will have the greatest degree of control, within the bounds of her existing international commitments. For this reason, priorities must be established in which high impact domestic policies have the highest priority followed by high impact changes in the external areas. In addition, while attempting to influence the external areas, the federal government must be ready to adjust to the consequent resulting outcomes, through possible changes as some domestic policy may also require governments to initiate dialogue in yet other areas as well. The next question is: Which are the high impact domestic and external policies? In getting this done, therefore, OECD (2001) brought out some key elements of how to arrive at an effective trade policy formulation process for developing countries to include the following:

i. a coherent trade strategy that is closely integrated with a country's overall development strategy;
ii. effective mechanisms for consultation among three key sets of stakeholders: government, the enterprise sector and civil society;
iii. effective mechanisms for intra-governmental policy coordination;
iv. a strategy for the enhanced collection, dissemination and analysis of trade-related information;

v. trade policy networks, supported by indigenous research institutions;
vi. networks of trade support institutions and
vii. a commitment by all key trade stakeholders to outward-oriented regional strategies.

Based on the OECD guidelines, the process of the trade policy formulation in Nigeria could therefore be as follows: Putting in place an executive trade policy organogram comprising all the relevant Ministries, Departments and Agencies of the Federal Government (Fig. 7.1); Designing domestic trade and external trade policies and strategies from the NERGP (Fig. 7.2); Establishing a trade policy dialogue and consultation process (Fig. 7.3) and Developing trade negotiation strategy and capacity for Nigeria (Fig. 7.4).

7.8 Sequencing and Negotiating the Various Trade Agreements Facing Nigeria

Nigeria's ability to effectively participate in both the various regional and the multilateral trading processes is largely constrained by the technicalities and the volume of negotiations she faces. While benefits in terms of trade expansion through enhanced access to the world market are apparent, the nation has not been able to benefit from these opportunities as the appropriate sequence in these negotiations has not been followed. As at now, Nigeria has the NERGP, but the trade objectives and strategies within the NERGP are yet to be thoroughly identified, neither is the trade policy dialogue and consultation process at arriving at a ***New Trade Policy*** is put in place. Without such a policy and effective trade negotiation sequence how best can Nigeria defend her trade interests in negotiating at ECOWAS, the AfCFTA, EPA and at WTO levels?

Effective policymaking on trade faces two problems: (a) tracking the complex effects of changes to trade policy and (b) participating in multiple negotiations most often at the same time. This makes it difficult to ensure that what is proposed and agreed in the multiplicity of negotiations is mutually consistent and, even more importantly, is line with a country's (say Nigeria) broader NERGP development strategy. This becomes even more difficult as negotiations move into highly technical areas such as:

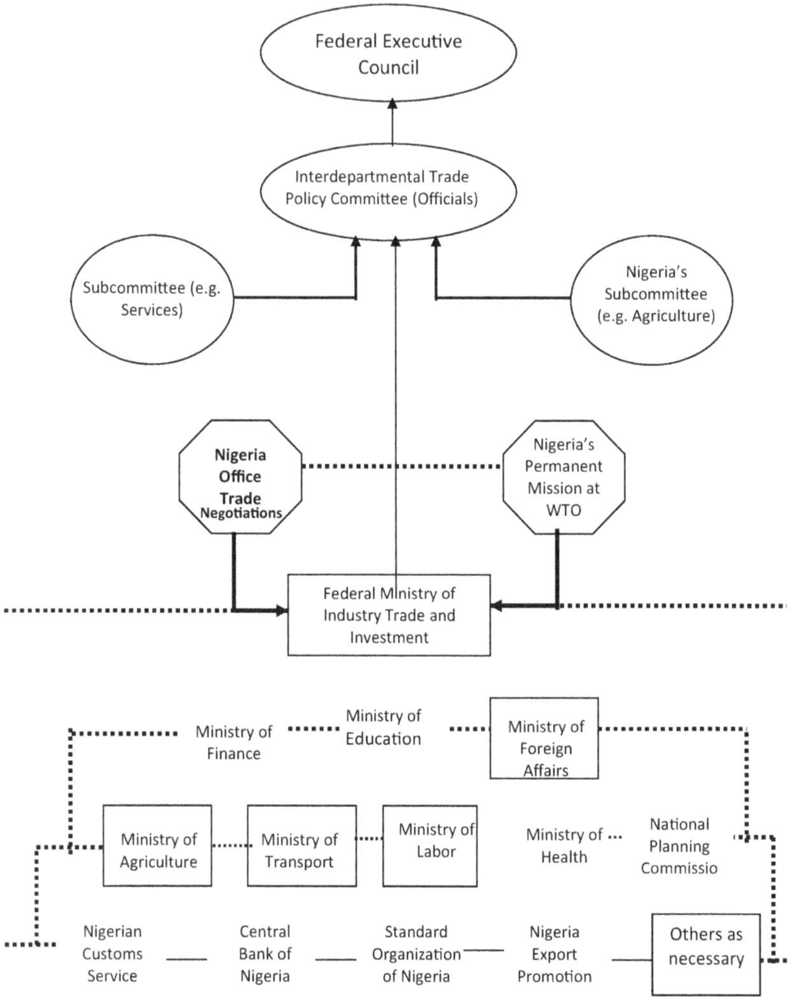

Fig. 7.1 Executive trade policy formulation organogram (*Source* Author's design)

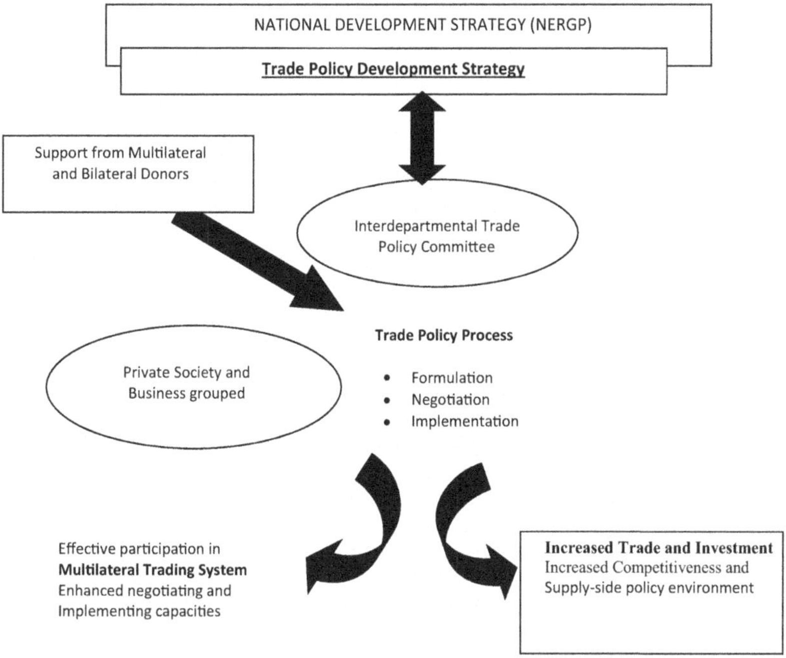

Fig. 7.2 Trade policy development strategy (*Source* Author's design)

intellectual properties, competition, investment, as well as plant and animal health. Further challenges exist in making sure that such a strategy has been formulated in conjunction with all the relevant public and private sector institutions and stakeholders. If the relationship between trade and development is weak, countries may wish to allocate a minimum amount of their scarce resources to negotiating and designing trade policy. However, if the relationship is strong, trade policy and its negotiations could be an important tool towards creating national development strategies.

7.8.1 *Sequencing the Trade Negotiation of Nigeria*

Trade Negotiation remains one of the most complex, challenging and, sometimes, controversial issues in contemporary trade policy. This is more serious for Nigeria which has no current trade policy. Despite this, the country is negotiating the following agreements: (a) ECOWAS Common

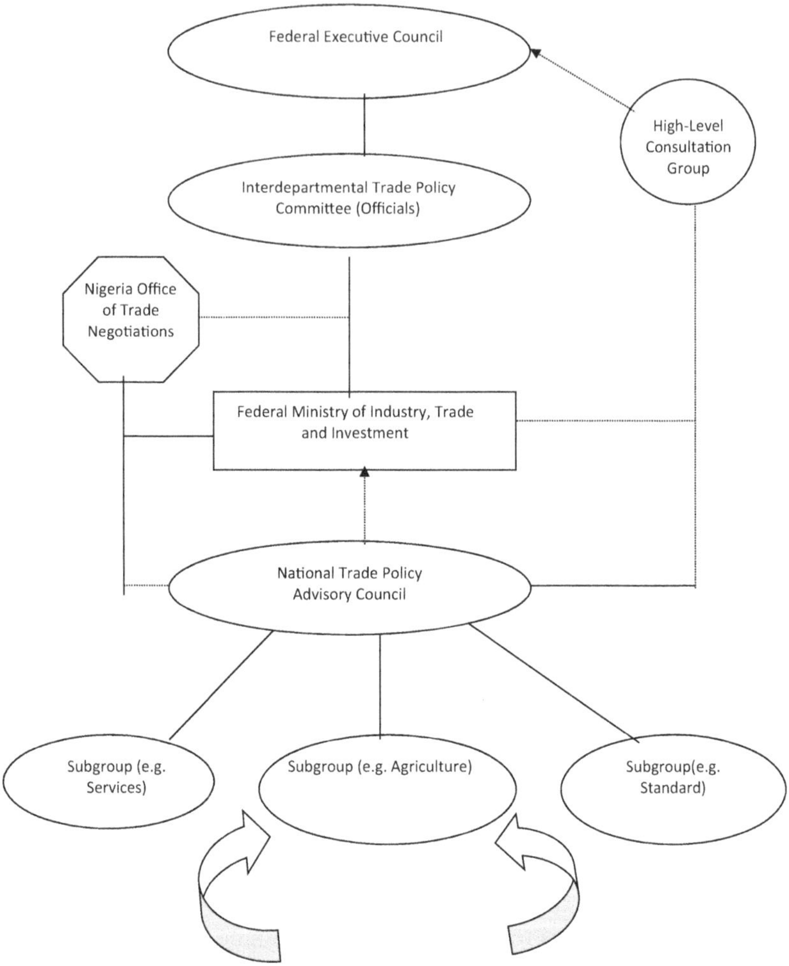

Fig. 7.3 Trade policy dialogue and consultation process (*Source* Author's design)

trade policy with the rest of the Member States; (b) ECOWAS/EPA with European EU; (c) AfCFTA with the AU Member States and (d) continuous engagement with WTO. The administrative burden of handling and negotiating multiple trade agreements, without a trade policy is a serious

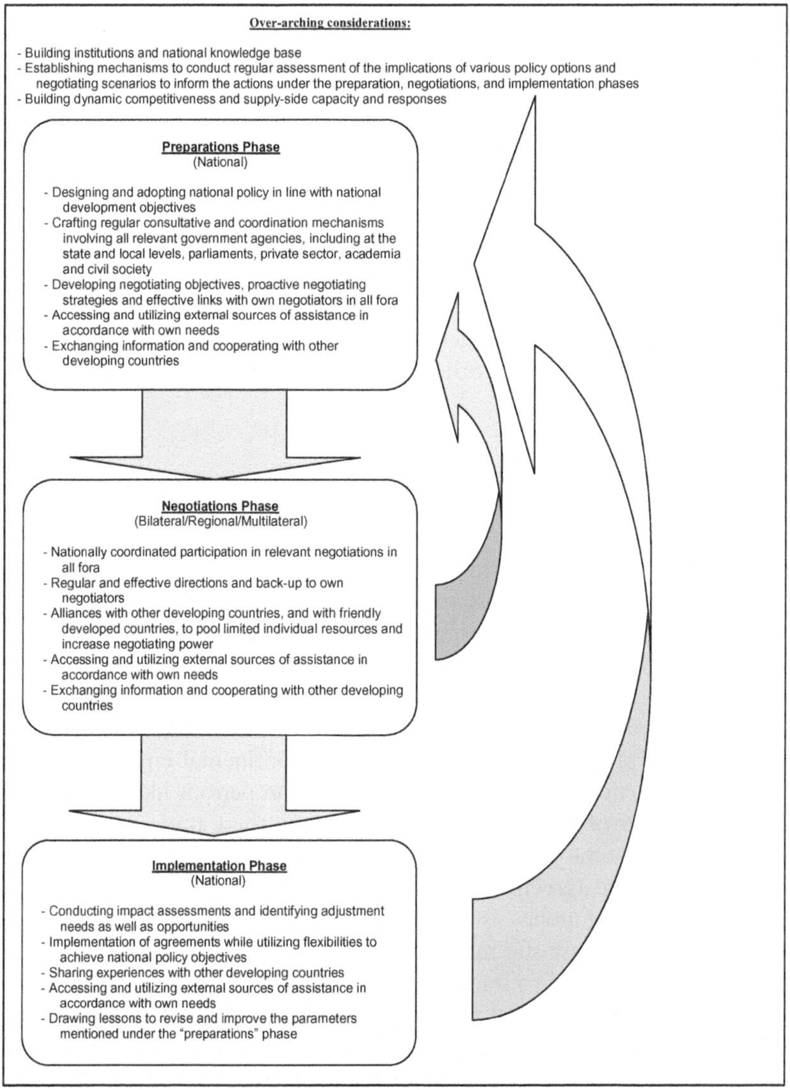

Fig. 7.4 Developing trade negotiations capacity in Nigeria (*Source* Author's design)

concern. Even as at now, the country still faces serious resource and technical constraints on the negotiation of multiple agreements that will serve her trade interests. Confronted with generally weak negotiating, regulatory and implementation capacities, the country is handicapped in her ability to engage meaningfully in all these negotiations.

To tackle these issues, an **effective sequencing and coordination strategy is urgently required**. Based on the varying degree of complexities involved in each of these negotiations, it makes sense to introduce the least complex and least costly/high benefit elements first, while leaving the more difficult, more costly and less benefit elements to a later time. It is advisable that Nigeria urgently concludes the domestic trade policy that will serve as a radar to other trade agreements to be negotiated in this order:

i. ECOWAS CTP;
ii. The AfCFTA;
iii. The EPA with EU and
iv. WTO.

This order of sequencing Nigeria's trade engagement permits progressive harmonization of various trade agreements that will avoid possible contradictions and discouragement that may occur if this order is not embraced. Due to lack of domestic trade policy the country may insert either interim provision in her regional and continental engagements as found in the Article XXIV of GATT or transition periods like it was done under the ETLS of ECOWAS when sequencing these trade negotiations; particularly for some of the more difficult issues. This means that some provisions of these agreements do not need to be applied fully until when the domestic trade policy is concluded. Such transition periods would allow Nigeria to phase the more difficult items of these agreements successively over time and to stagger their entry so that all difficult issues do not need to be dealt with at the same time. Given the timelines attached to these agreements, interim or transition periods of varying length will greatly facilitate the benefits of sequencing as well as implementing the provisions of these multiplicity of trade agreements.

While Nigeria may end up formulating its trade policy, equally important is the implementation initiatives of each stage of the sequence. In addressing the trade negotiation sequence, therefore, a matrix comprising 6 interrelated questions comes up:

i. ***What?*** This question highlights the issue of fundamental premises and challenges that serve as prerequisites towards achieving the objectives of trade policy and its sequential arrangement of negotiation.
ii. ***Why?*** Seeks the specific objectives for following a particular sequence of trade negotiation.
iii. ***Where?*** Aims at the definition of targets underlying trade policy objectives as the basis for the sequence selected.
iv. ***How?*** Once the sequence has been agreed upon it is necessary to determine the activities through which the sequence of negotiation can be achieved for the purpose of their prioritization.
v. ***When?*** *R*efers to the benchmarks and time frames for the implementation of the negotiation sequencing.
vi. ***By Whom?*** The final question refers to the line of responsibilities on the major issues involved in the sequence of trade agreement negotiated (that is, who does what in the trade negotiation sequence?) This calls for clear division of labour among various stakeholders at all stages, from trade policy and sequencing formulation, through implementation to monitoring and evaluation.

7.8.2 Capacity Improvement and Formation of Coalition

To complement the sequencing the power imbalances in trade negotiations, particularly at WTO, could equally be attended to through capacity improvements of the Nigerian Negotiators, and coalition building among other countries in the world. Because of their deficiency in negotiation capacity, Page Sheila (2003) said it is difficult to ascertain whether developing countries are victims or participants in the current international trade negotiation. Therefore, availability of efficient negotiating capabilities through capacity improvements as well as coalition at the national level is the foundation of effective participation in the various negotiations confronting the country. Such coalition building will facilitate Nigeria's ability to work together with other countries on common interests, influence agenda-setting and decision-making in their favour, and substantially affect the negotiating outcomes.

7.8.2.1 Capacity Improvement

Complex trade negotiations (whether at the bilateral, regional or multilateral levels) require that Nigeria to develop and improve human, technical, financial and physical infrastructural resources necessary to have sufficient capacity at the various negotiations. The country, like many developing countries continues to face challenges and resource limitations towards developing negotiating capacity for effective and substantive participation in trade negotiations. Such negotiating capacity has two aspects: the first—its institutional and technical mechanism to achieve the policy objectives through the negotiations and second—its political competence—which comes from being able to use negotiating capacity to address and influence the balance of economic and political power among the negotiating partners and so shape the negotiating outcomes.

To this end the country requires well organized and coordinated institutional mechanisms that can provide: negotiating experience; technical expertise both on the issues and on negotiating tactics; policy research and analytical preparation and support for appropriate negotiation strategy; the physical and financial infrastructure necessary to ensure that the country's negotiators have sufficient information about their negotiating counterparts' positions and interests, technical resources and actual physical negotiating presence to enable national trade negotiators to effectively develop and carry out their negotiating strategy.

Nigeria Office for Trade Negotiation (NOTN) was set up in August 2017. Up till now, the legal statue to back up its established is yet to be put in place. The lack of appropriate institutional and technical aspect of negotiating capacity often results in a diminished negotiating capacity at the technical and institutional levels particularly in the areas of:

i. difficulties in defining and promoting a clear national negotiating policy position in trade negotiations due to lack of coherence in both national policies and national policymaking institutions;
ii. lack or insufficiency of coordinated involvement of relevant MDAs and stakeholders in the policymaking and consultation processes;
iii. lower level of technical preparation with respect to trade negotiations due to the limited resources made available to support national trade negotiators;
iv. lack of coordinated national policymaking institutions and mechanisms and coherent national policies as well as inadequate preparations;

v. incoherent national economic and trade policies making identification of negotiating needs and priorities unclear and
vi. poor inter-agency coordination in policymaking which often is the result of unclear, conflicting or uncoordinated lines of decision-making authority within and among agencies over a given issue.

7.8.3 *Coalition Building*

In trade negotiation today, the need for strategic and united collective action, known as coalition building, (Kahler and Odell, 1989) on the part of Nigeria as well as other LDCs and the DCs in the regional international arena is very important. Both of them see coalition building as an effective means of countering the negotiating strength of the developed countries in the WTO, when it is pursued through the elaboration and articulation of common positions by the countries of the South. The establishment of South-South political and economic cooperation mechanisms such as the G-77, the Non-Aligned Movement (NAM), the various Southern regional cooperation and economic integration organizations, are all reflections of this recognition of the need for South-South unity and cooperation. However, a major challenge on this strategy remains the need to agree on the content of such strategy for South-South so that it could serve as a basis for an elaborating more specific regional, sub-regional and national programmes of cooperation that is equally sustainable.

However, collective South-South action presupposes that individually, developing countries have already identified its own individual strategic national developmental policies, priorities and negotiating interests which could then serve as the basis for their individual engagement in South-South coalitions and groupings in the WTO negotiations as well as in the other negotiations like the EPA between EU and the ACP countries. To this end, significant resources and political will may therefore need to be invested in establishing such coordinating mechanism for trade policymaking and negotiations at the national level.

Having an effective and coordinated trade policymaking and negotiations mechanism at the national level that has the support of the country's political leadership as well as trade stakeholders in Nigeria is necessary before engaging in such coalition. Such an approach will provide a clearer match between the country's strategic objectives in trade, the negotiating strategies and tactics used by its negotiators and their engagement in and use of South-South coalitions or groups in the WTO negotiations. It must be noted that the weaknesses in Nigeria's technical preparedness in trade negotiation s can to some extent be mitigated, **but cannot be substituted** even with coalition. Southern-defined, and technically sound negotiating positions might need to be adopted and put forward by Nigeria with other developing countries through their coalitions and groupings. This would however need to be discussed, agreed upon for all to be aware of their individual as well as group "***walk-away***" negotiating positions.

7.9 Conclusion and Recommendation

Trade governance has been subjected to multilateralism and regionalism over the years. While the structure of multilateral trading system had been governed by the GATT since 1947, this was later reinforced with the establishment of WTO in 1995. Despite this development, regionalism has deepened over the years in the form of different categories and phases of economic integration. The phenomenon of economic integration agreements since the end of twentieth century has implied a partial shift of political and economic power in trade negotiations from individual nation states to regional institutions. Further is a myriad of new bilateral trade negotiations and establishment of new interregional institutions and partnerships, like EPA between the EU and the ACP.

Simultaneously with multilateralism, regionalism and bilateralism, the global production system has been substantially restructured with the activities of TNCs and their affiliates networked across continents and operating in various economic integration arrangements. Their activities are shifting production across the world based on factor-determined endowments; and this is currently changing the pattern of international production, international trade structure, direction of trade as well as negotiation with them through their home countries and developing countries. These developments are having repercussions on national, regional and even international trade policy formulation processes and contents.

Most multilateral and regional trade agreements make all signatories treat one another the same based on the content of such agreements. Such **level playing fields** may be critical for LDCs and DCs because many of them are smaller in economic size, and in most cases less competitive. In spite of this, such agreements still have some advantages like: (a) they are expected to increase trade for every contracting participants as their companies would enjoy low tariffs; (b) they do standardize commerce regulations for all the trade partners, making companies to save legal costs since they follow the agreed common rules and procedures across all Member States in the agreements and (c) countries can negotiate trade deals with more than one country at a time, as the trade negotiation agreements do undergo a detailed approval process that are synchronized into national trade policies of Member States.

However, accompanying these benefits are other cautions which DCs and LDCs must understand in these negotiations, they include: (a) multilateral and regional trade agreements are complex and time-consuming to negotiate; (b) most times the details of such negotiations are particular to trade and business practices, most of which are often misunderstood by the public leading to lots of press, controversy and protests; (c) if the trade negotiations are not properly entrenched into national trade policy, some companies, countries and even regions may experience negative consequences arising from trade liberalization and (d) lastly many multilateral and regional trade agreement give competitive advantages to the TNCs who are already familiar with operating in a global environment, making small firms unable to compete and thus lay off workers to cut costs while others move their factories to countries.

Nigeria's experience within the various regional economic groupings as well as the multilateral trading system of the WTO has been less than satisfactory because of the lack of competitiveness of its. This has resulted in little enthusiasm for adopting a more activist trade policy posture within the government, think tanks and the trade policy community. Notwithstanding these challenges and doubts, joining RTAs such as AfCFTA could bring immeasurable benefits to Nigeria, in terms of making the economy more competitive, in the production and exportation of goods and services; as well as expanded **trade creation** in line with the foundational theories of economic integration.

In addition, the real challenges in Nigeria with respect to AfCFTA are: (a) the lack of full understanding of the benefits of trade liberalization at continental level in line with the Abuja Treaty of 1991, (b) domestic policy paralysis on trade and (c) consequently the lack of political will. Crafting a successful trade policy for Nigeria requires an understanding of geopolitics and global economic trends (particularly on trade) and the ability to negotiate to the advantage of the country. Again, effective/efficient trade negotiation under the NOTN is possible only if the government has the confidence and capacity to execute the necessary corresponding domestic reforms—some of which require painful adjustments as well as engagement of competent staff and intensive /extensive training for them.

With various regional and sub-regional FTAs within the same multilateral trading system currently facing Nigeria, to maximize opportunities within them, Nigeria will have to do the following:

1. establish an appropriate “Trade Policy Development Strategy” that agrees with the ERGP of the country, as suggested in Fig. 7.1;
2. urgently use the strategy to formulate an acceptable trade policy (Nigeria currently has no trade and investment policy), that will take note of issues in this lecture, among others, using Executive Trade Policy Formulation Organogram in Fig. 7.2;
3. review the existing the Enlarged National Focal Point on Trade Matters (ENFP) of the country in line with the “Trade Policy Dialogue and Consultation Process” as shown in Fig. 7.3;
4. put in place an effective/efficient trade negotiation strategy and sequence to enhance a better economic relationship within these multiplicity of trading agreements;
5. conclude the legal issues confronting NOTN, put in place technically competent negotiators in the Office, and develop their trade negotiations capacity in line with Fig. 7.4 to answer to the demand of current and emerging trade negotiation realities facing the country;
6. ensure that both the trade policy and the sequence of negotiating the numerous trading agreements facing the country are synchronized with the country’s development strategy under the ERGP;
7. review the country’s position in the various economic integration such as ECOWAS, EPA, AGOA; AfCFTA and develop an appropriate sequencing road map that will not marginalize the country;
8. carry out an extensive sensitization on future trade negotiations to secure the buy-in of the relevant stakeholders;
9. without delay accede to the AfCFTA Treaty by submitting her ratification instruments to AU Chair Person) and review the various domestic policies in line with her AfCFTA commitment and
10. engage in appropriate coalition with other countries in future trade negotiations at regional level as well as at multilateral level.

References

Adam S. (1776); *The Wealth of Nations*, Reprinted by Global Grey, 2018.

Arashiro Z., C. Marin, and A. Chacoff (2005); *Challenges of Multilateralism: The Explosion of PTAs*, Institute for International Trade Negotiation, Sao Paulo.

Aremu J. (2005); *Attracting and Negotiating Foreign Direct Investment with Transnational Corporations in Nigeria*, Marketlink Communications, Lagos.

Bergsten C. F. (2002); "A Competitive Approach to Free Trade", *Financial Times*, 5 December.

Bhagwati J. (1993); Regionalism and Multilaterals: An Overview in J. de Melo and A. Panagariya (Eds), *New Dimension of Regional Integration*, Cambridge University Press, New York.

Bjornskov C. and L. M. Kim (2002); Where Do Developing Countries Go After Doha? An Analysis of WTO Position and Potential Alliance, *Journal of World Trade*, 2002.

Coughlin C. (2002); The Controversy over Free Trade: The Gap Between Economist and the General Public, *Federal Reserve Bank of St. Louis, Review* 84, February.

Das B. L. (2002); *Strengthening Developing countries in the WTO, Trade and Development Series*, No 8, Third World Network. Viewed at www.twnside.org.sg/title/td8.htm.

Ethier W. J. (1998); Regionalism in a Multilateral World, *Journal of Political Economy* 106 (6), 1214–1245.

European Union Commission (2009); *Aid for Trade Fact Sheet*, September.

Grassley C. and R. Wyden (2019); *Approaching 25: The Road Ahead for the WTO*, Chairman Us Senate Committee on Finance, Tuesday 12 March.

Kahler M. and J. S. Odell (1989); Developing Country Coalition—Building and I Trade Negotiations in John Whalley and Ann Arbor (Ed), *Trade Policy and the Developing World*, University of Michigan Press, 146–170.

Kanal S. (2005); *Article XXIX of GATT: Good, Bad, or Both*, Department of Economics, Southern Methodist University, Dallas.

Krishna P. (1998); Regionalism and Multilateralism: A Political Economy Approach, *Quarterly Journal of Economic* 113 (1), 227–251.

Morrison S. P. (2017); Mercantilism in Economic Nationalism, *National Economic Editorial*, 30 March.

Odell J. S.; (2003); *Developing Countries and the Trade Negotiation Process.* UNCTAD, Conference Paper, Palais des Nations, Geneva, 6–7 November, x.

Page Sheila A. (2003); *Developing Countries: Victims or Participants: Their Changing Role in International Negotiations*, Overseas Development Institute, London. Viewed at www.odi.org.uk/iedg/index.html.

Pomfret, R. (1986); "The Effects of Trade Preferences for Developing Countries", *Southern Economic Journal* 53 (1), 18–26.

Vijayasri (2013); *The Importance of international Trade in the World, Research Scholar*, Department of Economics, Andhra University, India.

Viner, J. (1950); *Customs Union Issues, Endowment for International Peace, Carnegie*, UN, New York.

UNCTAD (2008); *Accra Accord, Addressing the Opportunities and Challenges of Globalization for Development*, UNCTAD, 12th Session, Accra, Ghana, 20–25 April.

UNECA (2017); *Brief on Regional Integration and the Continental Free Trade Area*, Prepared by African Trade Policy Centre, 18 March 2018.

Wilson, J. S., and Portugal-Perez, A. (2010); Export Performance and Trade Facilitation Reform: Hard and Soft Infrastructure. Policy Research Working Papers. https://doi.org/10.1596/1813-9450-5261.

WTO (2006); *Operationalizing Aid for Trade*, Panel Discussion at WTO Public Forum, Geneva, 26 September.

WTO (2005); *WTO 5th Ministerial Declaration*, Hong Kong, 13–18 December.

Zartman I. and William Zartman (Ed) (1987); *Improving North–South Negotiation*, Transaction Books, New Brunswick, NJ.

CHAPTER 8

Conclusion and Policy Recommendations

Gbadebo Odularu

8.1 Accelerating Nigeria's Innovation and Digitization Agenda Toward Benefiting Maximally from AfCFTA

Today, trade and production are heavily dependent on moving, storing, and increasingly deploying digital information (data) across borders, therefore making it a strategic component for trade facilitation automation. As Nigeria plans to domesticate the African Continental Free Trade Agreement (AfCFTA) in this digital age, this requires a systematic investment in knowledge, innovation, and an incubation ecosystem. In view of this, the adoption of innovative business models has generated more complex global trade transactions and policy issues. The Nigerian Government is strategically positioned to unlock these AfCFTA potentials and catalyze the adoption of digital trade and scaling up the latest commerce innovations, enabling trade inclusion for a significant population, both youth and women, and paving the way for a smart economy.

G. Odularu (✉)
Department of Economics and Finance, Bay Atlantic University,
Washington, D.C., USA
e-mail: g.odularu@ahusc.net

G. Odularu (ed.), *Strategic Policy Options for Bracing Nigeria for the Future of Trade*,
https://doi.org/10.1007/978-3-030-34552-5_8

The aim is this chapter is to propose workable and forward-looking policy solutions for adopting digital tools in preparing Nigeria for the future of trade. Based on its young and growing population, vast natural resources, and year-on-year economic growth, the role of digital revolution cannot be overemphasized in realizing the nation's enormous growth potentials. It is imperative for Nigeria to strengthen its business ecosystem in order to capitalize on the global digital economy opportunities which are valued at about $60 trillion revenue by 2025 (August/September 2019 African Business Magazine).

It is crucial to note that digitalization is rapidly coming to Nigeria's commercial and development landscape, thereby profoundly posing significantly positive impacts on its economic sectors. Increasing the roles and enhancing the capacities of social enterprises that build and share digital technologies will make Nigerians become more active and increasingly digitalized citizens. For example, since the creation of Konga, as an increasingly digital retailing platform, related apps like ThriveAgric, Farm-Crowdy, CrowdyInvest, etc., are now being fully embraced, and Nigeria's tech wizards are turning their focus on developing digital tools to improve governance, business, economics, democracies, health, farming, banking, transportation, communication, etc. In fact, from WhatsApp to Instagram to Facebook to Twitter, Nigerians are using non-profit platforms to inform socioeconomic and political policy processes, thereby making the most use of digital tools to facilitate trade, commerce, business, politics, economics, and governance. At this current and increasing rate of digitalization of trade, Nigeria could catch up with the leading players on the global digital stage. Thus, Nigeria needs to empower more social enterprises to serve as digital national, regional, and global communicable enablers, thereby providing connectivity services across all business sectors including agriculture, manufacturing, commerce, education, healthcare, etc.

In other words, innovation in agriculture, banking, healthcare, education, commerce, etc., have continually provided the fertile space for the adoption of digital tools. For instance, farmers are increasingly leveraging on digital technologies to become more empowered by accessing information about every stage of agricultural value chain, and also communicating via text messages and are also applying mobile apps to access vital information toward enhancing their productivity and profitability. In addition, remote patients can instantly access medical advice and blood bank as part of Nigeria's contribution to the increasingly digitalized global community.

Further, there is the need for more interoperability with other platforms and networks (especially for digital trade services like financing, loans application, payments settlements, telecommunications, business servicing, trade facilitation, etc.,). This will give all actors increasing opportunities and access, thereby enhancing the policy ecosystem for more digital transformations.

It is important for Nigeria to increasingly manage data as the backbone for leveraging digitization for optimizing resources allocation, enhancing efficiencies in public services, and facilitating trade activities within an enabling business environment. In order to rapidly reap the benefits of digitalization, Nigeria needs to quickly develop more effective network of data-related infrastructure such as assimilation of data collection culture across all levels (including government institutions like data bureaus, educational agencies, economic organizations), data centres, wireless communications, and fibre optics.

Well-targeted retooling and continuous learning by businesses should remain the new normal. In other words, government and the private sector should maximize the great opportunities of digitization by focusing on retooling and relearning digitalization skills, terms, tools, parameters, processes, and related technologies in this fast-changing global and digital business arena. To this end, for business, especially MSMEs, and including governments to survive in this increasingly competitive and rapidly digitizing markets, businesses must ensure that its employees are specifically equipped with customized arsenal of skills toward achieving organizational goals, therefore resulting in desired business goals. As future businesses become more digitalized, continuous learning, and targeted retooling remains an indispensable tool for bracing for the future of trade in Nigeria.

Digital transformation is a continuous business evolution that requires government and businesses to engage selected professional advisory firms to prepare Nigerian businesses to thrive in this digital world. These preparations range for strategy development, to technology enablement to cultural change. This also requires harnessing the power of engaging technologies and digital transformation to translate data into actionable insights.

Nigeria needs to strategically position itself by providing digital products that will innovatively influence the regional digital marketplace within the continental free trade agreement. Thus, the future looks bright as Nigeria is signatory to the AfCFTA, where the regional markets and landscape will be increasingly influenced by technological changes, especially gradual adoption of blockchain technology within its e-commerce space and other related online services and content to capture more markets opportunities on the continent.

Financing the Future of Digital Trade: Nigeria should strengthen plans to develop its silicon valley or innovation city by accessing the Africa 50's $871m funds which is aimed at deploying early-stake risk capital to lure local and global talents to Africa by giving early-stage startups and hi-tech ventures the financial freedom to test out ideas, access money, prove their concepts, and finally grow to create wealth and provide jobs for the domestic economy.

Taking actions toward seizing the gains and exploiting these development opportunities through digitization prism: Innovative regional policies and programs are crucial to enhancing growth capacities for inclusive economic transformation. Digitization remains a unique phenomenon, which is of immense importance to scaling sustainable development impacts. Being one of the last signatories to the CFTA due to the fears overflooding the country with unwanted commodities,[1] optimizing its implementation process within an effective digitization policy space, so as to realize its enormous potentials as a regional competitive force and digital engine for Africa's socioeconomic transformation.

E-commerce represents confoundingly novel and shape-shifting challenges that digital markets bring forth for competition regulations and laws. As these trends play out in the coming years, more novel STIs will emerge as crucial tools for designing, deploying and catalyzing the adoption workable tools for bringing digital experience to consumers, and also preparing for the future of trade facilitation in Africa. Digital trade could be the new growth engines to offset a cooling continental economy as recession rages on. E-commerce policy should deal with issues of cross-border data flows, especially on issues pertaining to the storage of data within certain jurisdictions. Data localization rules should also be

[1] As a result of palpable loopholes in its trade policies over the years, in which government impose protectionist policies but failed to simultaneously provide the enabling ecosystem (good infrastructure, steady supply of electricity, proactive regulatory policies, efficient ports, etc.,) for domestic industries to compete with foreign counterparts, and satisfying the local demands.

a core part of e-commerce policy to regulating cross-border data flow. Connected to this is the essential role of cybersecurity in this data-driven high-tech world and the need to strengthen cybersecurity training that protects our personal privacy, as well as enhance entrepreneurs' capacities with focus on national security and socioeconomic health outcomes, especially in the face of national shortage of highly skilled cybersecurity professionals.

From a strategic standpoint, every node of the commodity (products and services) value chain is ripe for disruption, thus, Nigeria should develop and implement a customized program to act as a catalyst toward creating an initial 5 million SMEs platform which will be deployed to engage with innovators, tech firms, agribusinesses, financiers over the implementation period. Focusing on logistics, technology can enable suppliers to aggregate producers demand for inputs, which can then be cost-effectively delivered to producers, thereby enhancing the effective use of digital technologies for commercial transformation in Nigeria. Thus, the proposed program should implement and expand innovative digital platforms to reach a large number of users that will unlock new opportunities for fostering an inclusive economy and regional synergies in areas like mobile or digital trade services.

- Nigeria has a comparative advantage in services, and services play a crucial role in enabling digital trade transactions in the sense that removing trade barriers for services is essential to promote market openness in this digital era.
- Identify the most promising digital trade innovations with the aim of getting five million SMEs onto a digital platform over the next 5 years.
- Create prosperity by strengthening the regional and global competitiveness of Nigerian digital commerce, promoting trade and investment, and ensuring fair digital trade and compliance with AfCFTA trade laws and agreements.
- Identify gaps in our understanding of the dynamic and complex Nigeria's digital commerce (trade, investment, and industry) and then fill these gaps by researching and developing new data products for rigorously/creatively improving and enhancing existing data production and accuracy, which are essential underpinning in this digital trade era.

- Though it raises a few policymaking challenges, digital trade promises new opportunities for firms and individuals of all sizes to benefit. Thus, understanding the drivers of this new paradigm for trade is key in designing the appropriate policy mix and making digital trade contribute inclusively to Nigeria's economic transformation and poverty alleviation agenda.
- Need to enhance the online digital capabilities of all MSMEs and SMEs, thereby offering various kinds of services and products on its online marketplace.
- There is the need to supply "digital commerce platform" towards providing needs-met services to merchants on catalog management, pricing, promotion, and other similar services.

This proposed program will be sustainable because it will provide a platform for connections, collaborations, ideas exchange, and sustainable financial services innovations. That is, harnessing the power of digitization to create opportunities for transforming how people access consumer commercial services.

Index

G. Odularu (ed.), *Strategic Policy Options for Bracing Nigeria for the Future of Trade*,
https://doi.org/10.1007/978-3-030-34552-5

The manufacturer's authorised representative in the EU is Springer Nature Customer Service Centre GmbH, Europaplatz 3, 69115 Heidelberg, Germany. If you have any concerns regarding our products, please contact ProductSafety@springernature.com

Printed and bound by CPI Group (UK) Ltd, Croydon, CR0 4YY

30/09/2026

02225644-0002